The Relentless Pursuit

Also by Kurt W. Zimmerman
Rare Book Hunting: Essays and Escapades

The Relentless Pursuit
of
Rare Books

Further Essays and Escapades

by

KURT W. ZIMMERMAN

Prologue by

Nicholas A. Basbanes

THE BOOK HUNTERS CLUB OF HOUSTON
2025

The prologue by Nicholas Basbanes was first published in
Fine Books and Collections, Autumn 2021.

The cover illustration "The Bibliofiends" by Oliver Herford
first appeared as the frontispiece and jacket illustration for
A.S.W. Rosenbach's *The Unpublishable Memoirs* (1917).

Copyright © 2025 by Kurt Zimmerman
All rights reserved
The author may be reached at
zbooks@yahoo.com
www.bookcollectinghistory.com

Dedicated to my wife Nicole.

My most serendipitous acquisition.

Table of Contents

	Prologue by Nicholas Basbanes	i
I	Organic Bookselling	1
II	Three Ardent Bibliophiles and the Greatest Book in the World	9
III	The Quarto Club: "A Few Harmless Bibliomaniacs"	15
IV	Clubbing with the Book Fellows	22
V	Extreme Book Collecting	33
VI	Use the Force: Barton W. Currie & John C. Eckel	38
VII	The Love and Pursuit of Books Unites Us	43
VIII	Dorothy Sloan: The Biblio-Rose of Texas	50
IX	McMurtry, Pass By	63
X	Revolution, Redouté, and Why Collect Books?	68
XI	Camaraderie and Competition. The Big Five Lincoln Collectors	75
XII	Booking in the Big Easy	83
XIII	A Portrait of the HRC Director Thomas F. Staley	90
XIV	Miss Stillwell and F. Richmond Goff	93
XV	Every Book Its Story	107
XVI	Good Books at the Florida Antiquarian Book Fair	121
XVII	Six Score and More: Wallowing in It with Bill Reese	132
XVIII	Feeling Good: Dr. Samuel Purple Makes a House Call	136
XIX	J. Frank Dobie Meets a Preacher, Gambler, and Book Collector	143
XX	William P. Barlow, Jr.: Personal Rewards and Public Benefits	151
XXI	A Blockbuster Deal Involving J. P. Morgan	158
XXII	In the Midst of It: Down the Cataloging Rabbit Hole	168
XXIII	Trafficking, Fossicking, and Noodling in Old Books	181
XXIV	Letting Go	186
XXV	A Biblio-Bender in the Northeast	190

PROLOGUE

Nicholas A. Basbanes

AS A WRITER whose roots are in journalism, my focus—and indeed my temperament as an author over the past thirty years—has always been trained on the experiences and motivations of other people, not myself, so the idea that I might in some way be "collectible" is a reality I have come to accept with what I hope is gratitude and humility. That said, nothing could have prepared me for Kurt Zimmerman of Houston, Texas, a self-described "book hunter" in the classic mode who gives fresh meaning to the expression "wanting it all," beginning with his zeal for having multiple copies of the same book.

At last count, Zimmerman had ten copies of *A Gentle Madness* (1995), my first book, on his shelves, and that is not even the most for any one title he has in a collection of 12,000 items relevant to the history of book collecting. Topping the list of duplicates on his shelves is A. Edward Newton's *The Amenities of Book Collecting and Kindred Affections* (1918), with nineteen copies, followed by A.S.W. Rosenbach's *Books and Bidders* (1927), at thirteen, and Charles Goodspeed's *Yankee Bookseller* (1937), eleven. Tied with my book at ten copies each are John Carter's *ABC for Book Collectors* (1952), Wilmarth Lewis' *Collector's Progress* (1951), and the Edwin Wolf 2nd-John Fleming biography *Rosenbach* (1960). Close behind is David Randall's *Dukedom Large Enough* (1969), nine copies, and Lessing Rosenwald's *Recollections of a Collector* (1976), at nine.

So why, you might ask, does Zimmerman covet so many copies of the same books? I put that very question to him myself, the occasion being the publication of his first book *Rare Book Hunting: Essays and*

Escapades (2021), a collection of the pieces he has written for his popular blog reflecting on his own experiences among the gently mad. "Each copy that I have of these particular titles is unique in some way," he answered without missing a beat. "Normally, they're inscribed to someone of interest, so that makes every copy unique. Sometimes I buy variant copies, but mainly I'm focusing on the associations. How many times have I contacted you and asked you what you remember about a certain inscription? Each book to me is a story."

In the instance of *A Gentle Madness*, Zimmerman continued, the fact that I profiled so many different people—not just collectors, but booksellers and librarians in equal measure, what the great Lawrence Clark Powell considered the holy trinity of the rare book world—made the book a prime "target of opportunity" for him.

"You surveyed not just the history," he said—and how cool is that, someone contextualizing the scope of my own work to me?—"but with your journalistic background, you captured the contemporary scene. No other book has done that. So it's a very important work in the history of collecting, which is what my collection is all about. And of course, you signed a zillion copies, too, and your inscriptions are always great, so there is that, too."

I became aware of Zimmerman's spirited activity about fifteen years ago by way of an email: he introduced himself, told me what he was up to, and wondered if I could tell him anything about a few of the inscriptions I had written in the copies he had acquired. The obvious ones I could recall without difficulty, a few of the others I had to think about—as he said, I have signed a "zillion" copies of that book since its release, more than a thousand at the ABAA fairs in Washington, Boston, New York, and Los Angeles in the first year of publication alone, and many hundreds of times since. (I have said more than once, and not entirely in jest, that the scarcest copies of the first printing of *AGM* may be the ones that are not signed or inscribed at all.)

I met Zimmerman face-to-face for the first time in 2014 at the California fair in Pasadena, where, aptly enough, I was signing copies of my ninth book, *On Paper*. He had heard that I was hoping to place my research archive with a major institution, which became a reality the following year at the Cushing Memorial Library and Archives at Texas A&M University. He wondered if there were any "extraneous biblio-related" materials I might consider parting with that were not part of that assemblage. I said that indeed there were, that I had hundreds of things not related to my *AGM* research, and they were ready to find a new home. Thus it was that he traveled from Texas to Massachusetts that August and spent three days poking about for items of interest; so much of it kept in an intimidating network of metal shelving in the basement known informally hereabouts as the "book warren."

My wife had arranged to be away, choosing to leave the two of us to explore by ourselves, though all the exploring was done by Zimmerman. There were a few breaks—I introduced him to the American Antiquarian Society in Worcester and the John Carter Brown Library in Providence, and we had dinner a couple times at a nearby Mexican restaurant—but most of the time he was on his own while I watched the Red Sox on television.

I had set the parameters of what was fair game, and what was off limits. Every once in a while Zimmerman would come by with a stack of things for me to look at, and in the absence of a bookplate—I don't have one—personalize the items I decided he could have with a prior ownership signature. "Got to have the provenance," he explained, so I signed and signed and signed.

Apart from the books was the ephemera he wanted, and which, truth be known, I was overjoyed to have him take. He was palpably excited by the spare copy of *Bostonia* magazine featuring the essay I wrote in 1988 that spawned the idea for *AGM* in the first place, along with some tear sheets of newspaper columns I had written during my Literary Features Syndicate days, and extra copies of reviews that had been published of my books. To these were added flyers and programs and promotional materials produced for lectures I have given, and sundry other curiosities he found relevant.

When it was time for me to drive Zimmerman to the airport, ten large cardboard packing boxes left with us—our first stop being the local UPS customer service center. I, for one, was exhausted—and he had done all the heavy lifting. I'd like to say the house looked empty after he left, but he had hardly scratched the surface.

❊ I ❊
Organic Bookselling

I'M SEATED in an outhouse thinking fondly of antiquarian booksellers. The outhouse is complete with wood board butt rest, bucket of sawdust for odor control, and a guest book. Book hunting can certainly lead to unexpected situations.

The outhouse is the inexplicable sole restroom for an otherwise fabulous, dodecagon (twelve-sided) home nestled on acreage in the beautiful Driftless region near Viroqua, Wisconsin. Driftless refers not to a land of unmotivated wanderers, but to a geographic area that lacks glacial deposits known as drift. The gorgeous landscape is composed of deep river valleys, steep hills, forest, spring-fed waterfalls, and cold-water trout streams intermixed with scattered farms.

I've spent the last three days in Viroqua in Driftless Books culling five boxes of goodies from the remnants of the reference collection of legendary Berkeley, California bookseller Peter Howard. Nicole has gathered four boxes of books related to Frank Lloyd Wright from another uncatalogued stash.

Nicole and I are staying with Eddy Nix, proprietor of Driftless Books, and Eddy's roommate, Theresa, a retired marketing executive who owns the home. Constructed in the early 80s by an eccentric astrologer, the home is designed for communal living with each bedroom having an outside entrance. The central living area has a massive stone fireplace, spacious kitchen, and a wall of two-story windows framing a forest and valley stretching to the horizon. Our first night's dinner is al fresco, and we enjoy the panoramic views at dusk—eating wild salmon cooked over an open fire by Theresa's visiting brother, Pete, along with fresh, roasted vegetables from Theresa's massive garden, and an ample supply of wine. The atmosphere is bohemian, the banter eclectic, and shoes are optional.

I first met Eddy Nix in 2012 at the Larry McMurtry book sale auction in Archer City, Texas. McMurtry had decided to sell much of his huge stock of used books due to health concerns. It was an on-site auction at his bookstore with books grouped in large lots. The sale attracted bidders from near and far, mostly fellow booksellers, or wannabe booksellers. I attended as an observer, made the mistake of registering to bid, and ended up taking home fifty boxes of material for my private collection. Eddy arrived from Wisconsin in a small Subaru. He returned home after hiring a semi-truck to transport his book purchases back to Viroqua.

Eddy is the architect of one of the best used bookstores in the country. His 500,000-volume shop is more than a business, it is a focal point of the community, even a live music venue on occasion, and now part of the local surroundings as much as the farms, trees, fields, and streams nearby. He has a penchant for bulk acquisitions, absorbing the stock of many defunct stores over the years, including a large batch from Peter Howard's Serendipity Books. Uncounted numbers of books fill boxes on pallets in an adjoining warehouse awaiting re-discovery.

Nix is now fifty-four, thin and wiry, and spends more time booking than eating, but can powerlift book boxes with the best of them. His long beard is as expansive and unruly as his bookstore. His dress code is relaxed, and one might not anticipate the depth of his knowledge or his keen insights. He has been an activist by nature since his youth, progressive in thought, but pragmatic enough to not lose sight of practical concerns. We discuss an ongoing effort to save a local historic building from destruction.

"You have to pick your battles," he says.

We talk about the influx of new people moving to his area from urban centers, most with good jobs who work from home, pining for a taste of small-town life and a slower pace. However, many are reluctant to join in the actual activities of the town, still holding onto habits of anonymity more common in crowded regions. Eddy is brainstorming ideas to bring the local natives and newcomers together, to blend the diverse elements and enhance the overall experience with books playing an integral part.

Nix's ties to the small community of ca. 5,000 residents run deep. A native of Wisconsin, he spent time in his 20s in Los Angeles pursuing an acting/theatre career. When that didn't pan out (how many do?), he eventually ended up back in Wisconsin, moving to Viroqua in 2009. He is on the local Historical Preservation Commission, the board of the Viroqua Museum, and involved in innumerable charity events. He has even hosted his own local radio show. People ask him to run for mayor. He demurs.

"That would cut into your time for books," I answer for him.

The three days we spend with Eddy are a master class in organic networking. He and I talk about biblio-matters, but I also trail along as his general sidekick as we visit the Co-op multiple times for food and craft beer, a town festival, a farmer's market, and other local venues, all walkable. *Everyone* seemingly knows him and wants to interact. They receive a warm greeting from him in return—always appropriate to the person—a joke, a hug, a serious remark, whatever flows naturally from the encounter. There is nothing stilted or rehearsed. Eddy introduces me to so many people my head begins to spin. Somehow at the same time it is a most relaxing experience. And how often does one meet an Amish woman writer of children's books? Her booth is at the Farmer's Market, and she hands Eddy her latest self-published works.

"Would you consider carrying these in your store?"

"Sure," he replies. For Eddy also offers the writings of local authors.

As we walk away, he explains she has written several other books that he has in stock.

We juggle her books back and forth as we take turns eating our homemade mini-pies just purchased. The air is a light breeze filled with the smell of fresh goods and vegetables. While at the Market, Eddy buys a plant from a friend who is a musician / horticulturist of some repute.

"Can you drop it off at the bookstore?" he asks, our hands already full.

His friend responds with a funny, expletive reply, but agrees.

Eddy is also entrepreneurial, the owner of a building downtown housing a secondary bookstore filled with Wisconsin history as well as an extensive mysticism section. Part of the building is rented to a comic book dealer who transplanted from California. There are rooms upstairs that can potentially be leased out. It is a work in progress, but somehow he finds time for many projects.

We next visit a beautiful tract of land he owns just outside of town where he plans to build a house. Eddy is also contemplating buying a building in a nearby town that has existing tenants. Part of it can be utilized for another bookstore annex, he says. Thus, like roots of a tree, his book offerings expand. Lest you think Eddy is a silver-spoon kid, this is not the case. He's grown his book garden with hard work, a bit of luck, and unusual business acumen. That and the price of real estate in rural Wisconsin remains relatively affordable.

Nicole and I are visiting Eddy for three days during a sixteen-day driving trip. The temperature when we left Houston in early August was 105 degrees. But escaping the inferno is secondary to our primary mission: books and architecture. Nicole is an enthusiast and serious student of Frank Lloyd Wright and related architects. Wright was from Wisconsin and first worked in Chicago, so the general region provides a plethora of homes and buildings to see. We did a similar tour years earlier, but we only scratched the surface the first trip. This time, we revisit such famous sites in Wisconsin as Wright's Johnson Wax Company complex and his home/studio at Taliesin. However, the intensity of this trip is cranked up several notches when Nicole maps out a journey through multiple states that takes us on ten scheduled tours, a further nineteen interior visits of buildings, and thirty-nine drive-by stops. It is a work of organizational genius, as many public sites have only limited hours, and our targets are scattered, and timing is everything.

We get up painfully early. We regularly exceed speed limits in our dash, eat hastily of fast food, curse mightily at occasional traffic snarls, but don't miss a single opportunity. It is exhilarating and exhausting. Many Wright homes are in private hands, so we are truly home-stalking, driving hither and yon, pulling up to the curb, out and about to take pictures for a few minutes, typically standing in front of the house, sometimes walking among bushes, side yards, and peeking over fences, all for the Wright experience. When I can take no more, I just sit in the car and wait.

Of course, we visit bookstores as well. Before we return to Eddy's story, a few bookish appetizers should be mentioned. While in St. Louis, I find Dunaway Books particularly fruitful. The store has been around for over four decades, has a nice patina, and is well-organized with a solid stock. I engage with the long-time store manager Vernon Bain. Bain is a friendly guy and finds my interest in books about books particularly exciting since they have a good section on the subject, seldom visited. I root around and discover two gems: the limited edition of William Dana Orcutt's *In Quest of the Perfect Book* (1926) inscribed to fellow bookman, collector, and biblio-author, Frederick W. Skiff. The second is the limited edition of A. Edward Newton's *A Tourist in Spite of Himself* (1930) inscribed to his close friend and fellow collector Barton Currie, who authored the classic *Fishers of Books* (1931). It is late in the day and the store is about to close. My last image of Bain is of him casually sipping a Pabst Blue Ribbon behind the counter as he organizes new acquisitions.

Other bookstores follow in rapid succession. Prairie Archives in Springfield, IL, opened by John R. Paul in 1973, is big and rambling. They sell cheeky t-shirts reading, "Abraham Lincoln: They'd have to shoot me to get me back to Springfield," and "Frank Lloyd Wright: I can design a building that would look good even in Springfield." John is kind enough to dig around for me once we talk about my interests. He tempts me with an inscribed book by famed Lincoln collector Joseph Benjamin Oakleaf.

I end up buying ten items, and Nicole finds a few architecture books. Our time frame is tight, so we leave not fully satiated. The main impetus of Springfield is seeing Wright's famous Dana-Thomas house. We do work in a bit of Abe Lincoln sightseeing as well. But how many travelers come to Springfield, which fairly exudes Lincolniana, and prioritize a Wright home and a used bookstore? We contemplate this over dinner; our initial self-concern soon turns to laughter.

Two other bookstores of note include Downtown Books in Milwaukee with a sprawling, active stock, super organized, but they pull their better books for online sales, and Prospero's in Kansas City, a three-story local mecca in an old building that is perfect for browsing.

Our cross-country dash is also filled with bookish people. In Oak Park, Illinois, we spend an evening with Geri & Francis Brennan, old family friends. Francis, at age 87, is still collecting books, prints, and autographs. He has been a member of the Manuscript Society since 1965. Francis eagerly shows me highlights of his Evelyn Waugh and Graham Greene collections, as well as the latest purchase for his large collection of Piranesi prints. He is a biblio-role model as I age. He is also the first book collector I ever met, at age four or so, without realizing the momentous occasion at the time.

Our second night in Oak Park is spent with book collector Tom Dannenberg and his wife Claire. They have a finely remodeled 1910 home just around the corner from Frank Lloyd Wright's original home and studio (now a museum). Tom reached out to me after reading my work. We discover simpatico interests and our exchange of emails establishes a congenial connection. He is in his late 40s and started collecting seriously a few years ago. Tom's primary focus is the nefarious English forger and collector Thomas J. Wise. There is an abundance of primary and secondary material available related to Wise. Tom has already gathered a startlingly good nucleus, including numerous association copies, and a copy of the most famous forgery, Elizabeth Barrett Browning's *Sonnets* (Reading: 1847, but really after ca. 1880). I congratulate and encourage him, although I'm envious of certain titles, as it should be when serious collectors get together. But I'm most envious of his huge, finished basement. (Houstonians can't have basements because of the high-water table.) I jokingly suggest I lease a portion for my own book storage. We part ways, newly minted friends, and I look forward to seeing him again.

Our last stop before Viroqua is in Baraboo, Wisconsin, original home of the Ringling Brothers, and now known for its Circus World Museum spread over multiple buildings. It is not only a museum but also features an active circus performance during the summer. We explore a plethora of exhibits and experience an exciting display of circus acts. This is not a simple tourist visit for us. Nicole in her younger days was a professional circus performer, a flying trapeze artist. Her circus friends Tim & Barbara Tegge live in Baraboo, and Tim has performed in circuses his entire life. Now in his 60s, he still tours the country as a ringmaster for various shows. His wife Barbara, besides being a college English professor, is a second-generation foot juggler.

Tim is arguably the foremost collector of circus memorabilia in the country with a collection of over 250,000 items, including an extensive library. His knowledge of the field is unmatched. We spend an evening with the pair, subsisting on wine and cheese, taking a deep dive into the collection—books for me, but also a visual feast of circus ephemera, costumes, and brilliantly colored lithograph circus posters, some dating back to the late 19th century. We stay the night in the nearby Ringling House Bed & Breakfast, former home of two of the Ringling brothers—another branch on our eccentric road trip tree.

The next morning is serene, and we are on our way to Eddy Nix. Visiting him and his bookstore was a primary impetus for the trip. Anticipation builds as we approach Viroqua. I try to tamp down expectations as we emerge from a meandering drive on country roads bordered by a mix of lush forest and immaculate farms, and then we spill abruptly into the town. And there it is! Immediately on our right—I recognize it from photos—the main building of Driftless Books. It is an enormous former tobacco warehouse of red brick, built in 1906, taking up a whole block. We park.

The wooden stairs leading to the weathered front door of the store are worn raw, a few weeds grow unchecked, the entrance discreet with no obvious signage. We enter a vestibule-like space, low ceilinged, compressed. The walls are filled with a startling array of visual paraphernalia: prints, photos, posters, stickers, a beer can collection, biblio-scat found in books. To our left is an office door, closed.

We move slowly down the narrow corridor, feeling somewhat

claustrophobic, a small room stuffed with books to our right, no sign of a checkout counter, and we enter a larger space, more books but still constricted, our hearts beating faster, and we see another doorway ahead, above it the sign "Driftless Books" and we step through it. Then an overwhelming feeling of release as the space expands exponentially. The wood beamed ceiling soars and surrounding us is a Valhalla of books as far as the eye can see. It is glorious. Eddy Nix is amidst stacks of books with a customer. He smiles at us in recognition and soon greets us warmly. We begin our hunt.

2023

❋ II ❋

Three Ardent Bibliophiles and The Greatest Book in the World

I AM re-reading A. Edward Newton's *The Greatest Book in the World and Other Papers* (1925) and the ghosts of bookmen past envelop me. Not only from the text of Newton's biblio-essays, but also from the copy itself—held gently, read closely, and treasured by three ardent bibliophiles, each with their bookplate on the front free endpaper and their scattered jottings crowding the rear pastedown. I see in the morning light the mild soiling on the tan boards from their hands and fingers—bookish fingerprints. The front hinge is cracked but sturdy. Newton has penned a humorous inscription to the first owner. A carbon letter of the owner's reply to Newton is attached to the front free endpaper by a dainty paperclip. 'Tis a well-loved copy—a copy that affected me emotionally when I catalogued it, surprising me in that respect for I have many association copies and this would not rank among the greats in an analytical sense. Then I felt a yearning to tell the book's story. So let us begin.

The Greatest Book in the World and Other Papers was Newton's third major book of essays following *The Amenities of Book Collecting* (1918), and *A Magnificent Farce* (1921). Newton as a writer, biblio-celebrity, and collector was at the peak of his powers in 1925. It is remarkable he was able to get any work or collecting done considering the sheer number of books he inscribed for fans, and the amount of correspondence he answered. But he loved it all and it fed his flame. The title essay of this work is a lengthy history of the Bible in printed form, highlighting the earliest, rarest, and most important editions. Newton explores other collecting areas in essays entitled "Colored-Plate Books," and "Sporting-Books." There is much on London and Newton's beloved eighteenth century of Samuel Johnson and related writers. He also writes of Dickens' *A Christmas Carol* in "The Greatest Little Book in the World," and ends with a touching homage to his friend and mighty American collector Beverly Chew in "The Last of His Race." Most of the essays have aged well and Newton's engaging style draws in the reader quickly and usually holds them. An abundance of illustrations add interest.

This copy is presented to its first owner, "Inscribed for a lawyer Mr. M[ark]. G. Holstein—but not a criminal—I hope. (see page 37). A. Edward Newton, Nov. 30, 1925." The page referred to cites the passage: "And I wish that trials for 'heresy' might cease—those tragic farces at which kindly old men of excellent character are goaded and made miserable by *criminal lawyers*—what a happy phrase that is!—at the instance of other old men."

Tipped to the front free endpaper is a humorous carbon copy reply dated Dec. 8, 1925 from Holstein to Newton thanking him for inscribing the book ("I have received from Mr. [Charles] Sessler my copy of 'The Greatest Book in the World'"), chastising him for making fun of lawyers ("I forgive you, both because of the pleasure which your book has already given me and the pleasure which I still anticipate"), and expressing his appreciation for Newton's writings ("My introduction to the author dates from the time when I first ran across the his papers on the 'Amenities' in the *Atlantic*, I may ... say that 'while my debt to him can be acknowledged it can never be paid'"). Mounted on the rear free endpaper by Holstein is a Feb. 25, 1927, column "Notes on Rare Books" reviewing *Essays and Verses About Books* by the late Beverly Chew—the collector eulogized by Newton in the book.

Already the book has gotten my full attention. For the book has been in the hands of Newton, of course, but also those of his friend and noted Philadelphia bookseller Charles Sessler (whose assistant Mabel Zahn was an ardent Newton collector). But what of Holstein? To proactively seek out not merely a signed copy but a personally inscribed copy and then write a reply to the author indicates advanced symptoms of the gentle madness.

I dig and find Mark G. Holstein (1873-1952), a New York lawyer, who published a number of biblio-essays on various topics. Notably, he contributed to *The Colophon* New Series, Vol. II, No. 4, 1937, "A Five-Foot Shelf of Literary Forgeries." In *The Colophon* "Notes on Contributors" we read, "Mark Holstein is president of the Quarto Club. He describes himself as an aging lawyer, who started collecting books in his teens and has kept it up with unflagging zeal for almost fifty years. He has collected more books than he will ever be able to read, and has a separate room devoted to Shakespeareana. If all the time he has spent in reading and marking [auction / bookseller] catalogues were placed end to end, it would reach far enough to round out several college careers."

Then a little voice talks to me, a faint recall, and I look in my *own* library catalogue and behold! I find I have Holstein's pamphlet *The Diversions of a Will Collector* (1929), a paper read to the Quarto Club in New York City, this copy inscribed to none other than legendary bookseller A.S.W. Rosenbach, "To Dr. R, with the season's greetings and the compliments of the author."

The association copy excitement I'm feeling now is rising quicker than my homemade pizza dough. There is more to explore with Holstein. I find a photograph of his library illustrated in another issue of *The Colophon*; I want to know about the Quarto Club he founded; I want to read more of *his* writings, but such byways will be pursued later. For now, this enthusiastic original owner of *The Greatest Book in the World* has been rediscovered if not fully resurrected. As to the dispersal of his library, the *New York Times* obituary of Oct. 19, 1952, records, "His will provides for distribution of his library among various public libraries." I also discover that "The Fine Library of Mark G. Holstein, Attorney at Law, New York City," was sold by Swann Galleries in 1953. I have yet to see its contents.

But I can hazard a guess that at Holstein's sale, if not earlier, Montgomery Evans II (1901-1954), the second owner of the book, acquired this copy. His bookplate is neatly placed under Holstein's. Montgomery Evans collected British author Arthur Machen with fervor, as Vincent Starrett records in his autobiography, *Born in a Bookshop*. I find references elsewhere to Evans' collection of Anglo-Irish writer Lord Dunsany. Evans knew Machen personally and wrangled letters and manuscript material from his favored authors. His ownership of this book was apparently a short-lived union, however, for Evans died in 1954, only a year after the Holstein auction. But the time he spent was memorable. In faint pencil on the rear pastedown Evans was moved to record and initial the following, "Read with great pleasure on Sundays in New York, May 1953." This simple note touched me. Could Newton have asked for a more concisely satisfying review?

From Evans the book found its way into the library of Abel Berland (1915-2010), a Chicago real estate magnate, who as a young Jewish man experienced discrimination and hardship, yet in Horatio Alger fortitude garnered a law degree and rose to the heights of business. Berland collected an exceptional library of English literature, incunabula, science, and philosophy. The highspots of this collection, including a fine set of the Four Folios of Shakespeare, were auctioned by Christies in October 2001 and brought $14,391,678. (The books would have certainly sold for even more had the events of 9/11 not happened shortly before the sale.) Yet Berland's collection contained many more books than his expensive rarities. By all accounts, he loved to deep-dive into the history and scholarship of his collection, and he was a voracious reader of biblio-books. This provided inspiration and gave him a sense of place in the long history of book collecting.

Berland was devoted to Chicago's The Caxton Club, a highly regarded organization of bibliophiles established in 1895. Berland served a term as president and recruited many new members. He was frequently featured in the Club's journal, the *Caxtonian*. Nicholas Basbanes profiled him in *A Gentle Madness* (1995). After his death, the April 2011 issue of the *Caxtonian* was dedicated to Berland and contained many reflections by people who knew him well. Fellow collector R. Eden Martin remembered Berland's friendship and guidance,

Abel Berland was Chicago's greatest book collector. Others have magnificent collections and are outstanding scholars in their fields. But Abel brought together wonderful books from a wide variety of literature and thought: copies of masterpieces of English literature . . . books from the early years of printing with movable type, and books of science and intellect. . . .

Abel would tell how as a child, after his parents had told him to turn out the light and go to sleep, he would read in bed with a special light. Or how, as a young man, he would bring home a book in its wrappings and place it outside a window in his house, so he could smuggle it in without having to provide an explanation. . . .

Abel introduced me to two prominent American dealers. He set up a lunch for me with a handful of Chicago's notable collectors. He regularly sent me copies of pages from auction catalogues. He spread his enthusiasm like a virus, which in a way it was. He helped me grow from an accumulator into a collector.

Robert Cotner, another close friend, recalled a particular visit, "The [library] room," Abel said that day, "is my library of the mind, the habitation of books literary, scientific, and historical that I consider important. I often read into the night and am stimulated by the great ideas of these remarkable people."

The ample bookplate of Abel Berland in Newton's *The Greatest Book in the World* largely covers—nay, overshadows—the earlier Holstein and Evans bookplates. It features a photograph captioned, "A Frank Lloyd Wright designed bridge as viewed from our library window." Heady stuff, but did Berland really read the book as he enjoyed the view? Did he spend time with it as Holstein and Evans had and draw biblio-nourishment from the contents? I wondered as much as I closely examined the book. The answer came on the rear pastedown, just below Montgomery Evans' faint penciled note, Berland had added his own, "Read in November 1968, and again in August 1981, and in April 97."

I then began my own re-reading that bright morning, holding the book as the others had before me, pausing occasionally to view our spring yard in bloom with fresh foliage courtesy of Nicole's efforts, the sharp sounds of birds and squirrels, and the focused efforts of our new cat, Ziggy, doing his best to hunt them, and realizing it was not unlike my own pursuit of books.

Dedicated to the memory of my friend and fellow bibliophile, Jerry Morris (1947-2022)

2022

❦ III ❦

The Quarto Club:
"A Few Harmless Bibliomaniacs"

CERTAINLY, cigars and pipes after. But first a meal of better fare, then adjourn to the private library. Oh yes, and drinks, pick your fashion. But overwhelmingly books, a few brought for show, but the focus on talk—lively talk—nothing perfunctory or mundane, for these bibliophiles are most comfortable in the details, the aura of the book itself bringing whatever one's pleasure. It is New York City, ca. 1926, and outside the world is roaring but within it is timeless, the same for the first bookmen long ago and the same now when I gather with my fellow bibliophiles. Today we admit all races, genders, and creeds but the fundamentals unite us.

This is a gathering of the Quarto Club, established in New York City by a small group of bibliophiles headed by lawyer Mark G. Holstein (1873-1952) who serves as president. You may recall meeting him in my essay "Three Ardent Bibliophiles and the Greatest Book in the World." He owned the copy now in my library of *The Greatest Book in the World* (1925), inscribed to him by the author A. Edward Newton, with a carbon of his cheeky reply to Newton tipped in (Newton had humorously disparaged lawyers.)

A biographical note on Holstein in *The Colophon: A Book Collector's Quarterly* begins, "Mark Holstein is president of the Quarto Club." The club's name is vaguely familiar to me. I research, and although I discover little secondary information about the club, I find three published volumes of papers (1927-1930) originally read by members at monthly club meetings. The club's effort to preserve them in book form saved the Quarto Club from almost certain historical oblivion.

The volumes are distinguished not only by the varied and interesting essays, but also by the involvement of many prominent printers. The first volume *Quarto Club Papers 1926-1927* (NY: 1927) was nicely printed by Club member Elmer Adler of the Pynson Printers in an edition of one hundred and ninety-five copies "hand set in Caslon and printed on mould made Glaslan paper." (Adler also established *The Colophon*.) The print run may have been an over-reach as we find that the second volume *Quarto Club Papers MCMXXVII—MCMXXVIII* (NY: 1929) was now limited to ninety-nine numbered copies. It is copyrighted by the Pynson Printers but printed by Daniel Berkeley Updike of the Merrymount Press in Boston. The third volume *Quarto Club Papers 1928-1929* (NY: 1930), was printed by William Edwin Rudge, another notable printer, with typography by Frederic Warde, and splits the difference with a print run of one hundred and forty copies. Then the major publications of the Club go silent, coinciding with the onset of the Great Depression.

The preface to *Quarto Club Papers 1926-1927* is illuminating. It reads,

> The Quarto Club was formed on the 17th of February, 1926. It is composed of a few harmless bibliomaniacs who meet once a month to talk about books and bookish things and to exchange ideas on all manners of literary subjects. There are no dues, no rules and the officers have no serious duties or enviable prerogatives. To stimulate discussion and to direct it along some well-defined channel, one of the members reads a paper at each meeting on some subject of his own choosing. During the first year of the Club's existence, eight papers were read and these are now collected and published in the present volume. The authors cherish no illusions about the quality of these essays but they have felt that here and there may be found some friendly reader who will peruse them with interest and perhaps discover something which may induce him to spend an agreeable hour in congenial company. It is however more than likely that those who wrote and those who listened to these papers will continue to remain their most sympathetic admirers.

An inspiration for the club and the atmosphere of the meetings is briefly recorded in the opening paragraph of the first printed paper in *Quarto Club Papers 1926-1927*, "Philip Quedalla" by Lois C. Levison, "The Quarto Club promises to become a very pleasant enterprise. It meets in an informal atmosphere of pipes and cigars, within book-lined walls. Its members are interested, as were the members of the delightful Saints and Sinners Club over which Eugene Field presided, that used to meet at McClurg's Bookshop, in the things that have to do with the writing and making of books."

The membership was small, befitting intimate gatherings for readings and discourse. The papers themselves are a delightful surprise. Between the three volumes, there are twenty-three contributions by thirteen members. I don't smoke a pipe or cigar, but I do enjoy a quality cocktail, and I had several over a few days as I read each volume cover to cover. These bibliophiles present a variety of topics linking books and authors to subjects ranging from literature and Americana to Arabia to prison to modern design; personal experiences to astute literary criticism; the chase of collecting to the re-discovery of forgotten authors. The papers vary somewhat in quality as one would expect from such a compilation, but all are well-written with a number rising to exceptional. The best-known paper is the first appearance of Newman Levy's "Alexander T. MacPherson," a minor classic spoof on book collecting that was reprinted several times under the title "Sandy MacPherson, Book Collector." This club may have been small, but members were talented, and their writings exceeded my expectations.

The Quarto Club appeared at first to have disappeared after these first three impressive volumes. But the club continued through the Great Depression until at least 1936 when a much more modestly produced but no less entertaining publication appeared: *How the Poets Celebrated the 10th Anniversary of the Quarto Club* (NY: Privately Printed, 1936). The foreword of this scarce work reads, in part: "The Quarto Club, which is composed of a small group of book-collectors who have been meeting monthly during the past ten years, recently celebrated its tenth anniversary. On that occasion, Mr. Mark Holstein, a member of the Club, read the following skit, which is now printed for the members and their friends."

It is a humorous romp, published in a petite 16mo pamphlet, containing supposed contributions by the likes of Shakespeare, Whitman, Wordsworth, Tennyson, Browning, and Omar Khayyam, each extolling the bibliophilic virtues and vices of the Quarto Club. Shakespeare's contribution will give the flavor. Entitled "A Book-Collector's Soliloquy," it begins,

> To buy or not buy: that is the question:
> Whether 'tis wiser, in these perilous times,
> To suffer the anguish of repressed desire,
> Or, throw discretion to the winds, and take
> A sporting chance. To buy,—possess,—
> To own the prize you have been searching for;
> And, by possession, rouse the envious spirit
> Of your fellow Quartos: 'tis a consummation
> Devoutly to be wished! To buy;—to buy;—
> Perchance get stuck; Ay, there's the rub!
> For in the world of books, unless you're wise,
> And really know your P's and Q's,
> You're apt to have the very hide
> Pealed off your mortal coil.

This was the last publication of the Quarto Club as far as I can ascertain. But I will seek out related items and further information as long as my mortal coil exists. The distinction and effort reflected in the Club's three publications of *Papers*, along with the overall quality of the contents, separates the Quarto Club from other efforts that left no written record. So does their relative longevity in maintaining monthly meetings during difficult economic times. The preface to the third volume of *Papers* provides a prescient conclusion, "These papers have at least pleased the members who prepared and read them and they now venture to offer them as their visiting-card to posterity."

Notes on Club Members

Many members were prominent in New York business and affairs. Some are well-known bookmen—collectors, printers, and publishers. Many are Jewish which adds a potential research angle as to the social nature/establishment of the Quarto Club.

Noted collector Mark Samuels Lasner wrote to me: "What you don't say, directly, but it's clear from the biographical details, is this was entirely a *Jewish* bibliophile group. My understanding, from someone who seemed to know what they were talking about, is the club was formed in part because Jews were not admitted as members of the WASP-only Walpole Society. If not the Walpole Society, perhaps some other collecting club. Not Grolier, which did not bar Jewish members. The publication program of Walpole and Quarto have some similarities; contributions by members and very nicely printed at considerable expense. It's also interesting that quite a few of the Quarto Club members had bookplates designed by Rockwell Kent."

Quarto Club Founders

Elmer Adler (1884-1962). Book Designer, collector, and graphic design educator. Founder of the Pynson Printers in NYC.

Mark G. Holstein, president (1873-1952). New York City lawyer and book collector.

Lois C. Levison (1890-1929). Harvard graduate, head of the commercial banking firm of Levison & Co., NYC. Committed suicide leaving note to wife that indicated depression issues; his lawyer said he'd been complaining of being ill. (NYT obituary).

Ralph E. Samuel (1892-1967). Investment banker. Established one of the first mutual funds in the United States in 1954. Involved in numerous Jewish philanthropies.

Amos Steinhardt (1886-1964). New York City. Brother of Maxwell Steinhardt.

Maxwell Steinhardt (1889-1977). New York City lawyer and book collector. President of the George Bernard Shaw Society of America. Active in various Jewish organizations.

Elected Subsequently

Bennett Cerf (1898-1971). American publisher, co-founder of Random House with fellow Quarto Club member, Donald Klopfer.

I. Edwin Goldwasser (1878-1974). New York Jewish-American teacher, principal, philanthropist, and businessman.

Ely J. Kahn (1884-1972). Commercial architect who designed numerous skyscrapers and residential buildings in New York City.

Jerome D. Kern (1885-1945). Composer of musical theatre and popular music; famous book collector.

Donald S. Klopfer (1902-1986). American publisher, co-founder of Random House with Bennett Cerf.

Newman Levy (1888-1966). New York City lawyer, poet, playwright and essayist.

Solomon Lowenstein (1877-1942). New York City Jewish-American rabbi, social worker, and philanthropist.

Victor S. Riesenfeld (1887-1964). New York City businessman, prominent in the Federation of Jewish Philanthropies of New York. His NYT obituary records he was a "capable painter and art collector ... He had an extensive collection of rare first editions, including Boswell's 'Life of Johnson.'"

Bruce Rogers (1870-1957). Famed book designer, typographer and type designer.

Alfred L. Rose (1886 -1981). New York City lawyer and former president of the Mount Sinai Hospital and Medical Center.

Howard J. Sachs.

Temple Scott (1864-1939). Rare bookman, publisher, author of many biblio and literary-related books / articles.

Alan Steyne.

John T. Winterich (1891-1970). Bibliophile, author, and collector. Wrote numerous books on books.

List of Quarto Club Papers from the
three volumes published 1927-1930.

Elmer Adler. "A Picture Story." 1926-7.
Elmer Adler. "An Adventure in Americana." 1928-29.
I. Edwin Goldwasser. "Hamlet: Act II, Scene 3, Line 191." 1926-27.
I. Edwin Goldwasser. "The Origin and Nature of the Literature of New England." 1927-28.
Mark G. Holstein. "Caveat Emptor." 1926-27.
Mark G. Holstein. "The Diversions of a Will Collector. A Dialogue." 1927-28.
Mark G. Holstein. "Some Famous Prison Books." 1928-29.
Ely J. Kahn. "Contemporary Design." 1927-28.
Lois C. Levison. "A Maker of Books." 1927-28.
Lois C. Levison. "Philip Guedalla." 1926-27.
Newman Levy. "Alexander T. MacPherson." 1927-28.
Solomon Lowenstein. "Chartres to Washington. The Virgin and the Dynamo." 1927-28.
Solomon Lowenstein. "Travels in Arabia Deserta." 1928-29.
Victor Riesenfeld. "Louis Becke." 1928-29.
Howard J. Sachs. "The Harrowing Contingencies of Human Experience. Some Reflections on Hardy." 1927-8.
Ralph E. Samuel. "The Bawdy Serving Man Disappears." 1926-27.
Ralph E. Samuel. "Lifting a Bit of Lamb." 1927-28.
Ralph E. Samuel. "The Well Known Name of a Little-Known Man." 1928-29.
Amos Steinhardt. "Something About Richard Jefferies." 1926-7.
Amos Steinhardt. "Number 30 Erewhon Place." 1928-29.
Maxwell Steinhardt. "An Appreciation of Mosher." 1926-27.
Maxwell Steinhardt. "A Devon Idyll." 1928-29.
Alan Steyne. "Norman Douglas." 1926-27.

2022

❖ IV ❖

Clubbing with the Book Fellows

I HAVEN'T done this much clubbing since college. But that is a far different story involving an energetic redhead, the thumping bass of dance music, and my free-form dancing skills that generated much laughter. Thankfully, no videos exist. But I digress. My recent excursion into the history of the Quarto Club of the 1920s-30s involved no such risk of injury or embarrassment. It was a pleasurable way to resurrect a nearly forgotten group of dedicated bibliophiles. But just as in those memorable college days, one clubbing experience was rarely enough and I was left wanting more. I pushed back further in time in my research, still New York City, but now the early 1880s. I recalled a book first spotted online years earlier, its importance not realized at the time. And thank the book gods it was still available!

I have on my desk now Frederick Locker's *London Lyrics* (NY: 1883) the first publication of The Book Fellows' Club (est. 1881), a tiny but influential wellspring that served as the genesis of the Grolier Club of New York, founded in 1884. Their club consisted of but three official members: the founder, Valentin[e] Blacque, and two biblio-friends William Loring Andrews and Alphonse Duprat. Their history is fragmentary and scattered but not lost. They left us two imprints and a story.

We begin with Adolph Growoll, indefatigable biblio-historian, who writes in *American Book Clubs* (1897), "In 1881 several book-lovers were in the habit of meeting at each other's houses, to compare notes and books, criticize each other's treasures and new purchases, to dine together and talk over their one hobby. Out of these gatherings grew The Book Fellows' Club. It was from the beginning, and remained until the end, a purely social and sociable organization. It had no constitution nor by-laws, nor any charter ... It was proposed to enlarge the club by the admission of many more members, among whom there seemed to be some whose qualifications for membership were open to doubt, and it was decided not to make such a formal affair of The Book Fellows' Club as would necessarily result from such an increase. This reluctance, in a measure, led to the formation of the Grolier Club. In the shadow of this larger, more completely-organized, and wealthier organization the 'Book Fellows' took a back seat—so far back, in fact, that they only continued to be sociable and published no more books."

More details are found in the earliest published account of the Book Fellows by Henri Pène du Bois (1858-1906), who knew the members personally. Pène du Bois, an American educated in France, was an ardent bibliophile, art critic, newspaper man, and flamboyant writer. The art and history of bookbinding was a particular interest. He is most remembered as the author of *Four Private Libraries of New-York* (1892), with one of the featured libraries being Valentine Blacque's. He also authored *American Book Bindings in the Library of Henry William Poor* (1903). (We will meet Mr. Poor later.) Pène du Bois' essay, "The Book Fellows' Club," appeared under the pseudonym of David Gamut in the September 8, 1889, *New York Times*. He writes,

> In 1883, when the lilacs were in bloom, the studious quarter of the Astor Library, Murray Hill, destined to be the most famous of patrician hills for its marvelous Grolier Club, Andrews, Avery, Hoe, and Ives Libraries, and every shop where two book fanciers meet, were conquered, invaded, and taken by a young bibliophilist as was Buda by Soliman in 1526. He did not commit this crime alone; he had accomplices; but they bore the impenetrable legend of The Book Fellows' Club, and as usually happens when imagination takes the place of reality, passed for an army larger than the famed one of Xerxes. The truth is stranger, for the truth is that Mr. Valentin Blacque, being possessed with much artistic discernment, an ardent love for books, and an impatient desire for more treasures than came of the Hotel Drouot and Sotheby's, one fine day invited to dinner Messrs. W. L. Andrews and A. Duprat, and there delivered a speech which is lost to the records of bibliomania, but may be re-

constructed in tenor, if not in exact diction, from the memory of its two auditors.

[Blacque] said that it would take longer than they could wait to found a club of a hundred book lovers without a publisher, bookseller, printer, or bookbinder, estimable people, but directly interested in the making of books. Then, that he was the founder and only member of a club called the Book Fellows, which at its first meeting made him President, as was his due; Treasurer, as was his penalty, and Secretary, executive, membership, and publication committees as was his pleasure. If they desired to become members he would pass upon their application at once. No initiation fee was required, but they were expected to share proportionately in the expense of the publication of the first book, which would be [Frederick] Locker's 'London Lyrics.' A month after came a portrait, a book-plate, and a poem in manuscript of Locker, and at the third dinner, two months later, the only officer of The Book Fellows' Club presented to its two members bills of the bookmakers for $560—public interest absolutely requires this indiscretion—in settlement whereof every one drew his check for $186.66 ... In 1884, the second publication of The Book Fellows' Club took the form of a square 12mo, bound temporarily, uncut, in blue cloth, entitled, 'Songs and Ballads by Edmund Clarence Stedman,' and illustrated by Bowlend. The entire edition of 100 copies was printed on Japan paper. . . .

Since then the Grolier Club has come and grown to one of the most influential clubs in the world; Mr. W. L. Andrews is the President; the Aldine has made a mark, and the prefatory poet [Henry C. Bunner] of 'Songs and Ballads' is one of its Directors ... but The Book Fellows' Club is not dormant. It sits at its library table, under a ceiling made of a gigantic Grolier binding, invokes the gods of India, Egypt, and other countries whose name it knows, to let it be modern, original, and American, plots to that end, and will make another conquest of all who dearly love the love of books, after its next dinner meeting.

Now *that* is a description, and it only gets more entertaining when Pène du Bois and Blacque rejoin us below. But first let us background the other two members.

William Loring Andrews (1837-1920) is the most well-known of the Book Fellows. His general fame as a collector and author of many privately printed biblio-books is not our topic now, so I'll limit his appearance to a relevant excerpt. Walter Gilliss writes in *Transactions of the Grolier Club* (1921),

> In any reference to the [Grolier] Club's early days, the first name that instinctively comes to mind is that of William Loring Andrews, our second president, whose name has always stood at the head of the list of Founders ... It was in his mind that there germinated the seed of the idea from which the [Grolier] Club sprang, and it was by him that the writer was told long ago that he was one of a little company of men, who, as early as the autumn of 1883, held meetings, having in mind the establishing of a Reading or Book Club ... It seems appropriate to record here that the little company of bibliophiles of which Mr. Andrews had been a member shortly before the founding of the 'Grolier,' and to which he often referred, was known as The Book Fellows' Club, and that it issued two books.

The second Book Fellows member Alphonse Duprat (1843?-1897), born in Holland, was a bibliophile, dealer, and publisher who started out as a Wall Street banker and spent much of his life in New York City. Duprat would publish several important biblio-books, notably the five volumes of *The Book-Lover's Almanac* (1893-1897), Pène du Bois' *Four Private Libraries of New-York* (1892), and O.A. Bierstadt's *The Library of Robert Hoe* (1895).

The last volume of Duprat's *The Book-Lover's Almanac* was announced in *The Critic* of May 8, 1897,

> The fifth volume of this truly artistic annual visitor lies before us. Its publication preceded by but a few months the death of its founder, Alphonse Duprat, who was happy nearly all his life, in that his profession was his avocation as well: for he was booklover by predilection and a bookseller and publisher by trade. Born in Amsterdam, Holland, only fifty-four years ago, Mr. Duprat originally came to this country to found a branch of his father's bank. His uncle had been a well-known collector of books and bric-a-brac. Mr. Duprat, soon after his arrival, entered the firm of Jay Cooke &

Co. as confidential man. Upon its failure he cast about for some agreeable occupation in keeping with his tastes and desires and entered into partnership with Mr. George J. Coombes as dealers in books. Subsequently he ran the business alone. His shop was a resort for book-lovers of the nicest tastes, and his publications were eagerly sought after by the wary collector. His taste in the fine art of book-making was most true, and both the collector and lover of the beautiful have lost a real enthusiast in his death, which took place on March 27.

Henri Pène du Bois writes of Duprat in the Dec. 8, 1895 *New York Times*,

> [He] was, until Pan visited Wall Street, a banker, an ardent book lover, the most active encourager of native artisans in furniture, pottery, bookmaking and bookbinding, rugs of Persia, magnificent tulips, unknown ivories, extraordinary books, and lived in an atmosphere of art, consulted in matters of taste, and regarded with reverence by experts and great collectors. When his bank failed and he became an invalid, motionless except in the expression of his eyes, he continued to be a Maecenas, not with money, but with ideas. He was one of the founders of The Book Fellows' Club, and the new spirit of book collecting inspired him as soon as it revealed itself to anybody. He presided over the development of private libraries of his friends with as much interest as if they were his own.

We'll finish this sketch of Alphonse Duprat by inviting him to speak to us first-hand via the February 10, 1900, *New York Times*,

> No reasoning or argument will deter the real book-lover from his charming pursuit. The love of books and their possession are to him pleasures that the man who reasons about their utilitarianism cannot feel, and his very argument is the best proof that he lacks the feu sacre [sacred fire] of the real book-lover.
>
> The collecting of books is pre-eminently the highest form of collecting, involving as it does more aesthetic pleasure than either the collecting of paintings, statuary, bric-a-brac, porcelains, or tapestry, against the folly of which no essays have ever been written. A book appeals to the intelligent collector not only by the art of the

author, be it prose or poetry, but also by the skill of the printer, the taste of the illustrator, and finally, by the art of the binder, and if to these are added the charm of provenance, or a dedication, or a fine ex-libris, you have a combination of pleasures not to be found in any other object within the domain of collectorship.

Finely stated, Mr. Duprat. You may be seated. Now we have come to The Book Fellows' Club founder, Valentin[e] Blacque (1851-1915), a New York City stockbroker, book collector, amateur artist, and musician. He was one of the early American collectors of contemporary French book design. Blacque's multiple interests reflect his varied background. He was born in France of an American mother from the prominent Mott family, and a Turkish father. He spent his early years in Paris. His father, Edouard Blacque, later became a Turkish diplomat stationed in Washington, D.C. Valentine Blacque's French roots stayed planted his entire life, permeating his avocations both bookish and otherwise, but he was primarily schooled in the United States, a graduate of Columbia University, and spent his adult years working on Wall Street in New York City before retiring in France. This theme of Wall Street work runs through the lives of many of these bookmen. An exploration for another time.

You'll recall Pène du Bois' early description of the Book Fellows gathering in a splendid room with a ceiling "made of a gigantic Grolier binding." A nice touch, surely metaphorical. But no, it was not! For Pène du Bois writes in *Four Private Libraries of New-York* this more lavish description of Valentine Blacque's library,

> The Trianon of a book-lover, coquettish as the Queen's. A room the ceiling of which, in red Morocco of the Levant, reproduces exactly the color, harmonious lines, and lyrical flight into azure of a wing of a book bound for Grolier. Tapestry of Beauvais; etchings of Rembrandt, Van Dyck, Visscher, Fortuny, and Lalanne; original drawings by Leloir, Du Maurier, Kate Greenaway, Blum, Chase, and Taylor; bookcases the crystal panes in the dark oak doors of which are lozenged ... At the table, carved in massive oak, on a Persian carpet of silk, in a casket of lapis-lazuli, pell-mell with the rubies, diamonds, sapphires, and emeralds, the treasure of the

> reliquary, a book of poems not to be described, illuminated by cherished artists with fugitive rays of sunlight, flame of eyes, and blushing pink of lips ... For there are no books in the cases not ardently loved; none prized because scarce although ugly; none admitted because necessary to a set or indispensable to a system. They are beautiful, and they have not a double elsewhere. All converge to the blue diamond book of poems of the reliquary in beauty and art. It is not an accomplishment that may be lightly given as an example to others. It is like drawing the bow of Ulysses, a feat of Ulysses impossible to our frail arms.

Pène du Bois might have been enjoying a wee bit of absinthe during writing time, but the imagination does run rampant contemplating *this* bookroom. It is a shame indeed that no photograph appears to survive of Mr. Blacque's library.

Pène du Bois was not the only one impressed. Famed French bibliophile Octave Uzanne visited New York City in 1893. Willa Silverman records in *The New Bibliopolis: French Book Collectors and the Culture of Print, 1880-1914* (2008),

> Uzanne found in the private libraries of Blacque and other American book collectors 'the best works of the present time, in extraordinary states, and bindings conceived in accordance with the exact principles that I have enunciated.' His stay in the United States convinced him that, far from being indifferent and unsophisticated as he had expected, American book lovers were in fact in many ways superior to their Parisian counterparts.

Glimpses of Blacque in the newspapers outline his character. The March 27, 1904 *New York Times* records,

> Vale Blacque ... is a well-known member of the Knickerbocker Club. He is quite a picturesque-looking personage on Fifth Avenue. He is very tall, and usually dresses in gray, and has the cast of countenance of the operatic Mephisto. But Mr. Blacque is one of the most genial of men. He is a collector of books and has one of the best selected libraries in town, and is an excellent musician and composer.

Another glimpse is found in the *New York Times* of March 18, 1906, after Blacque's retirement. He and his wife are spending much time in Paris:

> Valentine Blacque has been in Paris and Mrs. Blacque goes over to be with him. At present he is making much success with the binding of books, an art and fad much in vogue on the other side ... [he] was for years a well-known figure in New York society ... He composed a mass which was sung at the Church of St. Francis Xavier, and a number of songs. Mrs. Blacque was Miss Kate Read. Both she and her husband have a wonderful gift as raconteurs.

This raconteuring couple must have been fun to spend time with. One of their circles of friends was fellow Wall Street advisor Henry W. Poor and his wife. Poor (1844-1915) was a fully immersed bibliophile, one of the great book collectors of his time, well-funded and apparently persuasive. Coinciding roughly with Blacque's retirement in 1903, Poor purchased Blacque's Cabinet Library consisting of seventy-two carefully chosen volumes for the mighty sum of $25,000 [approximately $850,000 today]. Poor's enthusiasm over the purchase soon resulted in the publication of a *Catalogue of the "V[alentine]. A. B[lacque]." Collection in the Library of Henry W. Poor.* (1903). Fortunately for us, Blacque's letter to Poor about his collection is reproduced and gives insight into Blacque's approach to collecting and his sentimental leanings:

> New York, March 14, 1903
>
> My Dear Poor,
> I am tremendously flattered at the thought that you are to make a separate catalogue of my books. I have brought them together with a great deal of pleasure, have lived with them and loved them. I have endeavored from time to time to make them more interesting and valuable by adding documents, prints, autograph letters—when possible I have secured a volume which is unique. By a 'unique book' I

mean one which cannot under any circumstances be duplicated. The mere insertion of autograph letters or portraits does not seem to me enough to render a book worthy of the title—unique. But the original drawings of the illustrator of the book, or a series of drawings made especially for it and inserted must stamp it as the only one of its kind. Another feature which I have tried to carry out is the historical interest (to a book-lover) of the volume itself. It seems to me a decided attraction to a book that it has stood on the shelves of one of the bibliophile epicures of the time past. The men who were the patrons of the writers, printers and bookbinders, choose for themselves the best, and the knowledge that such a volume figured in their catalogue, bears on the fly leaf their book-plates and has since belonged to other collectors of note, marks it as being worth having ... It is a historical document with a title of nobility justly earned.

It is a pleasure to know that you will keep them together in one case, alongside of each other. I have kept them so long and so closely together that it seems to me as if they would mourn if separated. I love to cherish the fancy that my favorite authors with their Heroes and Heroines and the owners, too, of the books they cherished so fondly, left something of their personalities between the leaves and in the binding; and that at some quite midnight hour, they would walk out and flock together and talk matters over, discuss the failings and foibles of their present owner, the comforts or discomforts of their abiding place....

Yes, I am glad you will keep them together, thank you for that, and again for the compliment you have paid me.

Faithfully yours,
V.A.B.

Henry W. Poor was at the peak of his collecting when he purchased the Blacque books. However, Dickinson writes in *Dictionary of American Book Collectors*, "Poor's own financial career was marked with spectacular successes and equally spectacular failures ... In 1908, when Poor's financial structure collapsed, Arthur Swann of the Anderson

Auction Company prepared a sumptuous sale catalog calculated to pull large bids out of sensitive buyers ... a new collector, Henry E. Huntington, took away most of the prizes. With the irrepressible book dealer George D. Smith leading the way, Huntington managed to capture almost one-third of the Poor library."

Arthur Swann's (?) anonymous introduction to *Catalogue of the Library of Henry W. Poor Part V* (April 6-9th, 1909), highlights Blacque's books and explains the French-influenced idea of a Cabinet collection,

> A feature of the highest interest is a small but remarkable collection of Association and Illustrated Books originally formed by Valentine A. Blacque and by him transferred to Mr. Poor. There are only 72 titles in the collection, but each item challenges attention on account of its extreme rarity and value.
>
> To understand the collection properly, one must measure it by a standard of the leading French collectors, in whose ranks are found the most critical connoisseurs and perhaps the best judges. With them quality and not quantity is the desideratum. A small bookcase, 'Le Cabinet,' holding from fifty to one hundred and fifty volumes is the usual feature, in which are preserved the jewels of the collection, and other books of not so great importance are relegated to the shelves of the library, if the owner possesses one, though most men are content with 'Le Cabinet' alone. Baron Rothschild had a small cabinet holding one hundred and twenty volumes valued at more than half a million francs; Baron Pichon had one of the same size and nearly as valuable, as had also the Baron Portalis. Charles Nodier's Cabinet was composed wholly of the rarest and finest Elzevirs to be procured; and the Valentine Blacque collection is in the same category—indeed many of the books were secured at the dispersal of some of the Cabinets mentioned.

By the time of the Henry W. Poor auction, Blacque was happily retired in Paris, still buying a book or two that proved irresistible, and apparently trying his own hand at bookbinding. His life of books ended prematurely in 1915 amid World War I while helping others: "Blacque ... since the outbreak of the European war, had been assisting the American ambulance work in Paris, is dead at his home at Rue Pierre Charron. His illness [pneumonia], it was reported, was brought on by overwork among the war sufferers."

Blacque's carefully selected library represented the significant French influence among American bibliophiles of the period. But his cabinet collection was scattered involuntarily into the "vast azure" even before his death. Blacque's lasting legacy is the founding of The Book Fellows' Club, three sympatico bookmen dining at his home under a Grolier-esque ceiling, Blacque's Cabinet of Books close at hand, good talk among raconteurs, perhaps Blacque's wife joining in the exchange, one book, then two, produced by these Book Fellows, and a bigger moment springing forth and the Grolier Club soon formed.

Despite Blacque's prominence as a book collector and bibliophile over the following two decades (ca. 1884-1904), it remains unknown why he never became a member of the Grolier Club like his other two Book Fellows. History incomplete but not forgotten.

2022

❈ V ❈
Extreme Book Collecting

EXTREMISM is trending nowadays — weather, politics, sports, food portions. Even travel, an area with a historically wide latitude for adventure, is trending extreme. At least it appears so on those ubiquitous, addictive YouTube videos where an armchair traveler may lose themselves for hours. I'm readying for an actual trip to Colorado, real mountains, breath-taking vistas, cascading waters, and a modest bit of hiking and jeeping. But do I want to hang precariously over a plunging precipice, my life attached to a thin cable as I dangle in the air like a circus performer, my well-paid guide, conditioned as an Olympian, encouraging me, his (or her) can-do attitude quickly wearing thin like my cheap pair of hiking boots? Do I need this kind of adrenaline rush / confidence boost? You can guess the answer. For I'm a book collector and the betting odds find me seated at a craft brewery simply enjoying the mountain air, thumbing through an old-school travel guide, and admittedly googling to see if there are any bookstores close by.

Yet is book collecting really a staid and pleasant past-time, intellectually rewarding, but free of extremes compared to the whirl of the world we live in today? I have a one-word answer to the uninitiated—*bibliomania*. Physical demise may not be at stake, but in any other form book collecting ranks high on the extremism scale.

Take my own case, for example. I realize self-analysis is dangerous waters but let's wade in for a moment. I've been *told* by family and friends over the years that *perhaps* my book collecting has reached extreme levels *at times*. I read this as positive feedback, reflecting many years of effort and yes, obsessiveness (let's call it focus), in creating a collection that brings pride, joy, and an ever-elevating quest for storage space. I've surrounded myself with bibliophilic friends with the same traits, thus confirming it as the norm more than an extreme. But let me confess a few things. I admit in retrospect that a number of my escapades could be construed as *somewhat* extreme. There was the time I unexpectedly acquired fifty boxes of material at a book sale and I was, honestly, afraid to come home. This resulted in calling my *parents* and asking if I could stash the boxes temporarily at their house until I could muster some sort of excuse to my wife. I haven't lived that one down.

But any extremism on my part as a collector is quite modest on the larger scale. To bolster this statement, let me provide some examples.

Two English bibliophiles set a bar that has been providing cover for the rest of us for almost two centuries. Richard Heber (1773-1833) developed an inordinate taste for book collecting during his undergraduate years at Oxford, much to the dissatisfaction of his wealthy father who wished him to concentrate on more academic concerns. No matter, the bug had bitten and there was no cure. Heber inherited substantial money and land holdings upon the death of his father in 1804. This really unleashed him. Heber went on a rare book acquisition spree until his death that remains almost unmatched in the annals of the venerable avocation. He was not just an accumulator, but a highly skilled collector, and the quality and quantity of his library was astounding.

Heber, one of the founders of the Roxburghe Club, an exclusive English book collecting group, was a friend of Thomas Dibdin and inspired Dibdin's famous work *Bibliomania* first published in 1809. Heber is remembered for his remark, "No gentleman can be without three copies of a book, one for show, one for use, and one for borrowers." Upon Heber's death, he left *eight* houses in England and on the Continent overflowing with books. The auction of his collection took 216 days, flooding the rare book market, and providing opportunities for other notable bibliophiles to enhance their own libraries.

Sir Thomas Phillipps (1792-1872) was one of those bibliophiles. His bibliophilic flame burned even brighter than Heber's, and he acquired books and manuscripts at a pace unmatched by contemporaries, buying in bulk from dealers and bidding aggressively at auctions, seemingly always in debt to the booksellers as he dissipated his substantial wealth. His early goal was to own a copy of every book in the world. He did not achieve that, but it wasn't for lack of effort. His early manuscript holdings, often on vellum, numbered approximately 60,000 volumes, many being rare and important. Despite his irascible nature and single-minded focus, it must be admitted he saved unique items from possible destruction. His long-suffering wife and daughters were literally squeezed tighter and tighter into their home as acquisitions poured in. Sir Frederic Madden, keeper of manuscripts for the British Library, wrote of a visit,

> The house looks more miserable and dilapidated every time I visit it, and there is not a room now that is not crowded with large boxes full of manuscripts. The state of things is really inconceivable. Lady P is absent, and were I in her place, I would never return to so wretched an abode ... Every room is filled with heaps of papers, manuscripts, books, charters, packages & other things, lying in heaps under your feet, piled upon tables, beds, chairs, ladders etc. and in every room, piles of huge boxes, up to the ceiling, containing the more valuable volumes! It is quite sickening ... The windows of the house are never opened, and the close confined air & smell of the paper & manuscripts is almost unbearable.

Phillipps desired to convey his collection to the English nation, but negotiations broke down with the cantankerous bibliophile. After Phillipps' death, it took over 100 years to disperse the collection via private sales, auctions, and dealers.

These two classic biblio-extremists had the advantage of wealth to fund their book collecting. A modern-day example of extreme book collecting shows what can be accomplished when a single-minded bibliophile of modest means risks economic annihilation in the pursuit of his subject. Collector Roger Wendlick gives a first-hand account of his passion in *Shotgun on My Chest: Memoirs of a Lewis and Clark Book Collector* (2009). Wendlick's Horatio Alger story of collecting Lewis & Clark material over a quarter of a century began in 1980. It is the best memoir I've encountered of a book collector immersed in the world of rare books in the 1980s and 1990s with much detail about the book trade, booksellers, and fellow collectors.

Wendlick writes, quoting Lewis & Clark scholar James Ronda, "Books change lives." For Wendlick this certainly was the case. With only a high school education, construction foreman job, and a growing enthusiasm, he began collecting Lewis & Clark memorabilia related to the 1905 Portland World's Fair. This eventually evolved into the relentless pursuit of rare books related to Lewis & Clark, guided by early mentors and booksellers George Tweney and Preston McMann. With a goal to form the best Lewis & Clark collection in private hands, Wendlick juggled as many as eleven credit cards and multiple home refinances in a feat of precarious financing worthy of a Wall Street gambler, buying rarities where he found them with the particular help of dealers William Reese and Michael Ginsburg. After a decade-long binge, some luck, and growing knowledge, he was leveraged to the absolute hilt but had accomplished his goal. Serendipitously, Lewis & Clark College in Portland, Oregon bought the collection for $750,000, saving him from bankruptcy.

These examples of extreme collecting certainly caused stress at times for the participants and played havoc with loved ones and friends, but in the end their efforts nourished scholarship and preservation.

Yet let us finish with a cautionary tale. For extremism in any form—even bibliophilic—can foster chaos and conjure the shaded side of human nature.

Stephen Blumberg, the most notorious book thief in U.S. history, stole approximately 23,600 books from over 268 universities and institutions during a nearly two-decade spree during the 1970s-80s. Many were rare books, and the estimated value of the items exceeded five million dollars. He was eventually caught, convicted, and sentenced to prison. (Nicholas Basbanes profiled Blumberg in-depth in *A Gentle Madness*.) Blumberg had the skills of a cat burglar and used all sorts of deceptive schemes to access the rare book libraries. But a primary reason he eluded capture for so long was that he collected these books with no intention of selling them. In his twisted mind, he stole to preserve the books from perceived neglect and gather them for his personal library. He even removed bookplates representing the various pilfered institutions and saved them in an album to memorialize his sordid conquests. Blumberg stands out as a leading example of biblio-extremism taking a nefarious turn.

This writing has become a catharsis for me. I'm feeling better already. I've no urge to join the dark side of the Force, my wife still finds me palatable, there is food in the pantry and a roof overhead, and book space is getting tight but that is a relatively minor infraction. My biblio-extremism is well in check. Perhaps before we leave on our trip to Colorado, Nicole and I should go out for a fine send-off meal. But it is a passing thought—I order instead a good book that just appeared in one of my want matches. I'd been looking for a copy for a *long* time.

2022

⚜ VI ⚜

Use the Force: Barton W. Currie & John C. Eckel

SOMETIMES you just have to take matters into your own hands. Like Luke Skywalker in the original *Star Wars* when he blows up the Death Star using the Force to guide him.

This juxtaposition of science fiction and book hunting will become clear soon. It all started after a very late night of Ebay searching followed by a chaser of *Star Wars*. I grogged off in the recliner and didn't awake until morning when my wife Nicole rattled me from my slumber.

It was Saturday morning so no rush. I began breakfast and leisurely checked my email. There was a notification from Ebay about an item ending soon. My find from the night before was being offered at live auction by the National Book Auctions of Freeville, New York. The book was an inscribed copy of Barton Currie's *Fishers of Books* (1931), an autobiographical account of his collecting during the Roaring Twenties, and one of my favorite books. The cataloguer could not make out the name of the recipient because of Currie's rather difficult handwriting but was kind enough to post a photo of the inscription. I deciphered it and got that bookish tingle of excitement that stirs the dopamine levels. My natural high shot to nerve-jangling heights when I clicked on the auction link and found out the auction was already in process! The Currie lot would be coming up within the half hour.

I was disconcerted to say the least. The burnt smell of my now forgotten bagels lingered in the air. In my space fog the night before, I'd not only whiffed on the urgency of the situation but also forgotten to submit an absentee/snipe bid. The only option left was to bid manually online during the actual auction. I couldn't recall the last time

I'd bid at auction in some sort of live fashion—either in person, phone, or online. I'd grown soft and lazy utilizing snipe programs or absentee bids. A bead of sweat formed. I imagined a book hunting Darth Vader swooping in from who knows where to blast me out of the auction sky.

"Get a grip on yourself," I whispered. "This isn't like you're trying to knock down a Gutenberg Bible against Bill Gates."

So, I made my run through that metaphorical canyon of the Death Star, my targeting computer off, the thought of a last-minute internet crash pushed from my mind, and the Force strong as my lot came up and I opened the bid. Resistance was immediate from a Stormtrooping floor bidder. I kept firing away—click, click, click—until I had vaporized this unknown assailant and the book was mine!

"Not today, you bastard," I yelled, "Not today."

"Everything okay in there?" my wife said from the other room.

"All is very fine, very fine indeed."

A moment of silence—"What did you just buy?"

A week later what I bought was in hand. The presentation copy of *Fishers of Books* reads, "Inscribed for John C. Eckel, to whom I am indebted for some of the more fortunate adventures that have occurred in the course of my book hunting. Barton Currie, Nov. 11, [19]31."

John C. Eckel (1858-1943), noted Dickens bibliographer, collector, and fellow Philadelphian, was a close friend of Currie. Currie, inspired by Eckel, developed a strong Dickens collection and features it prominently in the book. Currie mentions Eckel and his writings numerous times in connection with Dickens and recommends his bibliography. Currie writes, "Even though you begin at the very bottom with a first edition (the book, not the parts) of *The Mystery of Edwin Drood*, hunt industriously until you discover a fine copy. Before making this modest purchase, buy a copy of *First Editions of Charles Dickens*, by John C. Eckel (London: 1913), and seek also for the Grolier Club *Catalogue of the Works of Charles Dickens*. Absorb all you can from these two valuable guides, then hit the trail" (p. 55).

Eckel's bibliography *First Editions of Charles Dickens*, first published in 1913, was revised in 1932. Eckel also wrote *Prime Pickwick in Parts*

(1928) with an introduction by A. Edward Newton, a good friend of both Eckel and Currie.

Eckel maintained regular contact with many members of the book trade including prominent Philadelphia dealers A.S.W. Rosenbach and Charles Sessler. He cited numerous other dealers and collectors for their help on both the first and revised editions of the bibliography. The majority of Eckel's library was sold by Anderson Galleries on Jan. 15-16, 1935, and scattered to the winds.

Eckel's position of prominence and respect in the rarified book world of his time makes this an important association copy: not only sentimental for the friendship it highlights but also for its broader appeal as an important artifact in the history of American book collecting.

Now back in the present, a number of my friends have recommended I see the Star Wars spin-off *Rogue One*. An excellent suggestion but you better believe I'll be checking any potential auction bids closely before heading to the movie theater.

Postscript:

On a chilly morning a few days after my blog post, I received an email from Richard Gresh. I didn't know Gresh but discovered that his mutual interest in Currie had led him to my blog. He collects the Cape Cod author Joseph C. Lincoln, a friend of Currie. Gresh was kind enough to notify me that there was a Currie letter to Eckel for sale on Ebay. (It turned out there were two letters.) The letters were listed as "buy it now" instead of at auction so I hadn't seen them.

I immediately swooped down like a Star Wars X-wing fighter plane at full throttle. Within a few moments both letters were mine. And what magnificent letters they are! Each referred directly to *Fishers of Books* and the signing of a copy for Eckel. The seller of the letters had nothing to do with the auction house where I got the book. The serendipity of this whole episode reinforced my belief in a benevolent Book Deity. In reality, it was a fellow collector generously sharing his knowledge with another. I have found such camaraderie to happen frequently, unless of course one has an interest in the same item. *Amor Librorum Nos Unit.*

Barton Currie's letter dated Oct. 12, 1931, reads in part, "Dear Mr. Eckel: Many thanks for your kind comments on my book [*Fishers of Books*]. I dropped in to [Morris] Parrish's twice to sign your copy but it was not there. I had a lot of fun writing the 'opus' but hardly thought it would have the spread of interest it seems to have developed. . . ." Currie writes again in a different vein on Oct. 28, 1931,

> You are a brave man to attempt to say anything good of my book after the reviews in the *Saturday Review of Literature* and *The Publisher's Weekly*. The latter calls it a *dangerous book*. The reviewer works for The Brick Row Bookshop and I have one or two veiled references as to how I was almost bilked by [Byrne] Hackett [proprietor of The Brick Row]. But the *Sat. Rev. of Lit.* goes out of its way to be nasty . . . Of course, I attacked the special pets of the review, and failed to include [Christopher] Morley as among the worth-while Americans to gather in, but I stated plainly enough that I reserved the right to collect whoever I damn pleased, and I never will include Morley . . . I'll get in to Parrish's in a day or so and write in your book.

So Currie did visit Parrish shortly after and inscribe the *Fishers* for Eckel now in my collection. Morris L. Parrish (1867-1944), the mutual friend of Currie and Eckel, was a fellow Philadelphian and famous book collector. Parrish focused on Victorian authors and was a condition fiend, allowing only the finest copies in their original state on his shelves. In doing so he established the legendary "Parrish condition." Parrish wrote a number of ground-breaking bibliographies of Victorian authors, the most famous being *Victorian Lady Novelists: George Eliot, Mrs. Gaskell, the Bronte Sisters, First Editions in the Library at Dormy House, Pine Valley, New Jersey, Described with Notes.* (1933), limited to 150 copies. His collection eventually went to Princeton University.

And serendipitously yet again—to end my story with a gilding of the edges—I happen to *already* own a copy of *Victorian Lady Novelists* inscribed appropriately by Parrish to Currie, "For 'Fishers of Books' from 'Victorian Lady Novelists,' 12th Sep. '33."

I am ready and willing for a sequel should it come. May the Force be with me.

2017

❖ VII ❖

The Love and Pursuit of Books Unites Us

IT'S A pleasant thought, isn't it? That the free-ranging, capitalistic mind, linchpin of our economy, pauses for a moment and rises to a larger cause. In this case, my book collection. Booksellers and book collectors share a symbiotic relationship. We are bound together by ecstatic moments and occasional torment. In the best of cases a fulfilling long-term union develops between us, in rare instances an acrimonious separation.

Most professional rare booksellers I've met tune in quickly to a serious collector's interests. I collect material about rare booksellers themselves, past and present, so this uncommon bypath usually is met with surprise and curiosity by those currently active in the trade. It is not often a bookseller gets a request for their *own* material—previous catalogues, perhaps a bibliography written by them, an essay contributed to a journal, and so on. I love this kind of stuff, and once we get through an awkward courtship period ("You really want my first catalogue, inscribed?") they often become enthusiastic supporters of my collection. And this is a good thing, for rare booksellers are always on the hunt.

I've acquired many items through the kindness and thoughtfulness of the rare booksellers. I don't see enough of these two traits mentioned in print. It's not always a merchant mentality of buy low / sell high. Placement of an item in the right home is a priority to many booksellers. Two of my recent acquisitions are good examples.

The first involves a long-sought desideratum of mine, the kind that nibbles annoyingly at your collecting subconscious for years, nay, decades in this instance. The book is William Reese's *Winnowers of the*

Past (1977), his Yale undergraduate thesis, published in an edition of 25 copies reproduced from the original typescript. The precocious Reese writes in *Winnowers* the most thorough history to date of the great nineteenth-century Americana collectors and dealers, with accounts of Obadiah Rich, Henry Stevens, James Lenox, John Carter Brown, and many others.

I already have two examples, but they are later copies, although not without merit. The first is a copy made ca. 1990 from the one in bibliographer Michael Winship's collection. He introduced the work to me when I took his bibliography class at the University of Texas. The reading of this work did much to stir my interest in American book hunting and was instrumental in sparking my collection.

The second copy reflects a special memory. While visiting Reese in 2015, I spotted a later, unbound copy housed next to his original. I asked if it might be available. He did not hesitate, and it passed directly into my hands. He was kind enough to add an inscription, "For Kurt Zimmerman, A later edition of my senior thesis at Yale, still useful in places! Bill Reese, Sept. 19, 2015, New Haven."

But these did not satiate my desire for one of the original twenty-five. Over the years, I've encountered only a single example for sale, but it bore no obvious provenance, and it sold before I could buy it. (I later found out Reese himself had purchased it!)

In November 2021, I receive an email from Nick Aretakis. Nick is the head of Americana at Reese Company, having taken over shortly after Reese's death in 2018. Big shoes to fill but Nick has done so admirably. Nick worked earlier in his career for Reese before going out on his own as an independent rare bookseller. His return to the Reese Company after Bill's death was a homecoming of sorts, albeit a solemn one. Nick and I have known each other for many years. We share common interests in bibliophilic history, the writings of collector and bibliographer Henry Wagner being one example. And we geek out over particularly juicy Wagner association copies as only two cognoscenti can.

But this email is on a different subject. It is short and succinct and makes me momentarily choke on my still warm blueberry muffin.

Nick writes, "I don't know if you've seen the recent list 'Occasional List R' issued by Dumont Maps and Books, but one of the items is the copy of Bill's 'Scholar of the House' paper, called 'Winnowers of the Past,' inscribed by Bill to Freddy White. Not sure if you have a copy of this already, but this one is a pretty great association copy. A scan of the relevant catalogue page is attached."

The muffin could wait. The recipient of the book, Fred White, Jr. (1946-1996), is one of Reese's earliest mentors and business partners. Reese writes in the preface to *Winnowers*, "Among many booksellers I am particularly indebted to Fred White, Jr. of Frontier America Corporation, Bryan, Texas."

I call Andre Dumont whose open shop Dumont Maps & Books of the West is in Santa Fe, New Mexico. I know of Dumont, having visited his store once years ago on a trip, but we don't have a personal relationship.

I introduce myself and cut to the chase, "Is the Reese still available?"

"No, I'm sorry that just sold."

I don't know if my deflation is audible (probably so) but Dumont sympathizes. I ask him out of curiosity where he'd gotten the book. He replies that he purchased it many years previously after Fred White's death and it has been in his reference collection ever since. We chat further about Reese, White, and bookselling. I establish my book collecting credentials.

"Did the book go to a dealer or private collector?" I ask.

"It went to a dealer."

A glimmer of hope, "Can you tell me who bought it?"

This is an appropriate question if the purchaser is a dealer. Probing about a private client is typically considered out-of-bounds.

Andre only hesitates briefly before he replies, "Andy Nettell bought it."

We finished our enjoyable conversation and you can guess who receives my next call. Nettell is not available but will return soon. His assistant takes my name and number.

Much like Andre Dumont, I know of Andy Nettell but have no

personal connection. Nettell also has an open shop, Back of Beyond Books, located in Moab, Utah. For over three decades it has been a fixture in Moab. It is a general shop with a specialization in Southwest material.

The much-anticipated return call from Andy comes and I'm fully focused, my senses heightened like the start of a job interview. I introduce myself and briefly explain the circumstances.

He replies with an ice-breaking laugh, "Oh, now you've put me in a tough spot." I take this as a good sign.

Andy explains he bought the book for himself having never read it and he is also an admirer of Bill Reese. I wax poetic about the book's attributes and describe even more poetically how much this particular copy would mean to me.

I hear him sigh, for he is a bookseller first and foremost, and a darn good one. "All right, I'll sell it to you. Once it gets here, I'd be glad to send it on."

No price is discussed. No details required besides an address.

Now I feel a little bad for Andy. The coin has flipped. Then a spark of inspiration on my part, "I'll make a copy of the *Winnowers* that Reese gave me and send it to you. I can also send you a copy of my own book *Rare Book Hunting* if you'd like."

He likes this idea very much and our deal is finalized.

When the book arrives, I savor opening it, taking my time as I cut away the mailing tape, resisting the Christmas morning urge of youth to rip and fling aside the packaging separating me from the prize. The book is nicely bound in quarter leather and marbled boards, certainly a presentation binding. It also has some related ephemera laid in. I wince as I unfold the invoice but find the price to be exactly what Dumont had originally asked for it. Kindness.

The second item is a proactive acquisition that unintentionally turns into a Holmesian chase across the Baskerville moor. My fellow collector, Douglas Adams, admonished me several years ago for not focusing enough on collecting my own contemporaries—collectors, dealers, rare book librarians, etc. active now. So, in that spirit, I acquire current items and have gotten fine inscriptions from notable book people, many I can call friends, or at least biblio-acquaintances.

I see the notice for the Grolier Club exhibition "Sherlock Holmes in 221 Objects: From the Collection of Glen S. Miranker." Glen and Cathy Miranker have gathered over four decades an astounding collection of material related to Sir Arthur Conan Doyle and Sherlock Holmes. Miranker, a computer scientist, started modestly enough both in collecting and employment and rose eventually to Apple's Chief Technology Officer, retiring in 2004. His collecting expenses and acumen rose as well. He has a bibliophilic spouse and that can make all the difference when rooms overflow and the book budget becomes busted.

I simply want an inscribed copy of the exhibition catalogue. I consider ordering a copy via the Grolier Club distributor, but it would be unsigned. It's often easier (and more fun) to acquire one from the collector directly with inscription included. I do not know Glen Miranker or his wife, but I do know rare bookseller Peter Stern, and Peter is not only a primary architect of the collection but also wrote an afterword to the catalogue. I reach out to Peter to see if he can facilitate and/or have any copies available. I want him to inscribe it as well. Peter is typically a quick responder to inquiries. His email style foreshadows the texting revolution—short, abbreviated and sometimes cryptic. (This is just the opposite of his in-person conversations when drinks are encouraged, and stories abound.) He provides Glen's email and writes to me, "It's an exceptional work. My contribution is minor. Glen and Cathy were responsible."

This help is appreciated, and I then email Glen Miranker, drop Peter's name, and wait to hear from him. In the meantime, I see a post that Nicholas Basbanes, author of *A Gentle Madness*, and many other books about books, is going to soon interview Miranker at the Grolier Club as part of the exhibition festivities. It's on Zoom, so a couple days later I settle in with a beverage and begin enjoying the exchange live. Then my lightbulb flickers—not in my room, the one in my head. I have Nick Basbanes' cell phone number; he and Glen are together *right now*; they are at the Grolier Club and there must be copies of the catalogue available onsite. I should reach out to Nick and see if he can snag me an inscribed copy. So, after a moment's hesitation I text Nick during the interview. (On reflection, this may have been an over-step.) I must admit when I sent the text, I watch and listen for any buzz or ding or reaction from Nick. None are forthcoming and indeed Nick has remembered to turn his phone off. He contacts me later and explains he had not seen my text in time, but he promises to reach out to Glen about my request.

Still no response from Miranker himself, and this is becoming more complicated than anticipated. At this point, Miranker has probably heard from Peter Stern and Nick Basbanes, as well as my email, and considers me some sort of book stalker. Shortly after the Basbanes interview, I make a random foray onto Facebook. (Who doesn't want to see what their old high school classmates have eaten for lunch or what fabulous trips they've taken recently?)

One Facebook friend is mighty collector and bookseller Otto Penzler, proprietor of The Mysterious Bookshop in New York City since 1979. Otto assembled over many decades one of the finest collections of mystery and detective fiction. At one time, his personal collection held over 60,000 volumes! The top 5,000 or so books were sold in a series of auctions. His book, *Mysterious Obsession: Memories of a Compulsive Collector* (2019) is a fascinating read.

Otto writes a post about Miranker's collection and Grolier Club exhibition and says that his bookshop has a few copies of the catalogue for sale. He also echoes a Peter Stern comment that the first printing of the catalogue is all but sold out. This spurs me to action: I better just buy a copy and figure out the inscription later. I email Otto that evening summarizing my pursuit. He replies: "Happy to get this inscribed for you. [Glen and I] are having dinner tonight . . . You are dogged and am glad you saw my Facebook post. I'm on Facebook very seldom and rarely offer anything for sale."

Otto's surprise reply of his upcoming dinner *that very evening* with Miranker ranks as one of my most serendipitous biblio-moments. The next day, Otto emails, "Hi Kurt—We had a great time, as we always do. Your inscribed copy is on the way. I told Glen that you'd been stalking him."

Indeed, Glen himself emails shortly after. I have trepidation about opening his message, but all is well. He writes, in part, "Any chance you will be in Oakland this weekend [for the ABAA book Fair]—I would like to have a whisky with you."

Alas, I would not be there, but I take a rain check that I intend to cash.

One last step remains. I box up the Miranker catalogue after receiving it from Otto and send it to Peter Stern. His inscription—certainly dashed off between selling exceptional books and perhaps taking a nap—makes me grin, "For Kurt—it is a rare occasion when I sign something other than a tax form or a check."

The practical result of all these twists, turns, and unexpected hurdles are two fine books on my shelves with stories to them. But much larger than that is my continuing appreciation of the rare book trade, sympaticos in the love of the book, and the kindness and thoughtfulness of a bevy of bookmen who could have easily deaccessioned my pursuits rather than help me.

2022

⁜ VIII ⁜

Dorothy Sloan: The Biblio-Rose of Texas

MY FIRST encounter with rare book dealer Dorothy Sloan (1943-2021) involved books of course, but also her garden of beautiful roses oddly juxtaposed with an open garage door revealing an overflow of scuba equipment. Dorothy loved to garden when not bookselling and her second husband Peter Oliver was a well-known scuba instructor at The University of Texas. The year was 1992 and Dorothy lived and worked at her house on the corner of 33rd and Duval Street in Austin, near the UT campus. The home built in 1919 was a spacious, stucco two story on a half-acre lot. It had been updated with some modern conveniences but retained much of its original charm. Custom bookcases were in almost every room. The natural, light wood finish of the bookcases blended harmoniously with the house as if they had been there from the beginning. But they had not. Dorothy had spent a small fortune on them. Her mighty reference collection, many thousands of volumes strong, filled much of the shelf space. Stock and consignments consumed the rest.

    I'd come to interview for a job. Dorothy was looking for a part-time cataloguer and assistant. She greeted me at the door with a smile and ushered me in, skipping any formalities, and asked if I wanted something to drink. She poured lemonade from a glass pitcher, and we sat down. She was about fifty years old at the time but looked ten years younger. Dorothy was medium tall, with blond hair highlighted with a hint of grey, an athletic, attractive figure, and she exuded an energy and restlessness that kept her from being seated for very long unless she was cataloging. I don't recall the details of our first conversation, but I do remember the spirit of it. Dorothy was witty and funny, and we bantered well together. In retrospect, I know she was testing me for compatibility. Dorothy tossed me some mildly off-colored humor and an occasional opinionated barb mixed in with questions about my book background. Being young and ignorant of her status as a rare book dealer, I showed no awe or adoration, just a keen interest. This first meeting must have satisfied her as I was invited back the next day to begin work.

Dorothy had recently acquired on consignment the massive stock of bookseller Dudley R. Dobie (1904-1982), cousin of famed Southwestern writer and personality, J. Frank Dobie. She was also cataloging the Texana collection of William H. Morrow, Jr. The books were overflowing the shelves, and Dorothy was basically a one-woman operation, typically with a single assistant (me at this point) along with help from her husband and family. I soon learned that Dorothy continually bit off more than she could chew in terms of volume of books. She had an innate drive for perfection in her cataloging descriptions combined with a strong desire to produce extremely high caliber catalogues. This regularly puts her behind schedule. This pattern would continue when she changed her focus from traditional book dealing to auctions. Some consignors were patient, some annoyed, and a few irate. Her letters / emails to consignors were often lengthy, all polished gems of explanation, excuse, flattery, and promises. They worked. To her credit, almost no one ever pulled a consignment, even when the sale was months, or years behind schedule. Success in the end overrode most objections.

On rare occasions an impatient consignor might show up unexpectedly in person. One memorable example happened shortly after I began working with her. William Morrow (1909-2002), who was in his early 80s at the time, came to check on the cataloging of his Texana collection, then about a year behind the original completion date. We all gathered in the living room. Morrow was old-school polite and quite a bookman himself, so I was fascinated with the introductory chat between him and Dorothy.

Morrow caught the collecting bug in 1929 after taking J. Frank Dobie's famous course "Guide to Life and Literature of the Southwest" while studying at the University of Texas-Austin. He went to law school and became an oil and gas attorney for Humble Oil. From the early 1930s he scoured the bookstores of Texas and beyond for rare and interesting Texana. He worked with notable rare book dealers such as Charles F. Heartman. Morrow recounted decades earlier trading a batch of items that cost him fifteen dollars in exchange for Heartman's unique issue of the famous Stephen F. Austin map of Texas (1834). The map was offered in Sloan's catalogue almost sixty years later for $30,000 and acquired by the University of Texas. Morrow was a living link to a bygone collecting era.

There was discussion of the Stephen F. Austin map, and comments by Morrow on the origin of a few of his books that he pointed out on the adjoining shelves. Then he suddenly asked if she was going to finish the catalogue of his books before he died. Nonplussed, Dorothy gently replied that she would. And she did, fortunate that bookmen often live long lives. Both the catalogue itself and the brisk sale of the books were beyond his expectations, and I recall his wide smile the last time we saw him. Recently, I bought a copy of the catalogue inscribed by Morrow to historian Harwood Hinton. It's the only copy I've seen that he signed. A rare Texana item, Zimmerman style.

Dorothy understood the mindset of a collector like Morrow very well, but she was fundamentally a dealer at heart. However, she tried her hand at collecting and assembled an extensive collection that focused on "Women in The Cattle Country," issued as her bookseller catalogue No. 3 under the same title (1986). She told me that she considered the experiment a success but collected no more after that. In the lead up to publication of the catalogue, Dorothy wrote about forming the collection in an essay published in the October 7, 1985 issue of *AB Bookman's Weekly*. She began,

> "Women in ranching? My dear, this certainly would be a new path in collecting, but three problems exist. First, I don't see why you would want to build a collection when there are only about 25 books on the subject. Secondly, most of the books are too recent to be of interest to a real collector. And finally, and most important, who cares even the least bit about such a subject?"

This summary dismissal by my dear departed mentor, Warren R. Howell, immediately became a personal challenge that led me to begin systematically collecting books on women in the cattle industry. Over a decade has passed since Warren and I had that conversation, and the collection has now grown to over 700 books, with a want list of about 75 as yet unlocated titles, plus the inevitable books of which I am not aware.

At the present time, my daughter, Julie, is preparing a catalogue of the collection which will be issued this year. It is gratifying to realize that despite Warren's initial negativity on the subject of women and ranching, over the years he became avidly interested in my collection and located for me some of the best and most unusual books in it.

What Dorothy loved and gathered without end was her reference books. She built a formidable reference library of approximately 8,000 volumes during a career that spanned over forty-five years. In flush times and lean times, she continually bought reference material. When I worked with Dorothy, I recall her husband Peter shaking his head over an unexpected invoice for another batch of reference books. Peter handled much of the finances and would gently admonish her to rein in spending. "But I *need* them," she would say. And that was the end of the discussion.

Dorothy began to hold auctions in the early 1990s and this gave her an excuse to expand her already large reference library. She reasoned (correctly) that an auctioneer would deal in a wider variety of material, including literature, fine press, science, medicine, *et al*. Although the internet eventually opened up further avenues of research, Dorothy understood that much knowledge was still found only in books and that an expansive reference library was indispensable.

The books were tools for her, and she was a master craftsman. She drew upon her library to catalog thousands of rare items, knowing not only what sources to access but also taking time to explore more obscure references. Her ability to utilize her reference material was exceptional. Dorothy was highly regarded for her detailed and accurate catalogue descriptions that remain an important source of information.

We were together day after day at her home, cataloging books and maps, her garden of roses just in view from a second story window. The experience was rewarding and intense. Dorothy's sense of humor could be wickedly funny, but she was all business when cataloging. Like a hummingbird, she would move quickly between bookcases, stopping for a moment to hover, pulling books to consult. Time was no object. The result of her efforts was an in-depth description with a focus on what made the book, map, or document important, enhancing both the historical and monetary value of many underappreciated items. I tried to keep up and learned much. But I would grow hungry, and it would be well past lunch hour. Food was a lower priority for Dorothy than for me. "I can make us some rice and beans," she would say, "that's a quick meal." I would grumble and eat, but after a number of these rice and bean specials I began to bring my own lunch.

Surprisingly, I learned that Dorothy was reluctant to express her own opinion in her catalogue descriptions. She structured them to be detailed and factual and always looked to quote or cite reference sources. They are models of their kind. She had many opportunities to interject her own thoughts about an item that would have taken the description to an even higher level. But she almost always deferred to the printed references. I noticed this right away working with her and encouraged her to make freer use of her knowledge — to no avail; her ways were set.

One day after another lean lunch she randomly said, "I should make you catalog a cereal box." I didn't know what to make of this, so I mumbled something. She laughed and tossed her hair back and explained that her reputation for being able to catalog anything had resulted in this early "assignment" by her male colleagues. She took their teasing in stride, but she was sensitive to being a woman in a predominately man's world of rare book dealing. This sparked memories. She shared her frustrations with me on the subject, but by the time I met her she had generally made peace with the occasional testosterone hijinks.

She did give me one example when the male-dominated world combined with her willingness to catalog difficult material certainly worked in her favor. When Johnny Jenkins acquired the Eberstadt stock in 1975 it was rightly hailed as a major coup. The best Western Americana and Texana material was sifted through and sold rather quickly. The Eberstadts had also specialized in Latin Americana, especially in their early bookselling career, and a great mass of Spanish language material awaited cataloging and re-discovery. It would be a complicated task. Dorothy was assigned the job as low woman on the totem pole. The Latin Americana turned out to contain many gems and Dorothy became an expert in the area. Through the cataloging and sale of this material she would meet numerous clients from the United States and Latin America. The rest of her career she acquired and sold many important Latin American items. One noted client was Mexican collector Roberto L. Mayer. I have before me an exhibition catalogue of Mayer's material *Mexico Ilustrado: Mapas, Planos, Grabados e Illustraciones de los Siglos XVI al XIX* (1994), inscribed, "For Dorothy with appreciation for helping me build up a collection and for your friendship, Roberto." Much of Mayer's extensive library was sold at auction in 2010.

Dorothy's rise to prominence as a rare book dealer was an improbable one. She was born in Houston in 1943. Marrying young, she eventually made her way to the University of Texas—Austin where she majored in American Studies. One of her professors was William Goetzman, historian and author of *Army Exploration in the American West, 1803-1863* (1959) among many other works. He encouraged her interest in books. In the early 1970s, Dorothy found her proverbial calling when she was hired by Warren Howell, proprietor of John Howell-Books in San Francisco. This famous shop on Post Street was founded by Warren's father, John Howell in 1912. Warren Howell served as a mentor to Sloan. "I was immediately thrown into the heady inside track on rare books, deals, dealers and clients," Sloan once said. "Every single day was exciting to me and I threw myself wholeheartedly into doing the best job I could."

I have Dorothy's annotated copy of the landmark John Howell—Books Catalogue 50, *California . . . The Library of Jennie Crocker Henderson* (1979) inscribed, "For Dorothy Sloan, My most apt student in the world of rare books. With love and affection from Warren R. Howell."

These heady years of book immersion were clouded by a complex personal life that pulled her in perhaps too many directions at once. She and her first husband divorced, and Dorothy returned to Texas in 1979, now an expert book woman and ready for a fresh start. She quickly found employment at The Jenkins Company in Austin, Texas. Johnny Jenkins was at the height of his biblio-stardom as a dealer in rare Texas material. He'd grown the business into one of the largest rare book operations in the country. It must have been quite a shock for Sloan to transition from the formal environment of Warren Howell's shop to the free-wheeling style of Johnny Jenkins. But Sloan once again dove in and soon played a significant role cataloging the wide-ranging material. She was responsible for a number of Jenkins catalogues including Nos. 140 & 146 *Latin Americana*, and No. 154 *Women* (1983). It is telling of the times that she is not credited within. She worked there for about five years before she went out on her own as a rare book dealer in 1984. I have Dorothy's working copies of Jenkins's influential *Basic Texas Books* (1983, 1988). She is acknowledged for her assistance and for reading the draft of the manuscript. The 1988 edition is inscribed, "For Dorothy Sloan, with high personal respect and regard—your genuine love and enthusiasm for the world of books has made all of us in the book world admire you. We miss having you at the Jenkins Company. John H. Jenkins, Publication Day."

Sloan's first catalogue under her name appeared in December 1984. It is dedicated to "the memory of Warren R. Howell, who taught me to love rare books." Designed by William Holman with a cover reproducing a Mexican-themed painting by her friend the artist Theresa Avini, it contains 213 books and maps for sale. The offerings are primarily related to Texas, California, ranching, Western exploration, Mexico, Latin America, and women's studies– a template of subjects that would dominate her catalogues and auctions as an independent bookseller. A few highlights included a Frederick Catherwood folio *Views of Ancient Monuments in Central America, Chiapas and Yucatan* (1844), a rare Hernán Cortés letter to the King and Queen of Spain,

Santa Anna's own copy of Suárez y Navarro's *Historia de México y del general Antonio López de Santa-Anna* . . . *1821 hasta 1848* (1850), the earliest known town plan map of any place in Texas (San Antonio, 1722), a second edition of Molina's *Vocabulario en lengua castellana y mexicana* (Mexico: 1571), an exceptional archive of Anaïs Nin letters, and many other less expensive but no less interesting items both well-known and newly resurrected through Sloan's research.

Between 1984 and the early 2000's, Sloan produced twelve numbered bookseller catalogues. This relatively modest number is deceptive as her Catalogue 10, *The Library of Dudley R. Dobie*, appeared in five parts over many years, including Part I, the *J. Frank Dobie Collection* (1993), Part III, *The Library and Work of Carl Hertzog* (2000), and Part IV in three volumes of the *Ranching Catalogue* through the letter "L". Her daughter Julie (Jasmine) was heavily involved in cataloging during the early years. After my relatively brief stint with Dorothy, Valerie Urban became her assistant. I have encouraged Valerie to record her own memories of the time.

Sloan's catalogues stand apart not only for their scholarly descriptions and content, but also for their high-quality production. Dorothy utilized the services of the Austin fine press printing community in the production of all her catalogues, notably David Holman of the Wind River Press, and W. Thomas Taylor. Eric Beggs did much of the photography.

Most of her bookseller catalogues contained items from various acquisitions. But single-owner collections offered in Catalogue 5 *The Library of Dr. Paul Burns* (1988) and Catalogue 11 *The Library of William H Morrow* (1994) set the stage for Sloan's transition into auctions.

Let's pause for a moment and explore an interesting sidelight. Amid growing her independent business, Sloan inadvertently ignited the greatest firestorm in Texas rare book dealing history. Her biblio-intuition about a suspect copy of the rare original printing of the Texas Declaration of Independence would have far reaching implications for her former boss Johnny Jenkins and the wider rare book world. W. Thomas Taylor tells the story in his well-known *Texfake* (1991). He begins,

The Relentless Pursuit of Rare Books

When Dorothy Sloan and William R. Holman approached the desk [at the University of Texas Barker Texas History Center] one morning in late June 1987, they were carrying a document that no doubt became the focus of attention. It was the original broadside printing of the Texas Declaration of Independence, which had been consigned to Sloan, a dealer in rare books, by a collector in Dallas. The collector wanted to sell the document; Sloan very much wanted to buy it. But responding to the sixth sense an experienced dealer develops when holding and examining a document, she was uneasy about it. She wanted to compare the collector's copy with the copy in the Barker Center's Vandale Collection, and she asked Bill Holman, a retired librarian with thirty years' experience with rare books, to accompany her. Holman is also a distinguished book designer and printer, with a keen eye for typographic nuance.

They carefully compared the two documents, and all seemed fine until Holman laid one copy on top of the other. At that moment he noticed that on the collector's copy the type area was perceptibly smaller—2 to 4 percent, he estimated. Combined with the fact that the printing of the collector's copy was noticeably fuzzy compared with the crisp blackness of the copy in the university's collection, this caused Holman to conclude that the collector's copy was probably a fake.

This discovery set off a chain reaction that eventually exposed numerous forgeries of rare Texas documents and their sales involving dealers Jenkins, Dorman David, auctioneer Bill Simpson, as well as other witting and unwitting participants. In the resulting fallout, both Sloan and Tom Taylor resigned from the Antiquarian Booksellers Association of America (ABAA), the national trade organization, unhappy with the lack of response to the scandal.

I'm fortunate to have Sloan's copy of *Texfake* in my collection. Taylor has inscribed it, "For Dorothy—a fellow-traveler from the beginning—now let's hope this is the end."

Her transition from bookseller to auction catalogues was the result of both frustration and accepting reality. Dorothy did not have enough working capital to buy and sell the rare material that she wanted. But consignment had worked well, albeit sporadically, with her regular catalogues. Auctions on the other hand were relatively clean cut—all or most of the items were sold in one go and then she could start over fresh. Also, the auction format appealed to consignors because of the nature of competitive bidding and possibly higher prices. From 1994 to 2016 she held twenty-four live auctions. Dorothy herself served as auctioneer of many of the sales. She was initially not comfortable in front of a group, and her early, somewhat halting style of auctioneering slowly evolved into a polished, relaxed presence.

In a major early coup, her second auction comprised the library of mighty California collector Henry H. Clifford (1910-1994). She had first met him at John Howell—Books. There is a photo in the *Los Angeles Times* of Dorothy sitting with and bidding for Henry Clifford at the third session of the famous Estelle Doheny sale in 1988. (Her heavily annotated Doheny auction catalogue recording Clifford's bids is preserved in my collection.) Sloan's three-part auction of Clifford's library was held from October 24-26, 1994, at the Biltmore Hotel, Los Angeles. The total for the three sales realized almost 2.1 million dollars (roughly 4.5 million in 2024). The first part contained Clifford's complete *Zamorano 80* collection based on the bibliography of the same name. The *Zamorano 80* publication (1948) identified important California books selected by a committee of the biblio-oriented Zamorano Club of Los Angeles. The Club is named after Augustin Zamorano (1798-1842), the first printer in California. Some of the books were relatively easy to acquire but many were scarce or rare. One famed item, *The Life and Adventures of Joaquin Murieta, the Celebrated California Bandit. By Yellow Bird* [John R. Ridge] (1854) is recorded in only two copies, one being the Cowan-Wagner-Streeter-Beinecke copy at Yale. The Clifford "Yellow Bird" sold for $69,000.

The auction catalogue itself mirrors the quality of her bookseller catalogues, finely printed and augmented with plates, some in color. The descriptions are extensive, and the preliminary material reprints an essay by Clifford himself on collecting, a biographical sketch, and a history of the Zamorano Club. Part II of the Clifford Collection, *California & the West*, was sold on Oct. 25, 1994, and Part III, *California Pictorial Letter Sheets*, Oct. 26, 1994. This last was issued in a fine press folio format of 275 copies, fully illustrated and produced and printed by W. Thomas Taylor and David Holman. It remains a key reference work.

For the next decade, Sloan averaged more than one major auction a year, bringing to market an exceptional array of rare books, maps, and documents from various consignors, all catalogued and marketed to Sloan standards. One major sale represented her special interest and expertise in cartography: Auction Ten, *Cartography and Views with an Emphasis on Texas and the West including the Collection of Mr. and Mrs. Stuart B. Gleichenhaus*, took place in Houston on March 2, 2001. This stunning, color-illustrated catalogue with an introduction by Robert S. Martin comprised 365 lots.

In 2003, she sold the Californiana collections of Daniel G. Volkmann, Jr. Volkmann had purchased the Henry Clifford copy of "Yellow Bird" and other items at the 1994 Clifford sale. Volkmann, with the acquisition of "Yellow Bird," achieved the collecting pantheon of assembling only the fourth complete set of the *Zamorano 80* (the others being Streeter, Beinecke, and Clifford.) This would be Sloan's second memorable auction involving the subject. She could have easily (and much less expensively) revised her Clifford *Zamorano 80* auction catalogue to sell the Volkmann collection. Her decision to do something special instead resulted in a biblio-masterpiece. She had two highly regarded California historians and bibliographers, Gary Kurutz and Michael Mathes, write lengthy new descriptions of the *Zamorano 80* items, updating the scholarly and historical importance of each and referencing new discoveries and insights. The result is a sale catalogue rarely matched for its combination of material, descriptions, information, and production value. It simultaneously became the definitive guide to the subject area.

As an interesting aside, the total realized for the Clifford *Zamorano 80* collection in 1994 was $603,106, and for Volkmann's collection almost ten years later $883,608. The "Yellow Bird" rose from $69,000 in 1994 to $86,250 in 2003. I rescued a VHS recording of the Volkmann auction from her dilapidated storage shed after her death. I had the VHS digitized. The recording was in only fair shape, but no matter.

For over two hours I relived the auction as she bantered with, cajoled, enlightened, and entertained an almost exclusively male crowd (including myself), drawing much laughter and most importantly, many bids.

After the Volkmann sale, she typically had a major auction once a year, often held to coincide with the West Coast ABAA Book Fair. The auctions occurred in various venues including a *Voyages & Travels* sale (Cat. 17) at Heritage Book Shop in Los Angeles in 2006, and later that year a sale of *Western Americana* (Cat. 19) to benefit the Buffalo Bill Historical Center in Cody, Wyoming, which took place at the Center itself. Other auctions were held in San Francisco, Austin, and Llano, Texas.

Her bookselling career after 2009 began to slow precipitously. In December 2009 she held a huge auction *Mostly Americana: Featuring High Spots of Texas, the West, Borderlands & Mexico* (Cat. 22) consisting of 576 lots. The catalogue itself resembles a phone book in size, all items catalogued to her exacting standards. It was dedicated to her son Anthony Sloan (1970-2009), who had died suddenly that May due to an undiscovered heart condition. She never quite recovered from this crushing blow. I attended the auction in person and immediately noticed that she had a somber cast that belied her spirited personality. This cast never fully dissipated. Two more auctions followed in 2013 and 2016 and another, long delayed, was in the works at the time of her death.

Dorothy's last years were beset with personal challenges. After her son's death, there was a withdrawal into a semi-reclusive life in a house on Lake Buchanan, near Austin, reflected in erratic behavior with those both close to her and the larger world, vividly recalled by recipients of puzzling, angry, combative emails and phone calls, until insidious dementia became apparent, and her keen mind fragmented. Ironically, as the dementia progressed, her final days were peaceful according to her daughter, the demons finally at rest. Unmoored from her beloved books, she mercifully did not live long. She died on March 14, 2021.

Dorothy Sloan's innate book sense often outpaced her business acumen. But this is not an uncommon occurrence in the rare book trade. When the chips were down, this book sense came through for her in the form of a private sale, a successful catalogue, or a resounding auction, all done her way, without compromise or cutting corners. Then she would exhale, savor the moment, tend to her roses, maybe give someone a piece of her mind, and begin again. She was undoubtedly one of the greatest rare book dealers of her generation.

Postscript:

In a sentimental mood after writing this essay, I reread my emails with Dorothy. We stayed in sporadic touch over the years. In 2015 she wrote to me, "I notice from time to time that you are still involved in the rare book world, and that is great. It is addictive, and for the most part not a problem (provided one has enough money). I do not have money and I never did! But oh, the books. I am satisfied."

2024

❋ IX ❋

McMurtry, Pass By

LARRY McMURTRY died recently, and both the writing world and the antiquarian book trade mourn his passing. McMurtry thought of himself as a bookseller as much as a writer, although that is not how he will generally be remembered. For he was a good and prolific author of fiction; a natural storyteller who also ventured successfully into history, screenplays, and insightful essays on many topics. I enjoy his essays the most. But I still have a tough time forgiving him for killing off Gus McCrae's pigs at the end of *Lonesome Dove*.

McMurtry scouted and sold used and rare books since his college days. These scouting adventures were loosely drawn upon, for example, in his novel *Cadillac Jack* about a rodeo cowboy turned antiques hunter. McMurtry had a predilection for buying whole book collections rather than cutting out the rarities of the herd and leaving the rest. He told me in 2012 he'd purchased the stock of twenty-six used/rare bookstores and over 200 private collections. So, he dealt mainly in quantities of better used books rather than focusing on rare ones, although he sold plenty of the latter over a long bookselling career. He would go on to establish used bookstores in Houston, Washington, D.C., and his hometown of Archer City, Texas. He eventually closed the Houston and Washington, D.C. stores and doubled down on the Archer City location. Here he filled a number of buildings he owned in the town square with over 300,000 books in all subjects. He may have had an American vision of Hay-on-Wye in mind. That didn't quite happen, but he did attract a steady stream of book hunters to the tiny north Texas town far from big city amenities.

I made my first book buying pilgrimage to Archer City in 2001. I arrived on a toasty August day, stopped at the Dairy Queen for an Oreo blizzard, and got situated in my room at the Lonesome Dove Inn. The Inn was owned by friends of McMurtry. They were used to having a variety of book hunters come through—in fact, I think book people were their primary guests. I still have my Lonesome Dove Inn tee shirt.

I wasted no time entering the main bookstore down the block from the town square. I was the only customer there. The rambling old building was packed with books and organized pretty well. This organization was greatly assisted by a couple of local women employees who kept shop. However, McMurtry was a hands-on bookseller and often in the store, even with the pull of his writing and its offshoots of signings, engagements, and general celebrity status. I could see McMurtry in the back room, a cavernous space, rapidly sorting and pricing huge stacks of book skyscrapers. By this time in his career, his occasionally cantankerous personality led to irritation when a fan showed up simply for an autograph.

I introduced myself and mentioned a couple of booksellers we both knew. His countenance changed and we had a pleasant discussion about Texas book people. I was anxious though to look at books. When I revealed my primary interest was books about books and bibliography, he stopped penciling prices and nodded approvingly.

"That's over in Building 4 across the square," he said. "Lots of stuff for you. I bought a whole group of bibliographic material from Brattle Books years ago, for example. There are also auction catalogues and pamphlets in Building 3."

Each of the auxiliary book buildings was boldly numbered on the facade for convenience. Before entering Building 4, I walked past the late nineteenth-century courthouse and Veterans Memorial in route, paused at the one stoplight downtown, and noticed the Royal Theatre made famous by *The Last Picture Show* in view just down the corner. I smelled barbecue cooking somewhere.

And what a sight I beheld when I entered the building! High ceilings and white shelves that stretched endlessly gave the place an airy feel. The building was well-lit and illuminated a rainbow of dust jackets and bindings. The bibliographic section was huge, encompassing a range of shelves at least thirty feet long. The whole Archer City complex was like that. Specialized subjects that would normally be represented in most stores by a few shelves of material were often found to have entire sections in Archer City — the result of decades of buying massive amounts of books—literally creating a bookstore of bookstores. Building 4 would be the site of the McMurtry book auction many years later.

An honest word must be said about the stock itself and McMurtry's pricing. Much of the collectible stock had been rode hard and put up wet. It was tired and picked over by professional bookslingers who had previously come into town and taken no prisoners. Many of the rarer books remaining were either overpriced or in poor condition. The general stock was aggressively priced as well, the result of a pre-internet mindset when uncommon books were harder to find. McMurtry was also known for the speed and bravado of pricing books. He rarely consulted price references and relied on his instincts. This could work to a buyer's advantage as we'll soon see, but often resulted in ranges of books that would require a needy retail buyer to magically appear in rural Texas to make a sale. But enough books were sold to keep things afloat, and if you didn't actually find as many books as you hoped on a visit to Archer City, you enjoyed the ambiance.

But for me on this occasion it was a unicorn moment. A cursory search of the biblio-section indicated it hadn't been scouted hard by a knowledgeable book hunter in recent memory. Over the length of a book hunter's career, there are rare opportunities when you find a bookstore for the first time with a section of books in your area of interest that yields great riches, much like discovering an unplundered Egyptian tomb. I began my bibliological dig, pulling each book and looking for interesting provenance and inscriptions, savoring the process. This took some time with the amount of material involved. It grew late in the day and my stomach growled, and my stacks of selected books soared.

Larry McMurtry's sudden presence startled me. I'd been so focused on hunting that I hadn't heard him enter. The setting sunlight from the wide store windows at his back cast a shadow of McMurtry across the floor, larger than life.

"We close soon," he said.

Before I could reply, he added, "But I'll just leave the building open for you. Stay as late as you want. Tell my friends at the Lonesome Dove Inn hello."

I stammered thank you and he smiled and left the building, in no hurry.

I didn't get around to eating until much later and I remained past midnight. It was quiet and dark outside except for the lights of an occasional passing car, the town square empty of people. It felt a little eerie being alone in the store, but I locked the door and continued the hunt. I'd found about 100 items that I wanted including a small stack of unpriced books. Within the unpriced stack was one gem I desired badly. It was a copy of Gabriel Well's *Gentle Reactions* (1923) inscribed to none other than Harry Houdini!

Gabriel Wells (1862-1946) was one of the foremost antiquarian booksellers of the early twentieth century, a rival of Rosenbach and George D. Smith; his clients included Huntington, Folger, Pforzheimer, Berg, J. K. Lilly, and many more. He was also a highly educated man, and according to Dickinson's *Dictionary of American Antiquarian Booksellers*, "spent three years at Harvard University, became a tutor in German and psychology and a protégé of the distinguished philosopher William James." His book *Gentle Reactions* was a collection of essays focusing on WWI and its aftermath.

Harry Houdini (1874-1926) needs no general introduction, but lesser known was his avocation as a book collector. He formed an extensive library on magic, spiritualism, and theatre. A contemporary account recorded that he had approximately 15,000 books and fifty thousand prints, along with literally tons of supplemental material. The Library of Congress acquired a substantial portion of his library after his death by bequest and the Harry Ransom Center at the University of Texas has significant holdings.

So, it was with trepidation the next morning that I carried the stack of unpriced books to the main store. McMurtry was not in yet, but I was told to leave the books and come back later. My intensive booking continued, and the hours passed like minutes. By the time I returned in the afternoon, McMurtry had priced and gone.

I sorted through the stack, saving the Wells-Houdini book for last. McMurtry's prices were haphazard. I put a few back as too much, others were priced within my reach. With the huge pile of already priced material I'd selected, my book budget was strained to bursting and choices had to be made.

Then, the Wells. I opened the cover slowly and kept a cool face as I stood near the bookshop employee, but my insides boiled over — $35 was freshly penciled by McMurtry on the front free endpaper above the inscription. An audible sigh and a slight smile.

I cannot think of another writer of his stature that was as dedicated a bookman. Yet his 2008 effort *Books: A Memoir* about his bookselling career was a disappointment when I first read it. The work felt rushed and unfocused, and I had higher expectations given McMurtry's writing ability and book experiences. But when he was persuaded to put his biblio-experiences on paper, they lost the verdant richness of immediacy, and certainly his full attention. I have eased into forgiveness about the book nowadays. McMurtry's life as a bookseller was as full and satisfying as his creative life. A life immersive and practical. For he always had more books to hunt, more to buy, more to price, and that gave him balance.

I settled up my bill and loaded the stacks of new acquisitions into my car. I stopped on the way out at the Sonic for a jalapeno cheeseburger, extra-large order of tots, and a fully sugared Dr. Pepper, grande size. Not my healthiest meal admittedly, but it tasted like true goodness in my euphoric state.

2021

✻ X ✻

Revolution, Redouté, and Why Collect Books?

The stray bullet shattered the hotel window narrowly missing the young American railroad engineer, Will Winterrowd. He would save it as a souvenir. It was February 1917 and Winterrowd was watching the plaza below from his hotel room in Petrograd (now called St. Petersburg). He recalled the chaos he witnessed "a hooligan with an officer's sword belted over his overcoat, a rifle in one hand and a revolver in the other; a small boy with a large butcher's knife, a soldier with an officer's sword in one hand, without the scabbard, and a bayonet in the other hand; another with a revolver in one hand and a tram-railer cleaner in the other; a student with two rifles and a band of machine-gun bullets around his waist. All were singing, shouting, and repeatedly firing off their weapons into the air."

The Russian Revolution had begun and what started out as relatively peaceful protests and strikes soon devolved into escalating violence. Winterrowd was Assistant Chief Mechanical Engineer of the Canadian Pacific Railway and traveling with George Bury, Vice President of the railway, having been invited to Russia as part of a commission to advise the government on modernizing their outdated railway system. Winterrowd recounted,

> We witnessed street fighting in Petrograd of a bloody nature. The first few days passed quietly enough, as far as bloodshed was concerned, but on the fourth day mobs gathering in the central part of the city were attacked by the combined forces of the police and of Cossacks and infantry hastily sent into the city to protect imperialism against the gathering storm.
>
> These attacks continued until the soldiery, disgusted at the sav-

age brutality of the police, deserted to the revolutionary cause. The fighting then developed into a battle between soldiers and civilians and well-armed police, who, before their capture, did deadly work with machine guns mounted on tops of buildings.

Mr. Bury and myself spent seven days on rations of black bread and coffee. During the height of the revolution all stores, restaurants, theatres and cafes were closed. No street cars ran and a large part of the city was unlighted at night. It was a mighty relief to us when, on March 16 [1917], Czar Nicholas abdicated and brought the revolution to a close.

Winterrowd and Bury escaped Petrograd shaken but unscathed, hopeful the new Communist provisional government would follow their recommendations for modernizing the railroads. His initial optimism of a more democratic system resulting from the overthrow of Imperialist Russia did not come to fruition. Winterrowd's account of his adventure was published shortly after their return home in *Leslie's Weekly*. But Winterrowd had another adventure awaiting him—one that didn't involve gunfire, revolution, or possible death—but nonetheless, changed his life. He became a book collector.

My introduction to Winterrowd is recent. Last week I acquired a copy of his pamphlet *Why Collect Books? To the Prospective Competitor in the Purdue University Book Collecting Contest* (1937), this example is inscribed to famous Chicago bookseller Walter M. Hill. I began to research Winterrowd's life and discovered his story about the harrowing trip to Russia. The next day I was in a high-rise condo in Houston, enjoying the panoramic views, thinking about Winterrowd as I appraised a group of interesting books for a client. None were from Winterrowd's library, mind you—nothing that serendipitous—yet another twist was added that would pull me back to the Russian Revolution. But first let's explore Mr. Winterrowd's essay *Why Collect Books?*

Winterrowd graduated from Purdue University in 1907 and became a stalwart alumnus, heavily involved in raising awareness and support for his alma mater. One activity that dovetailed with his personal interests was the sponsorship of a book collecting contest for students. Winterrowd's own book collecting was inspired by A. Edward Newton. He writes, "I became imbued with [the collecting spirit] many years ago after reading Newton's *The Amenities of Book Collecting* (1918). That book fired an interest in me that is unquenchable. In addition, it stimulated my interest in good books, books that are veritable treasure houses of wisdom, knowledge, inspiration, and interest. Read Newton's book if you dare. It will make you understand what I mean. It is in the University Library; at least I hope it is."

Winterrowd and Newton eventually became good friends. Winterrowd would write a sympathetic and touching introduction to the second sale volume of the A. Edward Newton auction catalogue (1941), recalling his visits with Newton at his Oak Knoll home. Winterrowd's sponsorship of the Purdue book collecting contest was certainly inspired by Newton. Newton himself was involved in sponsoring an earlier contest at Swarthmore College in the 1920s-30s.

Winterrowd explains in *Why Collect Books?* that he gathered a solid library related to engineering as his early career progressed. Then he writes,

> I made the important discovery that many successful men have culture. When I made that discovery I changed my plan of reading and study to include cultural subjects. It was one of the wisest things I ever did. Not only has it helped me acquire much valuable knowledge, but it has helped me in dealings with my fellowmen. In addition it has brought to me a joy and interest all its own, particularly in the field of good books. God help the man or woman who does not know that in good books one has the most constant friends in life! Good books are always at one's beck and call ready to afford knowledge, comfort, pleasure, and inspiration ... [Collecting] often helps you make good friends, and good friends in life are one of man's most valuable assets....
>
> I established the book-collecting award at Purdue with the hope that I might stimulate you to discover, before you pass beyond the campus gates, something that will be of untold value to you in after years ... May I tell you that in book collecting it is not quantity that counts? It is quality. I emphasize that point in order that you will not think you must own a whole room full of books in order to be a well-qualified competitor.

Revolution, Redouté, and Why Collect Books?

What books should you collect? Well, I am not going to give you a list. Part of the fun and pleasure you have in store for you is in appraising the value of books you read and add to your collection. Some technical books if you wish, but may I suggest that you do not overlook the fields of Biography, History, Art, Economics, Religion, and Literature. Why not have a book chat with the University Librarian, or some of your interested instructors? They can give you valuable suggestions and you will learn at once that knowledge of able men is most interesting, inspirational, and desirable.

And if you do not win the prize? Well, I hope that you do win it, not so much for the financial reward but for the knowledge and happiness it will bring you. If your collection does not win an award, may I assure you that in the years to come you will look back upon your initial book-collecting efforts with an ever-growing knowledge and appreciation of the fact that no prize could ever have been compensated you for what you have gained through the ... love of good books.

I have found little information about the Winterrowd sponsored contest—who entered, who won, did he continue to even sponsor a contest? And frankly, did many even read his pamphlet? But the seed was planted at the university, and later references show that in the 1960s Purdue had a vibrant annual collegiate book collecting contest sponsored by another collector, James Thielman, "noted Indiana book collector from Terre Haute ... Besides the local award from Thielman, the winner in the undergraduate division will automatically enter national competition for a $1,000 prize, the Amy Loveman National Award." A $1,000 award in 1965 was serious money. A brief research detour revealed that Loveman (1881-1955) was a founding editor of the Saturday Review of Literature and heavily involved in the Book-of-the-Month Club. The national award was created by the Women's National Book Association, together with the Saturday Review and Book-of-the-Month Club to honor the late Amy Loveman. The award was first given in 1962 for a collection on "Ancient and Primitive Man." About 100 submissions a year were received until the award was discontinued in the early 1970s because of high administrative costs.

All this new biblio-information was swirling haphazardly in my brain the next day when I began my book appraisal in Houston. I hefted onto the dining room table the large paper, folio copy in contemporary red morocco of Pierre-Joseph Redouté's *Choix des plus Belles Fleurs* (Paris: L'Auteur, et al., 1829), a magnificent work so rare in this format that very few have had the opportunity to even see one. The book contains 144 botanical plates, color-printed and retouched by hand, possibly by Redouté himself. Redouté (1759-1840), a Belgian painter famous for his watercolors of roses and other flowers, is generally regarded as the greatest botanical illustrator of all time. The owner had inherited the Redouté book along with a small selection of other illustrated books from a long-deceased Swiss aunt who came from a family of European book and print collectors. The books were purchased in the 1930s-60s. I recognized quickly that this cache of items had been collected with the developed taste of advanced collectors acquiring not just a copy, but the right copy. Most of the collection had been gifted to the Swiss National Library decades earlier. These were odds and ends retained by the family. But what odds and ends! Other fabulous items included a 1635 Blaeu Atlas, a choice copy in contemporary French red morocco of *La Fontaine's Fables Choisies* (1755-1759), and a signed set of Marc Chagall's illustrated edition of *Daphnis & Chloé* (1961).

As I examined the Redouté, I immediately noticed an armorial bookplate with the motto *Ferram, opes patriae, sibi nomen* ("I shall win riches for the fatherland, and for myself, a name"). I also found a small library stamp with Russian markings on the title page. Great books often have an interesting thread of ownership, sometimes straight, but often tangled.

That evening I identified the bookplate: Earl Grigory Alexandrovich Stroganov (1770-1857)—a Russian diplomat, an ambassador to Spain, Sweden, Turkey, a prominent state and public official in the epoch of Alexander I and Nikolas I, an official representative of Russia at the coronation of Queen Victoria in 1838, and a friend and relative of the Russian poet Aleksandr Pushkin.

The library stamp was more challenging. I enlisted the help of my friend and fellow collector William Butler. Butler, a distinguished law

Revolution, Redouté, and Why Collect Books?

professor at Penn State, has a particular expertise in Russian. He combines this with a passion for book collecting and bookplate collecting. After a couple of email exchanges, the mystery was solved. The stamp was of the Imperial University of Tomsk, the first institution of higher education in Siberia. With this key in hand, the door opened to the rest of the story and once again the Russian Revolution became vivid. The collector Stroganov, a cosmopolitan man who spoke many languages, had a wide variety of interests. He gathered a huge, valuable library with a focus on French books, both historical and illustrative, but he also acquired works in Russian, English, German, and Spanish. After his death, his sons gifted his 22,000 (!) volume library to the Imperial University of Tomsk. So, it appeared that the Redouté had either been deaccessioned by the library at one point or stolen—but the answer was more complicated.

As Winterrowd dodged bullets and witnessed first-hand the beginnings of the Revolution in 1917 in St. Petersburg, Stroganov's books sat comfortably ensconced at Tomsk in Siberia, apparently out of harm's way. But it did not last. By the 1920s, the Soviets were strapped for cash and began to sell cultural treasures from museums and libraries. Tomsk's remote location at first shielded the library from depredation. But in April 1930 a special government Sovnarkom "shock brigade" arrived in Tomsk from Moscow. The primary task of the brigade was to identify books in the library—principally in the Stroganov Collection—that might be of value to the Western book market and to designate these rare volumes for withdrawal. Over the objections of the local university community, eight hundred and thirty rare items were selected and transferred to the Soviet regime and eventually sold, among them the Redouté *Choix des plus Belles Fleurs*.

Winterrowd would not have been aware of these forced deaccessions as the details were kept secret well into the 1980s and beyond. His last published writing was the introductory essay to A. Edward Newton's 1941 auction catalogue. It was "more personal than bibliographical but I have spoken from my heart." This sentimental railroad engineer did not outlive his mentor Newton by much. I was saddened to learn that in December 1941, at the age of 57, Winterrowd was driving home and was involved in an accident, colliding with a trailer-truck. At first recovery looked promising, but a week later he suddenly collapsed and died.

What began for me as a rather straightforward look at William Winterrowd's pamphlet *Why Collect Books?* expanded into an intriguing saga of friendship, revolution, upheaval, and the mercurial nature of a book's passage through history. During my search for the elusive Winterrowd and the provenance of the Redouté, I found not only my own answer to Winterrowd's question, but a reminder of the durable power of a personal library.

2021

❋ XI ❋

Camaraderie and Competition: The Big Five of Abraham Lincoln Collectors

AN unsuccessful bid on a group of Lincoln biblio-books from the collection of Louise Taper leads me here. That and a rediscovery last week among a group of books I acquired shortly before moving my library three years ago. Both instances germinated an idea into an essay—the early collecting of printed material on the Great Emancipator.

Works by and about Abraham Lincoln, called broadly "Lincolniana," have been avidly sought by collectors since the Civil War. Lincoln's life from homespun roots to statesman to martyr has drawn interest from every conceivable angle. Publications abound. As early as 1910 there were already more than 125 separate published biographies.

Often when I am doing biblio-research, I'm the first to clear a path (or follow one much overgrown). I soon discovered this was not the case with Lincoln. The early collecting of Lincoln has been documented directly by collectors such as Daniel Fish (1848-1924) and Joseph Oakleaf (1858-1930), and in secondary essays, most notably J. L. McCorison's "The Great Lincoln Collections and What Came of Them" (1947).

So, a brief overview is at hand without a lot of hacking through the underbrush. This will be interwoven with my own story of a terrific find. The early groundbreakers in collecting Lincoln material included Andrew Boyd and Charles Henry Hart. Boyd and Hart compiled the first major bibliographic work, *Memorial Lincoln Bibliography* (1870). These men and others like William Herndon, Lincoln's law partner and biographer, laid the foundation for subsequent major collectors to follow. The next group of enthusiasts, labeled the "Big Five," each built fabulous collections during the 1890s-1920s. Despite the fierce competition among them, they all interacted as friends and colleagues, each to varying degrees willing to help the others and share new discoveries.

McCorison writes in his essay,

> Following Herndon and Boyd, the collecting of Lincolniana entered upon its most exciting period—a period dominated by the so-called 'Big Five.' This period was to witness the more careful definition of what comprised Lincolniana, the rise of specialized collecting, and the creation of those monumental accumulations which have since enriched lesser labors and permanently influenced all subsequent collecting. It is improbable that any one of the collections brought into being by Major William Harrison Lambert of Philadelphia; Judd Stewart of Plainfield, New Jersey; Charles Woodberry McLellan of New York City and Champlain, New York; Daniel Fish of Minneapolis, and Joseph Benjamin Oakleaf of Moline, Illinois could today be duplicated, admitting for the moment that such an endeavor would be desirable. These men were contemporaries and helpful competitors. They were also individualists and each assiduously followed his own bent. Individually and collectively the achievement of these men is so phenomenal that present day collectors look back upon it with wonder and wistful envy. Together, they dominated the field of Lincolniana, almost but not quite—to the exclusion of serious outside rivalry.

Joseph Oakleaf explains in the introduction to his *Lincoln Bibliography* (1925) just how this unusual confluence of like-minded collectors interacted: "We five concluded to, and did, establish a 'Clearing House,' with Mr. Stewart acting as the corresponding secretary, and new finds by any of us would be reported to Mr. Stewart and Mr. Fish. Thus we knew what each one was adding to his collection, and helped each other in various ways, in order to make the collections as complete as possible."

I know of no other instance where such a significant group of major private collectors cooperated in similar fashion—a truly extraordinary circumstance in the annals of American book collecting.

The five collections would all go on to enrich Lincoln scholarship and later collectors. The Lambert and Burton collections were dispersed by auction; the McLellan collection was purchased by John D. Rockefeller, Jr., and presented to Brown University, Providence, Rhode Island; the Stewart collection was purchased by Henry E. Huntington for his library; the Fish collection was acquired by the Lincoln Historical Research Foundation at Fort Wayne, Indiana; and the Oakleaf collection found a home at the Lilly Library, Indiana University.

Daniel Fish and Joseph Oakleaf were the most bibliographical of the group. Fish's *Lincoln Literature: A Bibliographical Account of Books and Pamphlets Relating to Abraham Lincoln* (1900, revised, 1906) was a groundbreaking work, influencing Lincoln collecting and bibliography more than any other early publication. Fish established definitions and standards for classifying Lincolniana.

Fish writes in "Lincoln Collections and Lincoln Bibliography" (1908), "Mine is a list of books and pamphlets (and no others) whose origin is traceable directly and exclusively to the life, acts, sayings and death of the man. Variations from the aim are blemishes. Failure to attain completeness in its execution, though unavoidable I suppose, is deeply regretted." McCorison adds,

> Fish was a Lincoln scholar of the first rank and his eminence was everywhere recognized. In his compilation of Lincoln books and pamphlets 'every reasonable effort' was 'made to exhaust the field ... The leading collections of Lincolniana' were freely opened to him. 'The chief libraries of both Europe and America were visited, 'extensive correspondence . . . carried on, and scores of catalogues examined.' His bibliography is therefore another benchmark of permanent significance and ranks among the three or four great works of its kind.

Daniel Fish was a busy family man, Minneapolis lawyer, and judge, active in numerous organizations, so it is impressive he found the time to heavily indulge his collecting and bibliographic passion. Here's how he explains the beginnings of his collecting:

The Relentless Pursuit of Rare Books

On my way home from the war in the summer of [18]65, while yet in the first half of my eighteenth year, I bought my first book, the very first that was paid for out of my personal earnings not a school book or else a dime novel. It was 'The President's Words,' compiled from Lincoln's writings and speeches by Edward Everett Hale, now venerable and beloved. If that volume had not been lost prior to 1892, it would have constituted at the beginning of that year my entire stock of Lincolniana. It was then that I was asked by a society of young people to address them upon a topic of my own choosing. The occasion seemed appropriate for a popular lecture on the revered Commander-in-Chief under whom I had served for a brief term as a boy-soldier of the Union. In preparation for that task I read two or three of the leading biographies. Whether my hearers were interested or not, my own enjoyment of the study was intense. Memory recalled the days when Lincoln's influence, surviving all the vicissitudes of war and politics, had become supreme, and, most vividly of all, the terrible anger of the troops when the news of his murder came to us in the camps of North Carolina. The sources of his power over men appealed to me as even more interesting than the mere events of the great struggle through which he had led us. I afterward bought such books about him as were readily accessible, and out of this came the desire to possess an adequate library on the subject. For a considerable time, however, I sought only biographies, of which there was an astonishing number. Often am I reminded of a first visit to the shop of that delightful old man Charles Woodward, in Nassau Street, New York, and his vain offer at a few cents a piece of a hundred or more of the pamphlet sermons and eulogies; treasures which have since cost me as many dollars. Needless to say in this presence, the craving for a complete Lincoln library became seated and I began the effort to find out what such a library should contain. A card catalogue resulted, embracing such Lincolniana as I could acquire or find; and that led to the printed list of 1900, of which 160 copies were made and distributed.

A leading purpose of that list was to bring to light the many uncopyrighted publications known to exist, but exceedingly hard to uncover. That aim was largely accomplished, but some other consequences followed not quite so pleasing from the collector's point of view. The enterprise of dealers was stimulated no less than the zeal of rivals. Both supplied me with desired information, but prices soared. I would be the very last to decry the services of that gentle mercenary, your merchant of second-hand books, but one of his virtues is slightly overdone; he appreciates the amiable weaknesses of a collector almost too keenly.

Joseph Oakleaf was the youngest member of the "Big Five", but he quickly proved himself worthy of his elders. Fish notes in his 1908 essay, "My friend Joseph B. Oakleaf, Esq., of Moline, Ill., is rapidly accumulating a fine Lincoln library. He is our junior, both in age and in the date of entry into this competition, but he is no laggard. From the late advices I judge that he is likely to surpass me very soon, his total being then 743 of the 1,103 published titles, only twenty short of mine. As the baby of our family, he demands, and of course receives the favors due that stage of development, and amply requites them."

Oakleaf himself tells of his fortuitous introduction to Fish and the beginnings of his Lincoln collection in "Hobbies: An Address on the Collection of Lincoln Literature" (1923),

> I thought I would like to have all the biographies of Lincoln, at least, and I then concluded that a hundred volumes would probably be the extent of my library. I began collecting in a modest manner and did not correspond with any one who was collecting, nor did I know of any one who had the hobby. I made notations from the foot notes of the work of Nicolay and Hay and I went to our Public Library and finally my name became known to the old book dealers and I received catalogues, and then my hobby really started ... My gala day came at the close of the year 1900. It was while visiting with genial Frank M. Morris of Chicago, in his famous book shop, that he informed me that a man by the name of Fish of Minneapolis had compiled a bibliography. Upon my return home, I wrote to the Hon. Daniel Fish, with a great deal of misgiving, and inquired as to his bibliography, and out of the goodness of his great heart he sent me a copy of Lincoln Literature. If I had known how extensive a complete collection of Lincolniana would be when I first began collecting, I am satisfied that I would not have had the heart to begin the work.

Oakleaf was tenacious in tracking down Lincolniana. He writes, "When I started in my collecting I had no one to go to for information, but if I heard that an item was printed in a certain place I wrote to the publishers for information, and if I got no reply I wrote to the postmaster of the town, and sometimes I wrote eight or ten letters for a commonplace item, but I generally got it. The pursuit of an item has been very pleasant to me." His collection would eventually contain over 8,000 volumes.

Oakleaf and his mentor Fish were soon exchanging bibliographical information and collecting news. Fish would introduce Oakleaf into the circle of the other four major Lincoln collectors. One was Judd Stewart. Oakleaf records,

> My collection of Lincolniana was known locally, and at one time I appeared before the high school of our City to say something about Lincoln. At that time I tendered the use of my library to any one who desired to make a research, and a young man by the name of Philip Joseph availed himself of the opportunity and delivered an oration entitled: 'The Fame of Abraham Lincoln.' The paper was well written, and I had it published for him and sent a copy to Mr. Fish, who asked me to send a copy to his good friend, Judd Stewart. This I did, and in that way reached the heart and hand of that genial Lincoln enthusiast.

The Fish-Oakleaf friendship deepened, and the two men visited each other and travelled together in search of Lincoln. Oakleaf refers all too briefly to "Hon. Daniel Fish, of Minneapolis, whom I have had the pleasure of entertaining in my home and with whom I have made a trip through Lincoln country."

Oakleaf sent a letter to Fish on July 28, 1920, after the untimely death of Stewart, "Now, you and I are the only ones left of 'The Big Five.' I don't want to lose sight of you, and I hope you won't forget me."

The culmination of the Fish-Oakleaf friendship would occur shortly after Fish's own death in 1924. Oakleaf had been working for years on compiling a supplement to Fish's bibliography. Oakleaf published it in 1925 as *Lincoln Bibliography: A List of Books and Pamphlets Related to Abraham Lincoln*. Oakleaf provided not only bibliographic material but also profiled each of the "Big Five" collectors with their portraits, rare photographic images of Lincoln from the collection of Frederick Hill Meserve, and an introduction by Henry Rankin, who met Lincoln at the age of ten and later became a law student in his office. Oakleaf's book is a highly sought item of Lincolniana in its own right (and scarce too, limited to 102 signed copies).

Oakleaf writes in his profile of Fish, "The passing of Judge Fish was a personal loss to the compiler, who expected to have him pass upon the manuscript of the bibliography before it went to press and to get the benefit of just criticism."

Some subscribers to Oakleaf's 1925 *Bibliography* assumed that the original Fish list would also be included. This confusion resulted in Oakleaf republishing at his own expense Fish's already scarce original edition as a companion volume a year later, *A Reprint of the List of Books and Pamphlets Relating to Abraham Lincoln Compiled by Daniel Fish of the Minnesota Bar in 1906* (1926).

Oakleaf explains in the introduction to the Fish reprint,

> I answered every one that I did not propose to filch from my friend, Daniel Fish, the honor that belonged to him and which is enduring, Mr. Fish being an outstanding figure in the book world as the original bibliographer of Lincoln Literature.
>
> Mr. Fish passed to the Great Beyond in February, 1924, and was laid to rest in a cemetery at Minneapolis, on Lincoln's birthday.
>
> At the solicitation of many subscribers who have been unable to obtain the Fish bibliography in separate form, I have concluded, with the consent of Mrs. Fish, to reprint it... This reprint, like my bibliography, is a labor of love; my work must be paid in gratitude, which I consider is sufficient compensation.

Oakleaf adds in his "Hobbies" essay, "Not only has the collection of Lincolniana been a pleasure to me, but the acquaintance that I have formed through my hobby is really worth to me many fold more than my collection."

As Honest Abe himself said, "The better part of one's life consists of his friendships."

None of this story was top-of-mind to me, nor apparently the seller, when I purchased during the midst of a move in 2018 a scarce first edition of Daniel Fish's *Lincoln Literature* (1900). I glanced at the book briefly before putting it into a box. But the distractions of moving my entire library vanquished the book from my thoughts. I was organizing some uncatalogued acquisitions from the time of the move and Mr. Fish made his welcome reappearance to great fanfare. (I let out a hearty huzzah!) For the copy bore the bookplate of Joseph Benjamin Oakleaf, his ownership signature, and his extensive annotations—certainly the copy sent by Fish to Oakleaf in 1900 that ignited their fruitful friendship and guided the early formation of Oakleaf's collection.

2022

❈ XII ❈

Booking in the Big Easy

MEMORABLE. The Big Easy is, especially at night. I am in the middle of Bourbon Street, leaning over, elbows on knees, head down. Lined up next to me are five other middle-aged white guys in a similar stance. The man beside me is groaning, saying his bad left knee isn't going to hold up much longer. A lively crowd surrounds us including our disconcerted wives. The smell of spilt beer and less amenable odors permeate the surroundings, the whole scene lit up by the neon glow of the Hustler Hollywood sign nearby.

Within a few moments there is a whoosh over my head and a lithe, athletic black man lands just past me. He has hurdled all six of us as the finale to a street show. He grins widely, shakes my hand, and thanks me for my participation. He and his other two cohorts have spent the previous minutes regaling us with gymnastic / break dancing moves, and energetic music blasting from a portable speaker. Their lead MC is a fast-talking comedian. He pokes fun at racial stereotypes, extolling the crowd to cheer louder, all the while appealing for generous tips.

I am selected from the revved onlookers to participate in the finale by the MC who is looking for "rich white guys." He's one for two in my case, but I'm rather tall and make the mistake of standing in the front row. The MC leads us in absurd dance moves before the mighty leap. I see a lot of phones recording. At the end of the show, I tip the enterprising trio all the cash in my wallet totaling $12, confirming their poor choice (I spent most of my cash on books earlier). I make my way to my wife Nicole who is wiping tears of laughter from her eyes and still holding the book bag.

This is our anniversary trip to the Big Easy—the first visit for us to New Orleans as a couple (Why did it take us almost twenty years?). More unexpected experiences await us including further pillage amongst a bevy of used bookstores.

Nature has never been kind to New Orleans, a city entirely below sea level, protected by a series of levies and massive drainage systems. The apocalyptic punch of Hurricane Katrina in 2005 and Hurricane Ida in 2021 has left scars not easily healed, even for a city used to disruption. Yet as frayed as the region is, the core remains, both in a physical sense and in spirit. Recovery may be fragmented, but progress is steady and visible, benefiting from a generally strong economy and a post-pandemic urge for travel and adventure.

We stay in the Garden District in a funky hotel called Creole Gardens. The amenities are basic, but the place has atmosphere: old house divided up, high ceilings, fireplace showpieces, dentil mouldings with many layers of paint, creaky wood floors, colorful, quirky furnishings, the walls decorated with history including inscribed photographs of musicians who stayed there and/or played the adjoining music hall. I see a picture from the late Seventies of a very young New Orleans native Harry Connick, Jr. and a couple of blues players. Who cares if our shower is a 3x3 stall, and the room heat is generated by an ancient space heater that could be featured in a public service announcement as a safety hazard?

The Garden District is magnificent to wander in, home to many astounding old-school mansions dating from the nineteenth century, most renovated, a few hanging on precariously. Parks, restaurants, sundry businesses, and Tulane University are interspersed throughout, and one must ride the famous St. Charles trolley cars to properly see the sites. Huge live oaks provide shade and atmosphere.

We eat at The Rum House on Magazine Street the first night, an irresistible mix of Caribbean fare and, naturally, rum-laden drinks. Nicole and I enjoy the ambiance and talk of book hunting the next day. This place is busy for a Monday night. We find that many of the restaurants require dinner reservations even during the early week. There remains a huge variety of dining options throughout New Orleans, many sporting upscale menus, any style of food you want from fancy French to gyro wraps. The irrepressible human urge to eat, drink, and mingle is on full display in the Big Easy, spare no dime, and be damned to any pandemic slowdown! Uplifting to the spirit. Yet the dichotomy of America is full front here—we pass a tent city under the freeway on the way to a trendy eatery, suddenly emerging in a poor area with blue tarp-covered roofs and rotted homes that abuts a street of brand-new townhomes under construction. A Porsche driver swerves deftly on a decaying street to avoid a mumbling, disheveled man pushing a shopping cart filled with his worldly goods.

We make our way the following morning to Blue Cypress Books on 8123 Oak Street in the Garden District. The first impression is clean, bright, and organized, almost too much for my taste but Nicole loves the attention to detail. A woman owns this shop, she says. And she's right: owner Elizabeth Ahlquist established the store in 2008. This is not a rare book shop and most of the stock is newer used items with a focus on fiction, poetry, and local material. Nicole heads upstairs to architecture and I browse the extensive poetry section—not my usual focus but each store has a feel to it, and I know my hunting is limited here and the voice tells me to spend time with the poets. Indeed, I pull out four scarce Latin American titles. But my collecting of thirty-three years outruns my memory, and I consult my Latin American catalogue on my phone. I already have three of them. I feel momentary disappointment and then satisfaction with my earlier collecting self. Nicole's hunt is more fruitful. Our total is enough at checkout to qualify us for not only a free store pen but also a handcrafted, purse-sized folding fan made from pages of a book.

Soon after, we inadvertently attend a wedding. We are in front of Faulkner House Books at 624 Pirate's Alley in the French Quarter. A couple is standing outside the entryway to the bookstore saying their vows, surrounded by a small group of family and friends. The biblio-part of me wants to push past and enter the store but I know that would be bad form. In contrast, I observe Nicole having an awe moment. This softens me and I take her hand. The vows are completed, a kiss, brief clapping and cheering and a small batch of confetti is thrown over the two lovebirds, and the wedding party dissipates into the masses.

An employee of Faulkner House opens the door and looks out, allowing us to enter.

"That was something," I said.

"Happens a lot," he replies.

The shop is small, a selection of carefully-curated used books focusing on fiction, with a nice display of Faulkner first editions and collectibles in the adjoining room, feeling more like an exhibition than a for-sale. Faulkner lived here while he wrote his first novel *Soldier's Pay* (1926). In 1988, retired attorney Joe DeSalvo, an admirer and collector of Faulkner and other southern writers, bought the building and opened the bookshop downstairs, while he and his wife Rose lived above. It has become a literary destination. Frankly, for general book hunting it is slim pickings because of the limited stock. But it is worth a visit, being just off Jackson Square and close to many sites. Around the corner, we have lunch at Finnegan's Easy, a no-frills pub with a cozy courtyard in back, the tasty pub grub enhanced by a pint of local Gnarly Barley Peanut Butter Porter. The famous Pat O'Briens is across the street but too crowded.

Sporadic music spills out all around us; even in the day, smatterings of jazz, blues, and other styles echo through the narrow streets. About ten young, carefree musicians play together on a corner for tips. Street shows of varying quality and palm readers in exotic dress tempt tourists in Jackson Square. The French Quarter still has *it*, that hard-to-define sensory experience which temporarily clears away the mundane and worry and opens the mind to a restorative breeze.

Nicole looks at me in the pub courtyard and says the Voodoo Museum is around the corner. This is wife code for we are going, but I'm a willing participant.

The museum, located at 724 Dumaine Street, was established in 1972. It is modest in size and consists of a small entrance area and two rooms. Objects, paintings, and bric-a-brac abound, the yellowed exhibit labels surprisingly informative. The ubiquitous Tripadvisor guide neatly summarizes, "There's just enough voodoo lore here to introduce you to the history and culture of this spiritual practice and to tempt you to bring home a love potion or voodoo doll as a souvenir."

We do not succumb to a voodoo doll, although Nicole brandishes the idea, but we did each write out a wish and leave it at the museum shrine honoring Marie Laveau (1801-1881). Laveau was a famous practitioner of voodoo as well as other forms of Native American and African spiritualism. Altogether an enlightening experience for us, but you know what soon beckoned.

We enter Crescent City Books on the corner of Chartres and Bienville Streets. This is a fine store of modest size, established in 1992, with expansive shop front windows that pull you in. The shelves are filled with a mix of well-selected and uncommon books, and a wall of older miscellaneous material that calls out to be scouted. Which I do. It is not often nowadays that one can simply handle an abundance of nineteenth century and earlier material in an open shop. However, I notice the manager eyeing me closely, observing my handling of the books. I'm on a book high. The smell and touch and atmosphere are invigorating after our voodoo interlude.

I speak briefly with the manager, so briefly I don't get his name. I compliment him on the establishment. He references my browsing.

"I could tell you enjoyed that," he said.

"Yes, I did." And I lit a virtual cigarette.

My actual finds however are in the Spanish section. I ferret out a Manuel Puig first edition and an early printing of Mario Vargas Llosa's *Conversación en La Catedral*. This two-volume work has a complex bibliographical history. To unravel it, I engage in a post-trip email exchange among fellow collectors Bill Fisher, David Streitfeld, and Carlos Aguirre.

Time is winding on and Nicole is impatient, having found nothing for herself. But there is Beckham's Bookshop, another venerable New Orleans bookstore, only a two-minute walk away at 228 Decatur St. They have been selling used books in the French Quarter since 1967. The store rambles and has a patina. The stock is varied and relatively cheap. A musty odor wafts strongly, strangely alluring to me, however. It is a time capsule of bookishness, a section of old glass front shelves running along the left wall upon entry, a stack upstairs of a remaindered title from the early 1960s, still seeking buyers, hopeful, but slowly disintegrating in the humid air. I go through the books about books section. Mostly a tired group, but one item comes home with me, an inscribed copy of my friend Kevin Graffagnino's *Only in Books* (1996), presented to a Luana Jareczek. It's an uncommon name, but Kevin doesn't recall the person offhand when I check in with him upon return.

That night is our anniversary, and we skip the white tablecloth dinner for a meal at Maïs Arepas, a Colombian restaurant near our hotel. The place is packed, and the hour wait time is filled by a visit to an Office Depot close by where I shop for a new office chair, sitting and spinning and leaning back in every floor model. I take photos of favorites to reference when we return home. Lest you think I've entered clueless man mode and dragged my wife there on a sentimental night, it was her idea, and she sat and spun with me. Efficient use of time, she said. Good for a laugh, one of countless we've shared.

The next day, Arcadian Books at 714 Orleans Street offers an experience in book hunting rarely met with—it's dangerous, exciting, and overwhelming. The proprietor Russell Desmond opened the store in 1986. He sits squeezed into a small chair by the entrance greeting visitors, his stock of overflowing books about to push him out into the street. It's as if he crammed the contents of a semi-truck into a VW Bug. Towers of precariously balanced books soar upward, the isles are narrow to non-existent, heaps of books fill every nook and cranny. One bump and an old folio could tumble and knock you out cold. If obesity statistics are to be believed, most Americans would not fit in here. This is tough hunting even for a grizzled book veteran.

I ask Russell the location of his books about books section. He points skyward and offers his chair to stand on. That's how I reach them, he says. I use all my limited skill set including full extension and ninja balancing to pull a couple of volumes from a pile. I return to ground and inquire about his Spanish section. He hands me a flashlight and points me past a huge assemblage of French material. Russell is a Francophile and has always specialized in French books. I'm not claustrophobic by nature but I'm getting there quickly.

I shine the light and root around, many books sprawled on the floor in front of crammed shelves. This is literally an archeological dig, and the deeper I go the older the stock gets. You could carbon date some of the stuff on the bottom. Russell's own description of the shop as being "organized chaos" is optimistic.

I do unearth a couple of minor Spanish items and Nicole finds a book before we retreat in self-defense. If anyone wants into an aisle, everyone else must shift. We chat with Russell as we pay. Echoing through the shop, two customers jokingly engage in a game of Marco! Polo! to find each other.

We have spent almost too much time at Arcadian Books and have to hustle to make our last excursion before we head home, a two-hour ride on a giant Mississippi steamboat paddle-wheeler. There is no better way to have fun with a thousand fellow tourists. We skip the optional meal and just enjoy the breeze from the top deck. The tour guide's voice trumpets through the speakers as we leave the skyline of New Orleans behind. We pass two huge navy cargo ships anchored downstream, then the Ninth Ward neighborhood which suffered tremendously from the breached levee in Katrina, and nearby the sprawling Domino Sugar Company, ancient and dilapidated in appearance but still in operation. The riverbank scenery takes a more natural turn. Music starts. The jazz trio Steamboat Stompers, mere feet from us, begin playing lively, well-crafted classics. They are an unexpected delight. Then there is a relative silence when the band takes a pause. I can hear the paddlewheels churning as we glide along, the wide river beckoning ahead, and for a moment, I'm Mark Twain.

Nicole gently squeezes my arm and breaks my imaginary meanderings. A deep breath, and I hug her. A fine wrap-up to a memorable trip.

"You look happy," she says. And I am. We are.

2023

✸ XIII ✸

A Portrait of the HRC Director Thomas F. Staley
(1935-2022)

LEAN and hesitant Kurt Zimmerman came from the hallway that led to director Thomas F. Staley's office. His bright white shorts and flip-flops matched uneasily with a buttoned, Ulysses blue shirt; for he was young, only twenty-two.

"Hello. Come in, Kurt," Staley summoned, springing forth from his chair. He robustly rounded his desk, dapper in appearance, fully outfitted with jacket and tie, hand extended for a firm shake. He appeared larger than his actual size.

"How are you? How do you enjoy being at the Ransom Center?" he said quickly, for he always spoke quickly, as I was to learn.

"I like it a lot. I'm volunteering with Frank Yezer, and I just made some preservation boxes for Sir Arthur Conan Doyle's spiritualism albums..."

"Yes, Doyle, interesting. Lots more to him than Sherlock Holmes. So, you like working with Frank Yezer? He has good things to say about you. Recommended you for this internship. I reviewed your application. Do you know the idea behind the internship?"

"I haven't..."

He patted me on the back and motioned for me to be seated. I almost lost a flip-flop in my haste to settle. He resumed his director position behind the desk. Most of his office was devoted to his collection of James Joyce, one wall of glass front bookcases housing rarities and another wall of shelves overflowing with virtually every secondary item ever written on Joyce and his contemporaries. I was intrigued.

He asked, "The Lilly Library—have you heard of the Lilly Library? At Indiana University, David Randall was the original director. In the early 1960s he established a one-year paid internship to foster and train rare book people—librarians, archivists, bibliographers, even rare book trade members. The Ransom Center internship will be two years. Five candidates will be selected for this first group. Do you have a particular interest or focus?"

"I've always liked books, Dr. Staley. I just graduated with my English degree, not sure which way I want to go. Professor Gribben brought our American Literature class to the Ransom Center last year and showed us some original Poe letters and Twain books . . ."

He thought: That shirt of Kurt's is really quite blue, like the cover of a first edition of *Ulysses*. I need more substance to make a final decision, *leaning no*, lots of applicants, and my board meeting with the executive staff is in an hour, review some notes, what am I supposed to pick up after work, call the wife, and this unread bookseller's catalogue, should have looked through it before having Kurt in, I really need to check that when I'm done with him, maybe Joyce's *Et Tu, Healy!*. But don't be ridiculous. No known copies. But.

"Frank tells me you have the makings of a collector," he said after a brief silence.

"I do like the idea of collecting books. However, I'm broke." I laughed, a bit too hard.

"So was I when I started," he replied with a smile. "Let me show you some things."

And before I could rise, he had darted to his wall of glass front bookcases.

I did not have to feign interest. The aura of collecting pulled me then as it pulls me still.

"Hold this," he said enthusiastically, gently placing a tome in my hands. "The first Spanish edition of Joyce's *Ulysses*. I found this quite early on." Then began the deluge—book after book related to Joyce—inscribed items, thin pamphlets, the weighty quarto of the thick first edition of *Ulysses*, one of 150 copies on Vergé d'Arches paper with a provenance I can't remember now. I could barely stay above water but

I did, his words coming as fast as his books. I asked lots of basic questions, and he took time to answer them. It was my first close encounter with a passionate book collector. There have been many such encounters since but none so important.

He thought: So Kurt's got the makings of a collector, very, very good, and he's a talker, hmm, not sure on that, and I'm going to be late for my meeting — and I still haven't checked the bookseller catalogue yet — but he's different from the others, potential here, and the answer then must be yes, yes, yes. But not now, formalities must be observed. And I must pee.

"Kurt, it's been a pleasure to meet you. I'm late for a meeting, and I really have to go. We will get back with you quickly on the internship decision. And perhaps I can show you some more Joyce if you are interested."

"Thank you, Dr. Staley. Thanks for considering me. It's been an experience seeing your books. And I am interested." We shook hands and I retreated from his book-lined command post, noticing a tennis racket at the ready by the door.

"One more thing, Mr. Zimmerman," he said, and I halted at the sudden formality, "If you are selected for the internship you will need to upgrade your beach casual look."

I stammered a reply and made haste down the hallway and out of his sight. Optimistic within, maintaining as much dignity as possible without. I was soon to find the violet never shrank.

Written as a memorial tribute to Dr. Thomas F. Staley (1935-2022), noted authority on Joyce and director of the Harry Ransom Humanities Research Center at the University of Texas—Austin from 1988-2013. He took a chance on me that changed the trajectory of my life.

2022

⁂ XIV ⁂

Miss Stillwell and F. Richmond Goff: The Recording of Incunabula in America

THE ABAA Boston Book Show at the Hynes Convention Center presented an array of delights to tempt even the most jaded book men and women. The brisk cold outside contrasted with the fervor of the book hunters within. I looked, I mingled, and when I could resist hunger no longer, I ate a meal at the Cheesecake Factory restaurant nearby. The calorie count displayed next to the menu items read like the prices in a nicely stocked dealer booth: 2,000, 1,800, 2,400, 1,200. The friends eating with me—Joe Fay and Bill Allison—paid no heed, and I was on a biblio-vacation, so damn the low salt diet. We pored over the extensive menu as one would examine a good bookseller catalogue; with astonishment and delight. I knew we were done for when we ordered the cheeseburger eggrolls as an appetizer. The food was surprisingly good but the book talk was even better. We staggered out after polishing off the obligatory cheesecake dessert. I wondered if the hotel gym had a Stairmaster.

This brief introduction only touches on what was for me a satisfying and varied trip. I found several biblio items for my collection, particularly from exhibitors Willis Monie and Brattle Bookshop at the main show, and from Peter Masi and Roselund Rare Books at the "shadow fair" held Saturday a few blocks away. But the most interesting acquisition originated from a bookstore. It was the result of a serendipitous encounter with a fellow collector George Ong who was conversing with ABAA bookseller Michael Laird. Laird, a long-time friend, texted me at the show from his booth and told me to come over pronto. Ong mentioned he had been visiting New England bookstores. One of them had a few biblio-association items outside of his collecting area. He described them to me. I was indeed interested and grateful for the tip. I soon after called the store to confirm the basics and with Bill Allison, my wingman for the trip, set out the next day to examine the books in person. It was a rainy, cold, dreary drive of an hour and half each way—a day most normal people would stay put—but not a collector in vigorous pursuit.

This leads us to Margaret Stillwell (1887-1984) and Frederick R. Goff (1916-1982), pre-eminent rare book librarians and bibliographers, most noted for their work with incunabula: books printed before 1501. Stillwell flourished, not without considerable struggle, in a male-dominated biblio-world. She records her triumphs and travails in *Librarians are Human: Memories In and Out of the Rare-Book Field 1907-1970* (1973).

For most of her career Stillwell oversaw the Annmary Brown Memorial Library located on the campus of Brown University. The Memorial contained the exceptional collection of incunabula formed by bibliophile and Civil War hero Rush Hawkins. Hawkins founded the Memorial to honor his wife after her death in 1903. He lived on for many years, hunting and gathering more books, and generally being an outspoken and cantankerous fellow, until he was hit by a car at age 89 in 1920 in New York City. Stillwell recounts her serendipitous first encounter with Hawkins in 1909 at Brown University. She was an undergraduate working in the library as an assistant to famed bookman George Parker Winship,

> One day I looked up to see a tall, handsome old man entering the room. 'My name is Hawkins, General Hawkins,' he announced. 'Is Winship here?' Mr. Winship was at the printers. Could I do anything? Would he not wait? 'No, no, nothing whatever. I wanted Winship. I have no time.'
>
> With that he whirled about, but halfway across the room he picked up Edmund Lester Pearson's *Old Librarian's Almanack* [1909], which was lying on a table. 'Have you read it?' he asked over his shoulder. Yes, and I had found it very amusing.
>
> 'Amusing! It's a regular sell.' And drawing out a chair he began to read to me its rhymes and pungent sayings, chuckling to himself

this while. 'A regular sell, a hoax that will fool the unwary, perhaps even some of the critics! John Cotton Dana and Henry Kent were in on this, you know. What a good time they must have had.' And he laughed in such a boyish way that I forgot he was the imperious, white-haired General who had appeared in the doorway half an hour ago.

It was a pregnant moment, but I did not know it. Seated before me was General Hawkins of New York, for over fifty years one of the world's outstanding collectors of incunabula, as the first printed books are called—a man so devoted to his wife that he recently erected a Memorial to her in Providence; a man who was notorious for writing frequent and furious letters to *The New York Times* about this and that; and whose reputation for swearing at his troops in Civil War days was so widespread that a pious aunt in Vermont gathered friends together to pray for the good of his soul. And I sat there at ease, reviewing these facts in my mind; intrigued by this courtly and handsome old man; amused by his running comments and studying him with a quizzical eye—unaware that one day he would influence me, and in a sense control my activities, throughout my long life.

The man Hawkins sought was George Parker Winship, a central figure in the world of rare books and special collections, who served first as librarian of the John Carter Brown Library (1895-1915), before moving to Harvard to oversee the Widener Library. Winship mentored Stillwell. She writes of him, "Mr. Winship, as I saw him, was essentially a teacher, a man of vision and keen perception. He worked always for cultural advancement. Everyone who came his way, from the most erudite scholar to a humble undergraduate, felt the eager touch of his helpfulness. Without self-seeking or thought of personal prestige, he threw himself into every bookish project which he thought worthwhile and worked to carry it through."

It was no coincidence, then, that when the Bibliographical Society of America in 1904 funded its first major bibliographic undertaking, a census of incunabula in the United States, Winship became involved. In 1919, the first edition of the Census was published with Winship writing the introduction. The Census provided information and locations of 13,200 copies of 6,292 titles in both private and public collections. Stillwell did not work directly on the first Census, but she had been thoroughly trained in bibliography by Winship while his assistant.

In 1917, Stillwell became curator of the Annmary Brown Memorial Library, selected personally by Rush Hawkins to oversee his collection. She was awash in incunabula and learning fast. When Hawkins died, his written will did not express his verbal intentions and the Memorial failed to receive the endowment he had promised her and the Trustees. This created consternation and hardship for many years, but Stillwell remained at the Memorial. Despite the difficulties, her expertise in incunabula continued to grow. 1925 would be a turning point. She writes,

> Mr. Winship came to see me in a state of considerable excitement. He was returning from New York, where he had learned that a German commission, which had been at work on a project for the last twenty years or more, was planning to publish the first volume of a complete catalogue of all incunabula—the *Gesamtkatalog der Wiegendrucke*. . . . In New York, Mr. Winship had attended several meetings and luncheons where this project and the forthcoming volume had been a topic of discussion. Everyone felt that the United States should be well represented in this record. And everyone, so he said, felt that I was the logical person to undertake the job. Some years before this, Mr. Winship himself had had a part in compiling the first Census, a tentative list of American-owned incunabula. But the one now contemplated would require a systematic search for copies, the results of which should be fed to the *Gesamtkatalog* and also eventually published as a record of early printed books available in North America. Knowing him as well as I did, I could see what a grand time he had had engineering all this and getting the New York group all worked up. The one thing he wanted to know, they wanted to know, was would I undertake it? This of course fitted in well with my scheme of things. Also, as usual Mr. Winship's enthusiasm ignited mine, and I agreed to take it on.

The project would become *almost* overwhelming and consume Stillwell for fifteen years until the second *Census* was published in 1940, a date selected to coincide with the celebration of the 500th anniversary of Gutenberg's printing press. She writes of the inherent difficulties,

> The mail which had accumulated at the Memorial was something appalling, especially that relating to the Census. Working with the letters en masse in an effort to sort them and to register the early printed books they reported, I became acutely conscious that something was very wrong.
>
> There was much new wealth in the country at that time. The market was flooded with books from Europe. New collectors were buying incunabula, but they knew little about what they had or how to report it. Although they bought the books in veneration for their antiquity or for their beauty or quaintness, the new owners had never been 'exposed' to incunabula. They knew nothing [bibliographically about them].
>
> In the reports from these new owners, author and title were fairly well stated. If they chance to have kept a clipping from the bookseller's catalogue from which a book had been ordered, this frequently proved helpful, especially when some bibliographical references were cited. Otherwise—having no bibliographic tools at hand and being unable to cope with the originals—my correspondents innocently created 'ghosts' by the dozen (that is, editions that had never existed). Since I now had several hundred correspondents, the effort to straighten this out became colossal. It became in effect a case of tutoring by mail.
>
> I became convinced, therefore, that if an authentic Census were ever to be produced, I had first of all to publish a manual explaining in simple form the method of identifying incunabula, giving lists of reference books, and including lists and tables which would present a nucleus of essential information, for use if proper bibliographic tools were not at hand. The selection of material which should go into such a manual became my constant thought . . . It was to be several years before I could make the manual become a reality, and in a form beyond my fondest dreams.

Stillwell's dream was realized in 1931 with the publication of her work *Incunabula and Americana, 1450-1800: A Key to Bibliographical Study*.

I was very fortunate to acquire many years ago the magnificent association copy inscribed by Stillwell, "To George Parker Winship, A tribute to the patience and skill with which he initiated me into the varied ways of booklore, Margaret Bingham Stillwell."

Laid in are letters from Stillwell to Winship. One dating Oct. 21, 1925, refers directly to the Census project,

> Enclosed is a prospectus with which I planned to kill two birds—to announce the 'Descriptive Essay' and at the same time to call the attention of collectors to the fact that incunabula should be reported here. I have had enough printed to be sent to each of the persons included in the first Census... I have a mass of material for the Census already and it keeps coming in all the time. I tried Mr. [Harry] Lydenberg again but he again refuses to give space in the [New York Public Library] *Bulletin*. That is a shame, I think, because the record could be so condensed and abbreviated that it would take but comparatively little space and the *Bulletin* is one of the logical places in which it might appear. So now we shall have to look elsewhere. What do you suggest? How about the Bibliographical Society of America itself? If the Census follows the plan which we made just before you went away—of coming out in sections following each volume of the *Gesamtkatalog*—the individual sections will not be so very long, and presumably only one a year. I am ready now to roll up my sleeves and whip Section I into shape.

Stillwell was over-optimistic in regard to time frame but never flagged in her efforts. Some of the difficulties she faced seem ridiculous today. The Annmary Brown Memorial Library was not originally designed for daily occupation but as a memorial. The heating system was inadequate, and Stillwell spent years literally freezing her butt off before the situation was corrected. During the first few years of her tenure, the building did not even have electricity.

Of equal challenge was the lack of reference material for the Census. When Hawkins died, his extensive reference collection was sold off as part of his estate instead of being transferred for use to the Memorial as planned. The John Carter Brown Library reference copies could not be loaned. But Stillwell persevered by borrowing material from the Library of Congress, Yale and Harvard. She writes,

> At the Widener Library at Harvard every possible aid was given me ... Here I would assemble the books as I went back and forth from the catalogue files to the shelves. At the end of the day an assistant would help to carry the books to the charging desk and out to my car. Much to my embarrassment, many of the books which I needed came from the shelves of the Cataloguing Room. Mr. T. Franklin Currier, the head of the department and later the Assistant Director of the Library, was among the best friends the Census ever had. He permitted me to take the books on an indefinite charge. He would let the Library's incoming incunabula accumulate to a point. Then he would send me a little note, asking if I would kindly return the reference books for two weeks, at the end of which time—the new acquisitions having been catalogued—I might have them again.

By a stroke of good fortune in 1934 she garnered a part-time assistant, Richard Currier, a recent Harvard graduate. He helped with preliminary work for about two years until he was offered the Librarianship of the Harvard Club of New York. This opportunity for Currier was to set in motion one of the most serendipitous meetings in bibliographic history. Stillwell writes,

> [Currier] had become acquainted, he said, with a junior at Brown named Frederick Goff, who seemed to be much interested in his work and might be willing to help me a little.
>
> So he brought his friend ... to the Memorial. And he was the youngest-looking junior I had ever seen. But he also looked keen, alert, and ready to tackle anything. His mother, he said, sent me her love. This threw me back on my heels, until he added that before her marriage, she had been Amelia Seabury. We had been classmates once upon a time, but I had lost track of her through the years. So, I was happy indeed to greet her son.
>
> Thus I acquired on my 'staff' Frederick Richmond Goff, who was destined to remain with me during the four ensuing years; to go on to the Library of Congress; to become presently the Acting Chief and the Chief of its Rare Book Division; and to compile the

Third Census of Incunabula in American Libraries, twenty-four years after my edition was published.

In due course, he began to talk about post-graduate work for a Master's degree. 'If I could arrange for you to receive credit for your work here,' I asked, 'would you like to major in incunabula? I think it could be arranged quite easily.' Then I explained that, for twenty years or more, it had been the custom of the Brown professors in certain departments—History, Mathematics, Education, Romance Languages and the Classics—to bring their students to the Memorial, whenever their studies could be appropriately linked with early printed books. I would put on a special exhibition for them and slant my lecture in the direction of their subjects.

At the same time, I always took occasion to discuss the invention of printing, the first printers, and the change which the art of printing had brought about in the world. The result was that every once in a while an undergraduate or a post-graduate student would want to know more about these subjects, or would show interest in bibliographic techniques. Even though I had no official connection with Brown, the University had allowed the students credits for such courses as I had given, and in several instances students had majored with me for the Master of Arts degree.

If it could be arranged that he could receive credit also for his work on the Census, that would be ideal. He would have his degree and I, meanwhile, would have a full-time assistant for a year. The scheme worked well. For his thesis he wrote a monograph on *The Dates in Certain German Incunabula*, which contained also valuable data on Saints' Days, on the Roman calendar, and on variable New Year's dates customarily used in Venice and other Italian towns. It was published by the Bibliographical Society of America both in its *Papers* and as a separate. And it is a valued bibliographer's tool today.

The offprint of Goff's first work was one of the items I acquired on my recent Boston trip. It was not just a copy but THE Copy, presented by Goff, "For Miss Stillwell, to whom I am greatly indebted for introducing me to the interesting and fascinating subject of bibliography. F. Richmond."

This stroke of acquisitive fortune sent a euphoric jolt through my system. Can there be a better feeling for a book collector? I particularly enjoyed Goff's signing as "F. Richmond"—something I've seen in no other inscription of his until now. The strong bond of friendship developed early on between Goff and Stillwell and continued throughout their lives.

Stillwell had Goff as her full-time assistant and two other part-time assistants (Harold R. Knowlton and Edwin M. J. Kretzmann) that contributed to the effort. She writes, "The three young men were buoyant and alert and, so it proved, excellent workmen. We would never take a client's word that he had the edition reported. Instead, we would check everything against the bibliographies involved, to make sure everything was right, or—as the modern phrase is—that everything 'clicked.' Often there was some question, and much correspondence resulted. On occasion we would take time out for a brief ice cream party, and the room would ring with merry laughter."

Stillwell writes in detail of the trouble getting Goff's position funded through a grant from the American Council of Learned Societies because of opposition to "grandiose projects" which had petered out previously. She also records that "The Secretary of the Council of Learned Societies . . . must have belonged to the faction that mistrusted a project headed by a woman. He sent me so many questionnaires relative to progress that the time consumed in compiling the required statistics became a serious matter. Finally, I explained to Dr. [Waldo G.] Leland that, unless the questions stopped, I would have to relinquish the grant from the Council. I do not know what transpired, beyond the fact that the harassment ceased."

The Second *Census* was printed for the Bibliographical Society of America by the Southworth-Anthoensen Press. Stillwell explains,

> In the course of the project I made three trips to Maine, to the Anthoensen Press . . . As I had devised a new format for registering the data, the type-setting involved new problems. As a result of my Winshipian days, I enjoyed these excursions into the midst of the thudding and throbbing presses. Having climbed to the top of a three-storied building, I would discuss with Mr. Anthoensen the type-selection and the spacing, while Mr. Skillings, his compositor,

would set up specimen-sheets for us to see. He was an expert workman, for he presently set the entire text single-handed and the book went through the press in seven months with minimum error. The resulting format proved so satisfactory to its purpose that it was followed in the 1964 Census compiled by Fred Goff. I understand it has been employed in Australia. And I have used it in two books recently published. Mr. Anthoensen's personal attention to every detail illustrates Mr. Winship's theory that intelligent typographical interpretation of a scholarly work is essential to its clarity and therefore to its usefulness.

Stillwell's *Incunabula in American Libraries: A Second Census of Fifteenth-Century Books Owned in the United States, Mexico, and Canada* (NY: The Bibliographical Society of America, 1940) detailed "35,232 copies of 11,132 titles owned by 332 public and 390 private collections. And of these 35,232 copies, 28,491 are owned by institutions, and 6,741 are in private hands."

This monumental achievement was not only a Census but also a holdings list, given that such a large percentage of the incunabula had a permanent home in institutions. The identification of material in 390 private collections, with full cooperation of the owners, is also a remarkable feat. The work was utilized by libraries, dealers, and collectors as a fundamental reference.

Stillwell would move on to other projects, but she continued to keep notes and updates regarding changes in the Census. Soon after publication, Frederick Goff garnered the position of chief of the Rare Book Division at the Library of Congress. It was Lawrence Wroth, librarian of the John Carter Brown, and a supporter of Goff and Stillwell, who made the recommendation of Goff for the post. The young Goff's career was off and running. He recalled later, "[Wroth] served as my mentor for nearly 30 years" and "indoctrinated me in the disciplines and pleasures of bibliography as applied to Americana just as Miss Stillwell had introduced me to the reference sources for the study of incunabula."

Wroth and his assistants gifted Goff an appropriate send-off: a copy of Winship's *The John Carter Brown Library: A History* (1914) inscribed by Wroth, "For Frederick R. Goff, from the staff of the John Carter Brown Library upon his departure for the Library of Congress. With the affectionate good wishes, Jeannette Black, Marion W. Adams, Lawrence Wroth, 28 June 1940." I acquired this association gem in 2001.

But a Census is never truly done, and in the early 1950s Stillwell writes,

> A note came one day from Bill Jackson [William A. Jackson]. He wished to know when I could come to Harvard. He wished to take me to lunch and he had a proposition to make. So we set a date. The proposition proved to be an invitation from the Bibliographical Society of America for me to prepare a new census of *Incunabula in American Libraries*, since my 1940 edition was very nearly out of print. Many copies of fifteenth-century books had been coming into the country. Other copies had changed hands. It was high time, so the members of the Council thought, that a new Census got under way. They wanted me to take over the project.
>
> "Oh, no." I said. "Not again!" And then realizing that I had spoken rather brusquely, I tried to soften my sudden vehemence. "It is very nice of them to want me to take it over. Please tell them I appreciate the invitation and am sorry not to accept. In my opinion, the job should be done by someone younger than I."
>
> And after a moment I added, "The logical person, it seems to me, is Fred Goff. He worked with me on the Second Census for nearly four years. He knows all the ropes. And being in Washington, he is strategically placed. I would have to resort to all kinds of devices, as I did before, to round up the new collectors and to get their reports. At the Library of Congress, he must be meeting new people all the time."
>
> "As a matter of fact," I went on to say, "some of the former subscribers have kept in touch with me. Yale has been buying incunabula right and left. Mr. Goodhart continued to report everything he bought, up to the time of his death. I have these records and various others annotated and on file. If they were turned over to Fred Goff, that would give him a good start."
>
> "Yes, but if you took on the work yourself, that would give you

a head start, wouldn't it? It looks to me you already have the Third Census under way."

"Oh, no, this is only the beginning. From the way it is shaping up already, I can see it is going to be a big job. I really think it needs a younger person. Also, I am fairly close to retirement and that in itself would complicate matters. As a matter of fact, I have two monographs, and possibly a third under way. I could not handle anything more. One I hope to finish before I retire. The other two I plan to finish later."

"Three monographs all going at one time?" he said incredulously.

"That is a trick I learned from Mr. [Wilberforce] Eames. He believed that in gathering data you should give priority to one topic but have two or three others in mind so that, when you saw something pertinent out of the corner of your eye, you could jot it down. 'Before you know it,' he said, 'you will have built up quite a foundation on each subject.'"

"Trust Mr. Eames to come up with a good idea," said Bill with a chuckle, "but a rather strenuous one."

So there the matter rested. I do not know whether my suggestion of Fred Goff as the new editor of the Census was responsible for the invitation sent him nearly four years later. A new President had come into office and there had doubtless been changes in the personnel of the Society's Council. So someone else may have come up with the same bright idea. At any rate, I got my wish. For Fred Goff accepted the editorship in January 1957; the annotated records which I had accumulated were sent to him; and with remarkable speed for so big a job, the Third Census of *Incunabula in American Libraries* was published in 1964, a volume of marked distinction which has already, in these fast moving times, found itself in need of a supplement.

Fred Goff writes in the acknowledgements to the Third Census,

My first obligation, of course is to Margaret Bingham Stillwell, under whose tutelage I served for nearly four years as an assistant in compiling the 1940 Census and in overseeing its progress through the press. In 1958, all of the reports that had been made to her subsequent to the publication of the 1940 Census were turned over to me. This carefully annotated record constituted an invaluable source of information for the new Census.

Stillwell's mention of the need for a supplement to the 1964 Census was fulfilled in 1972 by Goff with the publication of *Incunabula in American Libraries: A Supplement*. Goff had formally dedicated the 1964 Census to his parents. This supplement volume was dedicated to Stillwell, "Teacher, Colleague, and Friend."

Lessing Rosenwald, the great collector of illustrated incunabula, among other areas, worked closely with Goff after Rosenwald gifted his magnificent collection to the Library of Congress. He writes of Goff and the Census in his *Recollections of a Collector* (1976),

> I made my first gift of books ... in 1943 and we have been close friends ever since. He has been a splendid advisor and had aided me in my collecting and in bibliographical knowledge. I have seldom gone wrong in following his careful advice ... Fred's scholarship has produced a reference book which is not only invaluable and necessary; it also was of great aid in my learning about my books. This work, *Incunabula in American Libraries*, is usually called the Third Census. It is a book of 798 pages literally crammed with information ... One stands aghast at such a labor and such accuracy.

Thoughts of Stillwell and Goff kept me excited despite the bad weather as Bill and I drove to the bookstore to follow my Boston Book Show lead. We entered the store and met the friendly proprietor. The books I sought were acquired from the library of former Brown University professor Roger Mathieson who had known Stillwell. And there they were sitting on a table awaiting my perusal—I recognized the red cloth bindings immediately—Goff's Third *Census* and the *Supplement* volume. The *Census* was well used and the backstrip detached but I liked it all the more because of its bookish aura. I opened the cover to the *Census* and my hopes were confirmed. Penned on the front free endpaper in Stillwell's hand was "Margaret Bingham Stillwell from Frederick R. Goff, 19 December 1964." A tremble and a hard moment to stay calm. A cursory examination showed Stillwell had marked all the incunabula found at Brown University and the Annmary Brown Memorial Library from Hawkins' collection. There were also some scattered notes. I gently set the volume back down, took a deep breath, and picked up the *Supplement*. It also was as I had hoped. The inscription reads, "For Margaret Stillwell, the dedicatee, inscribed with affection by—F. Richmond."

I bought a few other things at the bookstore and had them shipped home. But Miss Stillwell and F. Richmond made the trip back in my carry-on wrapped securely in a favorite sweater.

2019

❖ XV ❖

Every Book Its Story

I'M cataloging a few of my recent acquisitions. They usually arrive one at a time and the backlog is manageable, but this last year has been a deluge. I'm way behind in bringing order to the chaos. Stacks of books everywhere in my office: desk, chairs, table. But with the big exception of pamphlets, I can find what I'm looking for as needed. My in-house catalogue goes light years beyond an orderly list-keeping: most of the items are association copies and each one merits at least a brief explanation that often expands with research into a mini-essay. But this is part of the fun for me—story upon story to discover, expound, resuscitate. I find time when I can to catalog, usually in the evenings and sometimes during the day when work is slow. It also can be an excuse when yard work is required or a welcome respite when life takes a stressful turn. The results of this thirty plus year pursuit of biblio-bliss is a current file of 1,301 pages in 10-point type, and 880,705 words.

The bookseller Dorothy Sloan, one of my early mentors, encouraged me to catalog my collection in some form. Thankfully, I listened, which has not always been my strong suit. Someday, I'll polish this mighty beast of a document up and formally publish it. But for now, the catalogue remains open on my computer screen 24/7, always beckoning me to add to it—to feed it new and exciting acquisitions. And believe me, I do, and I also back the file up to the cloud with religious regularity.

So, what of it the last couple of weeks? What books and stories have found the top of the stack to input? They range from blockbuster associations to more minor items in my biblio-opera. Come along and catalog with me and get your mind off an upcoming meeting, a thankless task, or an irrational person.

The book I now hold in my hand is Edmund Pearson's playful hoax *The Old Librarian's Almanack: A Very Rare Pamphlet First Published in New Haven, Connecticut in 1773 and Now Reprinted for the First Time* (Woodstock, Vermont: The Elm Tree Press, 1909). Published as The Librarian's Series, No. 1, edited by John Cotton Dana and Henry W. Kent, two prominent bookmen, the tongue in cheek *Almanack* received a few serious notices at first—that is until people started reading it closely. The prospectus states: "Only two copies of the pamphlet are known to exist and no previous reprints have been made. It presents, somewhat in the style of Poor Richard or the Old Farmer's Almanac, the opinion and counsel of the librarian and book lover of 140 years ago. It is of interest to the librarian today for its striking contrast with modern ideas of library administration."

Pearson's preface provides an enlightening biographical sketch of the "author" Jared Bean, the librarian for many years of the fictional Connecticut Society of Antiquarians, "who never accepted the results of the American Revolution" and retained his allegiance to King George III. "He believed with Sir Thomas Bodley, that a librarian should never marry, and he died a bachelor. His character is so well displayed in his Almanack as to require no other description."

One example, among many, of Jared Bean's long list of rules, lists, and instructions:

> Let no Politician be in your Library, nor no man who Talks overmuch. It will be difficult for him to observe Silence, and he is objectionable otherwise, as well. No Astrologer, Necromancer, Charlatan, Quack, nor Humbug; no Vendor of Nostrums, nor Teacher of false Knowledge, no fanatic Preacher nor Refugee. Admit no one of loose or evil Life; prohibit the Gamester, the Gypsey, the Vagrant. Allow none who suffers from an infectious Disease; and none whose Apparel is so Gaudy or Eccentrick as to attract the Eye. Keep out the Light-witted, the Shallow, the Base and Obscene. See to it that none enter who are Senile, and none who are immature in their Minds, even tho' they have reach'd the requir'd Age.

The text has just enough veracity to seem plausible, but the "advertisement" at the end of the almanack is a glowing red flag for those taken in so far: "A Sure and Certain Cure for the Bite of a Rattlesnake Made Publick by Abel Puffer of Stoughton" with a long description of its application, including this: "Then require the Sufferer to move his Limbs about, at first slowly, now with increasing speed, till he do thrash them about with all the Vigour and Rapidity in his power. After this, let him rise, and run in a circle, or nearly so, first giving him to drink half a glass of Jamaica Rum."

This was Pearson's first book, followed by a couple of novels, a number of excellent books about books including *Books in Black and Red* (1923), and most remembered nowadays, books on true crime, including *Studies in Murder* (1924) and *The Trial of Lizzie Borden* (1937). Bibliographer Michael Winship introduced me to Pearson while I was in library school.

Presentation copies of *The Old Librarian's Almanack* are rare. I discovered this example the old-fashioned way on the shelves of the Lyrical Ballad bookstore in Saratoga Springs, NY during our summer trip to the area. I recognized the spine label immediately from a distance and soon eased the thin book off the shelf and opened the cover, ever hopeful of an interesting association—and damn if it wasn't inscribed. A gleeful, private moment that all collectors share. I gave it a possessive squeeze. The association is not obvious, and the cataloging research requires us to dig more than anticipated—but success! My description,

> Inscribed, "For Miss Cobb (whose picture I have seen) with advice to be an Old-Fashioned Librarian—for she will never be an Old Librarian. E. L. Pearson, Dec. 27, 1909." Bookplate of Marguerite Buxton Cobb (1888-1971). Only the second presentation copy encountered, dated well before Pearson formally acknowledged authorship. This awkward inscription hints at a young writer smitten by a pretty photograph. I miraculously located two photographs online of Cobb in the 1910 yearbook *Microcosm* of Simmons College, Boston, MA. She graduated from Central High School in Washington, D.C. and attended the School of Library Science at

Simmons, being very active in student activities, including President (of her class?), President and Secretary of Student Government and in the Vice-President Guild. Cobb married Edgar Whittington Adams (b. 1885), an electrical engineer and patent lawyer. I haven't found evidence of her utilizing her library degree.

This book is an example of weighing time versus reward. I have many items to catalog, some more important than others, and often I must draw an end to my research and move on. Yet, the characters of the story have been identified and the book is once again alive, perhaps waiting for another (or myself) to expand the story later.

This same trip to upstate New York also yielded treasures at Willis Monie Books in Cooperstown. Nicole and I were among the few that skipped the Baseball Hall of Fame nearby to go to a bookstore. I certainly wouldn't have found this next item in the Hall of Fame gift shop. It was plucked, along with a couple dozen others, from Monie's expansive books about books section. The store, run by father and son, contains a massive, open-shelf stock that is jam-packed and well-seasoned.

My find comes from the library of Marcus McCorison (1926-2013), librarian and later director of the American Antiquarian Society (AAS) in Worcester, Mass. from 1960-1992. McCorison was one of the noted bookmen of his time and helmed the AAS admirably, expanding the collections and promoting scholarly access to one of the great libraries of historical material in the country.

After McCorison's death, the AAS received over 300 boxes of McCorison's library as a gift. Much of this was his reference library. The AAS culled the books they wanted, and the rest were sold—some more expensive items at auction but most going to Willis Monie Books. The AAS had also approached me to buy the bulk of what they did not want. It was too big a pie for me to swallow. However, I did purchase numerous McCorison association items from Monie via their online listings, and I also bought a selection of items directly from the AAS.

I never met McCorison in person, but we did become friends through an unlikely connection. In 2000, he was clearing shelf space by selling a few early Grolier Club exhibition catalogues on Ebay. I bought them, and it wasn't until we exchanged information after the sale that I realized who he was! A very pleasant correspondence ensued which continued until his death. Shortly after our initial contact, I found a copy of his book *The 1764 Catalogue of the Redwood Library Company at Newport, Rhode Island* (1965) inscribed to Edwin Wolf, a close friend of McCorison. Wolf, the legendary bookman best remembered for his *Rosenbach* biography, later served as director of the Free Library of Philadelphia, a sometime rival to McCorison and the AAS for acquisitions. Who could resist sending it on to McCorison to be re-inscribed? (I didn't mention who the original recipient was to heighten the surprise.) He inscribed it to me on Christmas Day, "Dear Kurt, this brings back happy memories! I must have signed it first at Edwin's home. Now—to you—Marcus A. McCorison, 25 Dec. 2000." I am pleased to report that I was eventually able to acquire a batch of material inscribed from Edwin Wolf *to* McCorison along with the manuscript of a eulogy given by McCorison for Wolf.

All these thoughts were swirling about as we entered Willis Monie Books on that cheerfully sunny day in late August, no hint of the afternoon rainstorm soon to come, but safely ensconced inside among the tomes when it did. I anticipated that not all the McCorison books had been listed online and I was right. Interspersed among the general books about books section were several McCorison items including a book by Clifford K. Shipton, *Isaiah Thomas: Printer, Patriot and Philanthropist 1749-1831* (1948). Isaiah Thomas founded the AAS, so McCorison having a copy is appropriate. I saw that it was inscribed to him by someone named Ted. Time was short and lots of shelves needed to be searched, so I didn't examine my finds closely. Instead it went like this: Stack, repeat, stack, repeat, lug to checkout counter hours later, please ship them, thank you, and their arrival in two boxes after returning home; open excitedly, skim, preliminary sort, more stacks, and I'll catalog them as soon as I can.

The Shipton book on Isaiah Thomas does not take long to research and sends a sudden shock through my system akin to installing a car battery cable improperly. Shipton was the AAS director before

McCorison and went by the name of Ted. Here is a mighty association copy that I *almost* overlooked on the shelves in Cooperstown (and a shudder to imagine a general reader buying it and spending the evening in their bathtub absorbed in the biography, and oops, the book slips from their hand as they reach for a glass of wine and it gets a splash, but no matter, it served its purpose and will soon be placed in the donate-to-the-library box or, egad, the recycle bin—such are the nightmares that sometimes haunt me). But I didn't overlook it. And I hold it now. Mentorship, friendship, and the passing of the torch can hardly be represented better. My description,

> Inscribed by Shipton, "For Mark, whom I chose to follow in Isaiah's footsteps [followed by small drawing of footprints], Ted." Bookplate of Marcus McCorison.
>
> The footprints by Shipton in the inscription are a nice touch. Phillip Gura writes in *The American Antiquarian Society 1812-2012* (2012), "To become librarian of the American Antiquarian Society was McCorison's dream job. As he put in a letter to his new supervisor [Shipton] when he was initially hired, he still had 'an aura of disbelief' about his good fortune. Seven years later, when McCorison was named Shipton's successor [in 1967], Councilor Walter Muir Whitehill claimed to be 'very happy at the thought, in fact, I would be very unhappy and irate at any other thought.' McCorison remembered his 'apprentice years' fondly. During that time he learned 'a great deal' from Shipton, with whom he had 'a close and very gratifying relationship.'

McCorison wrote a moving tribute to Shipton in the AAS *Newsletter* and contributed an extensive checklist of his works to the Festschrift *Sibley's Heir: A Volume in Memory of Clifford Kenyon Shipton* (1982).

I have many McCorison books with interesting stories; however, I am attempting to stick to recently cataloged items—one more of which also deserves mention. The book is Ricky Jay's *The Magic Magic Book: An Inquiry into the Venerable History & Operation of the Oldest Trick Conjuring Volumes . . .* (1994), inscribed to McCorison and signed by Jay and the book's artists.

Famed magician Ricky Jay (1946-2018) wrote extensively on magic and its history. Jay collected rare books and manuscripts, art, and other artifacts connected to the history of magic, gambling, unusual entertainments, and frauds and confidence games. The AAS, while under McCorison's leadership, hosted an exhibition drawing upon Jay's collection published as *Many Mysteries Unraveled: Conjuring Literature in America 1786–1874* (1990). (Where did the McCorison copy go?) The crème of Jay's collection was sold at Sotheby's by my friend Richard Austin, head of rare books and manuscripts, and his highly regarded associate Selby Kieffer for $3,835,694. The colorful catalogue is online, but I wanted a printed version and got it. It has introductions by David Mamet and Steven Martin, and besides, how much longer will printed catalogues be produced?

I can state that it is uncommon for me nowadays to find important material in bookstores that I visit. Most of my best material is acquired online. This next example I hold was not found in a bookstore; however, a book I located in Asheville, NC on the shelves of Battery Park Books directly resulted in its purchase. Before we dive into specifics, a word about the store. The general mood is set upon entering—it is located in the Grove Arcade, the first American indoor shopping mall, a 1920s era masterpiece of design and detail, lovingly restored. The bookstore is also a champagne and wine bar. Disconcertingly, tables spaced closely among the bookshelves are filled with visitors and tourists sipping the fruit of the vine, gaily munching on charcuterie and similar offerings. I've never had to squeeze behind/around seated drinkers with excuse me's and sorry's to hunt books before.

I find respite on the quieter second floor. My wife Nicole is also upstairs, diving deep into the architecture section. I wander around. To my amusement, I find in the farming section a signed copy of Bill Reese's bibliography *Six Score: The 120 Best Books on the Range Cattle Industry* (1976). The adjacent hunting and fishing section catches my eye with an inordinate number of nineteenth-century bindings. It becomes apparent that the store has acquired a solid collection of sporting books and has not taken the time to research them properly. I can't resist buying two books, one of which leads us to our story. This is Henry Thomas' *The Rod in India: Being Hints How to Obtain Sport with Remarks on the Natural History of Fish, Otters, Etc. and Illustrations of Fish and Tackle* (Mangalore: 1873). Yes, I know, quite obscure (but rare!) and why would I want that? Well, because it bears the bookplate of John Gerard Heckscher, one of the great American sporting book collectors. I don't have anything representing Heckscher in my collection and that is reason enough, I reason.

I returned home and dutifully cataloged the Thomas. I also search online for any inscribed Heckscher items. I fish one out of the great biblio sea—and a fine story emerges involving a duel and early baseball:

(John Gerard Heckscher). "Ellangowan" editor. *Sporting Anecdotes*. London: Hamilton, Adams & Co., 1889.

> Bookplate of Heckscher. Inscribed, "E. B. Talcott, with John G. Heckscher's compliments, Dec. 16, [18]98." Tipped in is Heckscher's calling card with the note, "Very sorry this book is not in better condition but I fancy the sporting stories will amuse you."
>
> Donald Dickinson writes of Heckscher (1835?-1908) in *Dictionary of American Book Collectors*: "As a sophisticated turn-of-the-century New York clubman, Heckscher owned racehorses, took an interest in yachting, and formed a large library of sporting books. He specialized in works on fishing, particularly those with engraved plates and watercolors. He owned all four early editions of *Walton's Compleat Angler*, a nearly complete collection of the sporting classics by English novelists Robert Surtees and Pierce Egan, Audubon's *Birds of America*, and a large assortment of dueling literature. A small portion of his library was dispersed at Merwins in 1906, but the major part did not come on the market until after his death. The sale of the first edition of *The Compleat Angler* to Daniel B. Fearing brought the estate $3,900, the highest price paid during the season for a single volume. Although Heckscher's private life was somewhat chaotic, as reported in the New York Times in October 1905, he was known as a gentleman and a connoisseur. Heckscher's sporting library was one of his chief ornaments."

Being curious about the "chaotic" reference, I pull up the *NYT* article. Heckscher at age 70 "but very well preserved" had secretly married his third wife the year before, a young widow "who was very handsome and accomplished." The article recounts with relish that earlier in his life a rivalry with a best friend over a young lady led to blows and eventually a full-blown duel! (Note the "large assortment of dueling literature" referred to above.) Neither man was injured but his friend won the day and marriage. Later this couple divorced, and Heckscher, ever the patient hunter, eventually took the woman as his second wife.

The recipient of this copy of *Sporting Anecdotes* was the young Wall Street financing whiz E[dward] B. Talcott (1858-1941), an early owner of the New York Giants baseball team and an enthusiastic baseball fan and sportsman.

I am fortunate to have booksellers and book collectors who scout for me while on their own hunts. Mighty bookman Joe Fay, formerly with Reese Co. and now a partner in McBride Rare Books, spotted a heavily annotated copy of Merle Johnson's *High Spots of American Literature* (1929) in John Bale Book Co., Waterbury, CT. I answered Joe's text message and picture posthaste. He did not buy the book and resell it to me, but simply passed me on to the proprietor, Dan Gaeta, whom I had recently interacted with, and I ordered the book. But Joe knew that a good steak dinner awaited on his next visit to our home. The book I'm holding is well-used but sturdy. I have a number of association copies of the title already, including Johnson's own working copy (the High Spot of *High Spots*!), but there is always room for one more unique item. It provides a brief but illuminating story that conjures the imagination of the collector's lair. My catalog description,

> Lafayette Butler's copy with shared references to items in his library mentioned herein. Note by Butler on the front free endpaper. Extensively annotated throughout. Many of Butler's copies were signed/inscribed, letters laid in, etc. He records condition, special features, occasional prices paid/provenance. On the rear free endpapers he has written a detailed list of his holdings, noting that he owned at the time 88% of the titles mentioned within (169 of 191). A fine example of a "working copy" utilized by an advanced collector to record/build his collection.

Lafayette Butler (1887-1975) was an industrialist and resident of Hazelton, PA. Stanley Weintraub recalls a visit to Butler in his essay "The Lafayette L. Butler Collection," in the 2000 *Annual of Bernard Shaw Studies*,

> In 1957, LaFayette L. Butler, then seventy, noticed a Sunday newspaper piece about my work on Shaw—possibly the first, ever—and wrote to me. He had a lot of stuff I might want to examine, he offered kindly. Hazelton was about three hours from Penn State, a rather easy drive even before Interstate 80 shortened the time, and I took up his offer to visit, sometimes taking a colleague or a grad student with me. Later, even my daughter, Erica, came along to play Butler's big grand piano for him, freeing me to explore the holdings crammed into the three levels of the large frame double house—long runs of first editions, musty and often more interesting books, and files of manuscripts, mostly on late nineteenth-century and early twentieth-century writers. By then Butler had become nearly blind, but stubbornly still collected. The visits did not make a Shavian of Erica, but I owe parts of several books, and some articles, to my work at the Laurel Street hoard. After Butler's death in 1975 his son Charles followed testamentary instructions and arranged for the Bertrand Library at Bucknell to receive several major collections from the Butler archives, the largest, perhaps, those on Shaw and on other Irish writers.

The Bertrand Library Special Collections reading room is named for Butler. The plaque records, "After his death in 1975, Butler donated several other manuscript collections and first editions from his extensive Fountain Lawn Library, including the works of George Bernard Shaw and early folios of Shakespeare's plays."

This last mention of Shakespeare and Folios leads us to the oversized pamphlet that sits cozily next to me on my desk. To win it, I had to do some recent flexing at auction. I found the item via the rarebookhub search system which monitors upcoming auctions for my saved wants (subscription required). Thank you, founder Bruce McKinney.

No more suspense: the pamphlet is A.S.W. Rosenbach's *A Description of the Four Folios of Shakespeare 1623—1632—1663-64—1685 in the Original Bindings. The Gift of Mr. P.A.B. Widener and Mrs. Josephine Widener Wichfeld to the Free Library of Philadelphia in Memory of Their Father Joseph E. Widener. (1945). This is an inscribed example and quite rare thus. The auction house, Alan Blair Auctions / Emerald Ventures in Richmond, VA, is unknown to me. A quick review of their site shows their focus is typically stamps. A seasoned collector or dealer immediately smells bargain when an out of the way auction house offers material not in their specialty. The answer is yes and no, hit or miss, and not as likely in the internet age. But I am hopeful. The books and autograph letters come from the collection of the omnivorous collector Dr. O. O. Fisher of Detroit. Fisher died in 1961 and most of his vast library was dispersed. (You'll read more about him soon enough.)

I identify not only the Rosenbach but also a few other items of interest in the sale including a H.P. Kraus catalogue inscribed to Fisher and a couple of letters by noted bookmen. The Rosenbach comes up first in this online-only auction. I sense trouble as there are multiple bidders early. But I wade in full tilt at the end, thrashing my sword, auction fever running hot, and knock down the pamphlet for about double what I'd originally wanted to pay. Irritated but thinking clearly, I do not cede the field on the other items I am chasing because of a blown budget on the Rosenbach. I stay in the hunt and secure all the rest for bargain prices, thus acquiring a fine lot of material at a reasonable price, albeit a much higher total overall than anticipated. Welcome to the mindset of a collector. In retrospect, I think the Rosenbach ran up in price because of the Shakespeare connection, not regrettably because of the presentation by the great Rosy. So, here it is as I described it moments ago,

> Inscribed, "For a *real* collector of Shakespeariana, Dr. O[tto] O. Fisher, from A.S.W. Rosenbach, Feb. 18, 1947." Penciled annotations by Fisher.
> Dr. Otto Orren Fisher (1881-1961), a Detroit doctor, was a renowned book and manuscript collector who at his death had assembled a collection of some 20,000 items in many subjects. He was a graduate of Miami University, Ohio in 1909. In 1949, he gifted

the university with his own set of the Four Folios of Shakespeare. Their library website records, "The crown jewels of that envied collection arrived in Oxford, Ohio, on Oct. 7, 1949, flown there personally by Dr. Fisher in his private plane. The gift he carried for his alma mater was simply too precious to be trusted to anyone else."

It does not appear that Fisher acquired his Folios from Rosenbach, but Rosenbach knew a serious collector when he saw one, thus the inscription. It is also quite possible that Widener's gift in 1945 to the Library Company of Philadelphia recorded here by Rosenbach inspired Fisher's own donation to his alma mater in 1949. Information about the Fisher Folios is available on the Miami of Ohio University library website.

And would our cataloging extravaganza be complete without an Ebay find? It turns into a two-for-one biblio special. I bought for a modest sum a well-worn copy of a California classic and "Zamorano Eighty" title, Soule's *The Annals of San Francisco* (1855). This example belonged to none other than Robert E. Cowan (1862-1942), famed bibliographer and bookman, and author of *A Bibliography of the History of California* (various editions).

I admit to being pretty stoked about this find. But why stop there? I searched for other available copies of Soule out of curiosity and found a beauty in the stock of Nat DesMarais, Portland, Oregon bookseller. The condition is superior in original cloth, the price reasonable, and the provenance spectacular. I have a soft spot for women collectors, and this is an exciting addition to the collection. My full description this time, just cooked and still warm,

(Jennie Crocker Henderson). Frank Soule, John H. Gihon, and James Nisbet. *The Annals of San Francisco*. NY: D. Appleton & Company, 1855. A superior copy of a book typically found quite worn/incomplete/rebound. This copy was offered in Howell Catalogue 50 of the Crocker Henderson collection, item 791.

Bookplate of Jennie Crocker (Henderson).

Jennie was born in San Francisco and spent much of her life in Hillsborough, California, just outside of San Francisco, adding much appeal to this copy.

Bookseller Warren Howell sold her famous Californiana collection in Catalogue 50 (five parts), 1979-1980. His father John Howell had also sold books to her and her brother beginning in the early part of the twentieth century. Warren Howell writes in the introduction to the catalogue,

"The library ... is the last of the great collections of Californiana to come on the market ... A granddaughter of Charles Crocker, who was one of the celebrated 'Big Four,' and the sister of Templeton Crocker, who founded the California Historical Society, Jennie Crocker naturally developed a strong interest in California history and culture in general, and in the history of the Central Pacific Railroad in particular ... [she] decided to create a definitive collection of important California material on her own....

Following her marriage to Malcolm D. Whitman in 1912, Jennie Crocker moved to New York, where for the next twelve years she actively increased both the size and the scope of her California collection. She acquired material both at auction and from the most prestigious American rare book dealers of the time: Dr. A.S.W. Rosenbach, George D. Smith, and Edward Eberstadt in New York, and John Howell in San Francisco. While Jennie Crocker was actively collecting Californiana, her brother Templeton was busily doing the same. They often bought from the same dealers. A friendly rivalry developed between brother and sister, as they found themselves frequently bidding against each other for particularly choice California items ... [Howell tells a couple of entertaining stories including Jennie outbidding her brother at auction for the first book printed in California, the famous *Manifesto* of the Mexican governor Jose Figueroa, printed by California's first printer Augustin Zamorano in Monterey in 1835].

The scope and the depth of this superb collection cannot be overemphasized. In addition to the Gold Rush journals and Bret Harte material already mentioned, the collection is strong in nearly every area of California interest. From the earliest European voyages of exploration to the emergence of the Golden State as an integral component of the modern American political and economic system, virtually every subject of importance is covered."

We've been cataloging now for quite a while. If you're still with me straight through, kudos. I am hopeful that the rest simply have become so inspired to catalog their own holdings that they've taken a temporary respite from my essay. I'll bring this to a conclusion, the outside world rudely intruding, my cellphone ringing insistently, and my stomach growling. But I'll be back to cataloging soon—there are plenty more stacks here.

2022

❖ XVI ❖

Good Books at the Florida Antiquarian Book Fair

"ARE you sure you want a beer guy to order the wine?" says friend and bookseller Jay Rohfritch, as I scan the vast and mostly incomprehensible (to me) wine list at Sauvignon Wine Locker & American Trattoria in St. Petersburg, Florida. It is Sunday night, March 12th, 2023, and the Florida Antiquarian Book Fair has just finished. Celebration is in order. I'm sitting with Jay, Dennis Melhouse of First Folio Books, and Bryan & Kelly Young of Grayshelf Books.

Dennis is a man who knows his way around a wine bottle. He asks if the restaurant has a sommelier. I've never heard this term actually spoken before. Only read it in books. We've already polished off the first bottle selected by Bryan & Kelly, a Napa red that I can't recall the name of, but I drink heartily. Bryan and Kelly are into wine like I'm into craft beer, so the selection is a good one.

But now I'm feeling cheeky. I intercede and say I'd like to select the next bottle. There is a brief look of consternation from the others. I insist and I find a moderately-priced (okay, relatively cheap) bottle of cabernet from Paso Robles. Dennis diplomatically says he has had some good cabs from Paso Robles in the past. I seal the deal by guaranteeing to drink the whole bottle if it doesn't meet expectations. The merriment continues as we talk books and Jay once again expresses skepticism of my selection abilities.

The waiter is an interactive, humorous fellow with hair like Albert Einstein. We don't know if this is a trending fashion look, or he was simply running late to work and forgot to comb his hair. He arrives with my bottle and ceremoniously *unscrews the cap*, no cork removal needed. Muffled laughter ensues and the waiter places the cap before me and pours a glass to have me approve.

Bryan states in my defense that many better wines have screw tops nowadays, but I know he is lying. I swirl the wine around, inhale the bouquet ("Smells like wine to me") and take a swig. Tastes pretty good, actually. The rest are soon swirling their glasses and sipping.

"It's getting better as it opens," Kelly says.

"I can drink it," Jay smirks.

"It's a bit tannin-forward," Bryan chimes in.

I'm not sure what to make of this comment, but Dennis, who is sitting next to me, leans in and clarifies, "That's not a good thing."

More funnin' continues at my expense, but I asked for it, and rather enjoy it. Just one of many memorable episodes from a bibliophile's escapade to St. Petersburg, Florida. But how did I get here? That is a serendipitous story.

Jay Rohfritch's bookstore Good Books in the Woods is the best open shop in the Houston area. Quality used books in all fields and a fine selection of rare and collectible material make up the approximately 50,000-volume stock. The bookstore is in an old home, now zoned commercial, and Jay lives upstairs. He's been in business fifteen years, and over time the shop has developed a cozy atmosphere, varied offerings, and bookish aroma that is nectar to book collectors.

Jay's full-time assistant is Jacob Imerman. He is a young man, sharp, excellent with customers, and has a strong back. Jay is thus free to travel more than in the early days, and he wishes to expand the antiquarian side of the business. He has this in mind when he takes up Dennis Melhouse's suggestion to exhibit at the Florida Antiquarian Book Fair. I first heard about his pending journey by chance (or serendipity?) when I was speaking with Jay on the phone.

"That sounds like a fun trip. Who's going with you?" I ask.

"I'm going by myself," he replies.

"That's a lot of driving."

"I know. But the show is supposed to be good, and I need . . ."

"What you need is a wingman," I quickly interject, my mind more nimble than usual since it involves books.

"Sure," he replies, after a brief pause. Our talk continues and enthusiasm builds.

What was a book business trip has now become an adventure. My wife offers no resistance to me going. In fact, she mentions something about it being easier to do home improvement projects while I'm gone.

A month later, I meet Jay in the morning at his shop and help load up his Mazda SUV: four collapsible bookshelves, a couple of flat display cases, and many boxes of books filled primarily with modern literature and 19th-century African travel and exploration, two disparate areas in which he has strong holdings. Our suitcases barely fit. Then we are off, heading eastward toward Mobile, Alabama, our stopover for the first night.

In the many hours spent together on the drive, we discuss every possible nuance of antiquarian and used bookselling. We then have time left to solve virtually all the world's problems if someone would just listen. The banter is lively, and there are few moments of silence. Jay and I over-indulge in fast food without regret, particularly DQ Blizzards. When Buc-ees is not available for a pit stop, we handle subpar bathrooms with aplomb, whereas my wife would certainly recoil in horror.

We learn things about each other during the hotel stays. He finds out quickly that I snore ("but not as loudly as my mother did on family vacations" he adds.) I discover that he snores, so we are even. Neither of us will dare enter the bathroom after one of us answers the call of nature. He forgot his hairbrush and must use mine. He notices, as I had not, that the price tag is still hanging from the handle. "I'm going to return it when we get back," I say.

Overall, our travel experience is amicable and easy, just two guys on a road trip, handling whatever comes our way. We do secretly worry that if we break down somewhere here in the Deep South that locals might utilize us for entertainment.

The Florida Antiquarian Book Fair has been going on for forty years, one of the longest running shows in the country. It is held at the Coliseum, a venerable venue built in 1924, that originally served as "The Best Ballroom in the South," with the likes of Glenn Miller and Tommy Dorsey performing. The building was later acquired and renovated by the city of St. Petersburg. It is well-nigh perfect for the fair: spacious with soaring ceilings, well-lit, and easily accessible. It also retains the charm of its past, a large stage providing a spot for live music during the fair on Friday and Saturday including a pianist. A nice touch by the book fair organizers.

The first day of the fair opens Friday March 10th at 5:00 pm. Exhibitors must be ready by 4:00 pm. Most arrive much earlier in the day to set up, including us. There are over 80 booths at the fair and we aren't sure how chaotic it will be during load-in. The organizers supply porters and equipment to assist. The fair is very well run with few hiccups—the result of seasoned people in charge, numerous capable volunteers, and the use of the same venue year after year. Jay notes that the booth cost of $500 is quite reasonable.

Set up is pretty quick. I concentrate on the manual labor so Jay can organize the booth. We fuel ourselves with organizer-supplied donuts and coffee. We are done by 11:00 am and many booths are still being loaded.

Set-up is often prime shopping time among dealers. Jay has heard that pre-fair sales are usually good at this event as several upper-end ABAA dealers attend and buy from the other dealers. In fact, many dealers count on these sales to make their fair successful. For example, Bauman Rare Books, with offices in New York, Philadelphia, and Las Vegas, is present. Their three representatives, Erin Mae Black, Steve Moosbrugger, and Tom Posey are roaming the booths, friendly book carnivores in search of a meal or two. They consult their in-house holdings on a laptop, occasionally confer with the mothership back at headquarters, and buy liberally in many fields. Several dealers sigh in relief as thousands of Bauman dollars are exchanged for some of their best wares. And not a single civilian has entered the building yet. Other dealers are shopping and buying. A 20% discount to fellow trade members is common, and sometimes a book will simply move from one booth to the next, price raised as it journeys up the book food chain.

A collector or special collections librarian may read this with a furrowed brow. Unfair, he or she thinks. I don't have a chance to get the book, or it will be priced higher when it does reappear. Yes and no. For some do not realize that a significant portion of sales in the rare book trade are between booksellers. Collectors and institutional buyers can be fickle or occasional, but booksellers in search of new stock are the steadiest customers. Does one bookseller briefly begrudge another when he or she sells a book for $1,500 to a fellow bookseller, only to find it priced at $3,500 a few minutes later? Maybe, particularly if the book sells quickly at the higher price. But this is the game, and the original bookseller knows his or her rent was just covered, or now there is money to buy another item.

The disgruntled collector must keep in mind that as sympathetic as a dealer can be with your interests—and one should always cultivate good relationships with dealers— selling is the thing for them, as it must be. So, in this spirit, as a collector or special collections librarian, if you are offered a freshly-found item directly from a dealer before it is offered elsewhere, hesitate not in your decision yes or no, and thank the book gods you have favored status.

Our own booth, however, sees few pre-show sales and Jay is feeling down and disappointed. (Although later, Jay *buys* two early Stephen King books, including a decent copy of *Carrie*, that feels he can sell easily to a customer back home.)

"Cheer up," I say to him, assuming the role of biblio-therapist, "It's early and the show starts in five minutes!"

We are situated in the back of the exhibition hall, furthest from the entrance doors, and we hear a rumble like the approach of a herd of wildebeests, and we soon watch the crowd spill haphazardly among the booths, followed by the din of activity: conversations ignited, semi-polite jostling to view books, and smiling booksellers, some already writing up sales receipts.

The quantity of the crowd is exceptional by book fair standards. (I am told later this is typical of the Florida fair.) I don't have attendance figures, but traffic is heavy over the entire three days, even on Sunday which is normally fairly quiet. This is uplifting to me; the interest in collectible books retains a solid heartbeat. What further amazes Jay and me is how many young people are present—real, live book enthusiasts in their 20s and 30s, some with small kids in tow. A stroller randomly bumps me. (But keep the young'uns out of the booth, please. No touchee, *rare* books.) The human form itself is apparently a canvas to this age group, as we can't help but notice the myriad tattoos on display, a rotating art gallery of sorts, as the crowd flows in and out of the booth.

The dealers at this show fall into roughly two categories: many are primarily used booksellers, with offerings in the $10-100 range, and then a smaller group offering antiquarian, rare, and collectible titles at higher prices. We quickly discern this fact as most lookers do not turn into buyers, because Jay has brought more expensive books. It makes no sense for him to bring cheaper material halfway across the country when he can simply sell those books in his store or online. But the local Florida dealers have more leeway in this regard.

There is some tension in our crowded booth as patrons handle expensive items with inexperience and Jay intercedes as politely as he can. I see some steam pressure building, but we have no explosion from him. We move a few more fragile items to safer ground.

Jay is a fine salesman and more patient than he claims to be. Soft-spoken, he asks a couple of polite questions to a potential customer, "What do you collect?" for example, and gauges their reaction. If there is a response he can work with, he quickly explains the importance of the item in hand, or of another item in the booth that is related, and tells some interesting tidbit associated with this copy, or the book's history. He's a good storyteller; no embellishment needed and simply brings the items to life. His blend of dry humor and almost instant recall of facts grabs the attention of customers of all stripes from rookies to jaded book people. I'm an advanced people-person myself, and watching Jay in action was impressive, although he'd never admit to any special skills in this area.

One exchange sums it up—I watch as Jay writes out a receipt and bags a fine copy of Ewart Grogan and Arthur Sharp's *From Cape to Cairo: The First Traverse of Africa from South to North* (1900), priced at $600. The book details a walking journey across the entire continent of Africa, involving love, bravery, and incredible happenings. The customer turns to me and says, "Jay's story about the book made me have to have it."

I naturally do my own shopping during the fair. There is not much in my field of biblio-books, but I do snag a copy of Norman Strouse's *The Pleasures of Packing a Library* (1968), presented to a Ford executive. Strouse was an advertising executive by vocation, and one of his main accounts was Ford Motor Company. He writes in the essay of a fellow book collector at Ford. So, a nice find! Then I stumble across *General Sir William Howe's Orderly Book at Charlestown, Boston and Halifax June 17 1775 to 1776 26 May . . . Collected by Benjamin Franklin Stevens . . . with an Historical Introduction by Edward Everett Hale* (London: Benjamin Franklin Stevens, 1884), this being the copy presented by Stevens to Hale with a letter laid in. Hard to beat that association. And of further interest, Benjamin Franklin Stevens, also a bookseller, was the brother of the famous rare bookman Henry Stevens. My only other find of note is literary—a copy of Eudora Welty's *Losing Battles* (1970) inscribed to author Linda Kuehl during the time Kuehl interviewed Welty for the *Paris Review*.

I seek out the Florida Bibliophile Society booth where I acquire several of their recent publications including the impressive *"I Contain Multitudes. . . ." Selections from the Ed S. Centeno Walt Whitman Collection* (2022). More impressive is meeting three of the club officers firsthand: Charles Brown, Ben Wiley, and Gary Simons. We have Zoomed together and exchanged emails on a variety of subjects over the last few years. I also gave a Zoom talk to the Club, introduced by the late, lamented FBS member and biblio-writer Jerry Morris. The FBS is a very active club and uses the booth to promote membership. As we bibliophiles stand and chat, it is pointed out to me that I am featured in the booth on a blown-up version of an FBS newsletter with my picture on the cover. It serves as one of the booth promotions. I like it, of course, but remain semi-humble, and I really hope Jay will not see it. But he does. (Okay, I showed it to him.) And soon he has the booth in stitches saying it would make a good dart board and exclaims this idea throughout the show to any other book person who knows me. He is my ride home, so I can only grin and take it.

While I'm out and about at the fair, Jay is selling books. On Saturday, I return to the booth after a hot dog snack at the concession counter and find Jay in unusually optimistic spirits.

"What happened?"

"I sold my group of inscribed Vonneguts to the Bauman crew. They also might have an interest in my book from Ulysses Grant's library."

Shortly after, he sells a couple of good books to collectors and gets a few leads for post-fair follow-up.

"I'm lazy about follow-up," he says.

"You better follow-up," I reply.

Saturday evening, immediately after the close of that day's fair, the organizers throw an on-site party for attendees, complete with substantial hors d'oeuvres, beer, and wine. We mix and mingle with dealers including Bryan & Kelly Young, and Bob Lakin, an eighty-year-old dealer from Chatfield, Texas, as well as Steve Moosbrugger and Tom Posey from Bauman Rare Books. We discuss many things, not all of them bookish, and enjoy the camaraderie.

The show has more modern literature than I've seen in a while (a specialty of the Youngs, for example), and the word among them is that the market for modern literature is making a comeback. The internet decimated the modern literature field two decades ago by flooding the market with more copies than buyers. High spot items in great condition by Hemingway, Faulkner, Joyce, etc. have continued to find customers over the years but much of everything else remained in the doldrums. Now it appears the continuous fishing of the biblio-pond for a long period has created scarcity once again for a broader range of titles. I use the term "modern literature" loosely in this context and include contemporary genre fiction, such as horror, science fiction and fantasy, which are also seeing a resurgence, especially among younger collectors.

The hottest current area is ephemera and original documents related to women, African Americans, and LGBTQ, or some combination thereof. Many dealers are looking for it and offering it. Prices are high, and much of this market seems to be driven primarily by institutional buying rather than private collectors.

The party winds down and the groups scatter. The party organizers do their best to foist upon departing attendees surplus Yuengling beers that are iced in a large cooler. Their efforts are successful.

On Sunday morning, Jay and I say hello again to the men in the booth next to us. I will not call them booksellers because they aren't—or at least this is a one-and-done experience for them. Both are retired judges. One has been a book collector for many years, the other a good friend helping him out but not a book collector himself. The collector has planned to sell vast quantities of his collection at the fair. His focus has been big-game hunting, African exploration, and related travel. He is well off, and this is not so much a money-making expedition as a space clearing one. The two men haul in full-size bookshelves and recreate a cozy library setting in their booth—the major issue being that the towering shelves completely block a view of our booth from one side. Jay fumes. This is poor bookselling etiquette and technically not allowed, but striving for congeniality we do not protest, and the fair organizers let it go.

Jay quickly scouts their booth during set-up and returns, "Most of the good stuff is way overpriced," he opines, correctly.

The two men spend the fair talking to many but selling little. They are friendly guys and are soon chatting frequently with us as well, seemingly fascinated by the whole process of selling rare books for a living. I'm on the receiving end of much of this conversation as Jay feigns other duties when one of them appears. I explain that I'm not a bookseller myself anymore, just a wingman, but this does little to slow the questions. The show turns into a grind for them. By Sunday, I hear the comment, "There is no way we could do this full-time." And later, "I'm going to see if I can sell my collection as a whole. This is too much work."

At the end of the fair, Jay and I quickly disassemble the shelving and load the SUV. Our booth neighbors are still struggling mightily to move the heavy shelving and figure out the re-boxing of books. We wish them bon voyage as they pack their oversized U-Haul trailer. We have the collector's contact information. Jay expresses interest in a few books at the right price. It won't surprise me if the collector reaches out to Jay at some point.

Jay is personally thanked more than once by the organizers for doing the fair, and he is happy overall with the results. He puts down a deposit on a booth for next year. Maybe I'll also be back for a reprise in 2024.

Midday Sunday, I borrow Jay's car to make a personal trip. My step-grandmother Betty lives in Bradenton, only about 30 miles from the book fair. (She has outlived my paternal grandfather by over thirty years.) The family stays in regular touch with her by phone, but I haven't seen her in person in a very long time. Betty's small, one-story house with carport, neat yard, and fruit trees, is much the same as I remember it, memories of our vacations as a kid to see Betty and my grandfather bubble up from deep recesses. Betty greets me warmly and we have a meaningful, if all too brief visit, highlighted by family talk, reminiscences about my grandfather, meatball subs shared at the dining table, and the surprise appearance of my Aunt Judy.

"There is something I want you to have," Betty says.

I soon hold in my hand a photograph of my grandfather in high school ca. 1929 posing on the athletic field in his leather helmet and football uniform. He played running back for his team. He has a hint of a grin and a mischievous look.

I drive back to the book fair Sunday afternoon, crossing over Tampa Bay to St. Petersburg on the Sunshine Skyway bridge, enjoying the brilliant day, the boat-filled waters beneath, the soaring seagulls, and the smell of the ocean breeze from my open car window. I can't wait to show my grandfather's picture to Jay and anyone else who will humor me—my favorite acquisition from a memorable biblio-escapade.

The two-day return trip is once again filled with lively banter as we discuss every aspect of the book fair, then we solve more world challenges. Our friendship deepens. We don't listen to music at all. But this goes unnoticed until we get back. Our most memorable stop is at a Dairy Queen in Rayne, Louisiana, self-proclaimed "Frog Capital of the World" with signs of frogs and statues of frogs dotting the tired town. Baffled and curious, we google and find the area was once renowned for shipping the highest quality frog legs to famous restaurants world-wide.

After a long second day of traveling, Jay drops me off at home. Nicole greets us warmly outside. Jay and I exchange *hasta luego*. We watch as Jay pulls out of the driveway.

"I really like Jay," she says.

"Yeah, great guy," I reply. And for the next few days, I have Jay withdrawals.

"Let me show you what I remodeled while you were gone," she says with a beautiful smile as I drag my book-laden suitcase to the door.

2023

⁕ XVII ⁕

Six Score and More: Wallowing in It with Bill Reese

I'VE been wallowing in rare books with noted bookseller Bill Reese. Not literally, but via the Rare Book School archived podcast of his June 15, 2016 talk, "Starting Out: My Early Days as a Rare Book Dealer." Bill's entertaining account of his biblio-youth in the 1970s focuses primarily on Yale and Texas, two seemingly disparate paths connected by his early interest in Western Americana. Reese discusses a brilliant sky of prominent bookmen and women who influenced him. He ends with an observation about his pre-digital experiences garnered at the Yale libraries and via the rare book trade,

> In the pre-digital age...one could really only learn and obtain knowledge of material by being absorbed in it and soaking in it. I had the great good fortune to have the ability to wallow in vast amounts of material and be able to soak in a huge amount of knowledge through it... One of the things that has obscured the digital age is the difference between knowledge and information. Information is now readily available all the time in every form, we think we can look it all up, and to a degree we can look things up in ways we never could before, but being able to look things up without the knowledge, and the knowledge that only can be obtained by literally wallowing in the material is I think the difference between true deep book knowledge and simply accessed information.

I'm familiar with this pre-digital wallowing. In my college days in the late 1980s I had free rein of the stacks of the Ransom Center at the University of Texas (and other libraries on campus) during a three-year internship. I combined this with frequent visits to bookshops in

Austin and San Antonio and all served as a marinade of biblio-learning that no amount of internet surfing can replace. Wallowing is still available by the way—libraries are still filled with books, bookstores are still out there, rare book classes and schools are flourishing, and most dealers are more than happy to share their experiences. One just needs to make a concerted effort to dive in.

Reese's talk is delivered to me digitally, but it feels like an old-school radio show with no video or a printed transcript as a crutch. I pause the recording for a moment to crack open a Live Oak Hefeweizen, settle back on the couch sipping my brew, pet the fat cat sprawled next to me, and close my eyes to listen. About twenty minutes into his lecture Reese discusses his four primary mentors at Yale: Archibald Hanna, Charles Montgomery, Donald Gallup, and Fritz Liebert. All but Montgomery are familiar to me as prominent bookmen. As Reese talks about Montgomery a flicker of recognition ignites in my mind. My eyes are open now and I listen intently.

Montgomery (1910-1978) was an "extraordinary character," says Reese. He began as a dealer in decorative arts and antiques and was hired as a curator in 1949 by Henry Francis DuPont to develop the Winterthur Museum and Library in Delaware. In 1954, Montgomery became director of Winterthur. After retiring, he came to Yale in 1970 to teach. Reese took a class from him and soon learned that Montgomery, like Archibald Hanna, "knew everybody and had been everywhere." Montgomery was "absolutely fearless in taking his classes out to see things."

Reese recounts an example when Montgomery took a group of students to the Frick Museum,

> There was this amazing Boulle table that even in those days was probably worth a couple million dollars ... Charlie was very insistent that everybody understand the woods involved and things like that. So, we're standing in the Frick's drawing room ... and Charlie turns to me and another and says, 'Bill, Joe, turn that table over'... Before the director could say anything we picked the table up and turned it over and I look up and the director of the Frick is standing there with his jaw hung open but it was too late to do any-

thing about it so we got away with it. That's the way Charlie was: you went in, you wanted to see something, you picked it up and looked at it. That was a great lesson, too.

"That gall could get you a long way," Reese says, finishing his recollection with a laugh. Charlie's "brashness" and knowledge made quite an impact on the young Reese.

The flicker of recognition becomes a full-fledged fireworks display, and I pause the recording.

"Son of a biscuit," I say loudly to the cat who is startled awake. I can still move quickly when motivated and motivated I am. I'm up from the couch and heading full tilt for the bookshelves in the master bedroom. There is no exact order to my books, but I know the general area to search. I can't find it right off, damn it –take a deep breath— and then success: the tall, thin tome is top shelf left, and I soon cradle it in my hands like a newly discovered relic. The book is Reese's precocious *Six Score: the 120 Best Books on the Range Cattle Industry* (Austin: 1976). I bought the book on Ebay in 2010 from a dealer in New Hampshire.

The inscription reads: "For Charles Montgomery, My first book— far afield from decorative arts, but another side of Texas from Miss Ima Hogg. Best, Bill Reese, July 27, 1976."

My original catalogue slip is in the book. I'd dutifully researched the information then available on the web to identify Charles Montgomery and sketched out a biography. I briefly explained Reese's reference to Ima Hogg, Texas philanthropist, patron, and collector of the arts, but I certainly didn't realize the full importance of the Montgomery association—until now.

I immediately phone Douglas Adams, my friend who tipped me off to the Reese podcast. "I just found an awesome association copy," I say excitedly.

"What did you buy?"

"Nada. *It is already in my collection*," and I tell him the story in full.

I gently place the book on the shelf and linger a moment admiring it from a fresh perspective. Now is time for a catalogue revision and a surprise email to Bill Reese.

I'm wallowing in it, indeed.

Postscript:

Bill Reese read the essay and was kind enough to reply,

A few further notes on your copy of SIX SCORE. I finished writing the book in late 1975 and gave it to [Texas bookseller John] Jenkins, who got it out in a boxed set with Ramon Adams' book in July, 1976. I spent that June and July cataloging books in Texas, including a lot of time at the Jenkins company going through Eberstadt books. I had the first copies with me when I came through New Haven briefly in the last week of July to organize my apartment for the next year. Charles Montgomery's wife Florence and I shared a birthday-July 29- and several years had a birthday dinner together. We did it early in 1976 because I was turning 21 that July 29 and was having dinner with my family, then going to Europe for the rest of the summer the next day. So I had dinner with the Montgomerys a few days early, on the 27th, which is when I gave Charlie the book.

As I suggested in my talk, Charlie was a great inspiration to me, and he and his wife became good friends as well as mentors. Sadly he died in the fall of 1978, of a heart attack.

2016

❈ XVIII ❈

Feeling Good: Dr. Samuel Purple Makes a House Call with Henry C. Murphy

DR. Samuel S. Purple (1822-1900) has made an unexpected house call. It is my house specifically, second floor, third shelf to my right, the newest delivery to the library. Dr. Purple did not author the work that just arrived; he owned it. The book is a tribute to his friend and legendary Americana collector, Henry C. Murphy (1810-1882). Once finely bound in half morocco and marbled boards with an elaborate gilt spine, the book's binding has been battered and rubbed over its long journey, apparently unappreciated by some previous handlers, but protecting the contents within. There is the faint scent of cigar smoke. I plucked it from the flotsam and jetsam for pennies, restoring the appreciation if not the binding.

The Murphy focus initially caught my attention. I've gathered a number of books related to him and I'm always on the lookout for others. I had no idea who Dr. Purple was but his amusing name, reminiscent of a knock-off soft drink, also intrigued me. This sammelband, assembled by Purple and bound to his order, contains three items: The first is an autograph letter dated May 16, 1871 from Murphy to Purple. Second is a copy of Murphy's privately printed *A Catalogue of an American Library, Chronologically Arranged* (ca. 1850), and the last item is a description of Murphy's library removed from a copy of Dr. James Wynne's *Private Libraries of New York* (1860). Two portraits of Murphy are included for visual appeal.

A Catalogue of an American Library is what first fired my dopamine receptors. It is *muy raro*, printed in an edition of only twenty-five copies according to bibliographer Wilberforce Eames although no limitation is found within the catalogue itself. Murphy, then about age forty, had it printed for private use and distributed copies to friends. I'm fortunate to own another example, inscribed to fellow collector J. Carson Brevoort. It is the only other copy I've seen in the wilds. The catalogue records 589 items of Americana in Murphy's library, many rare and important. It concludes with the statement, "End of First Part" but a second part never appeared.

Murphy was a busy man and probably didn't have time to issue a supplement. Don Dickinson writes in *Dictionary of American Book Collectors*,

> As a lawyer, then as a politician in the Brooklyn city government Murphy was eminently successful in the early part of the nineteenth century. His appointment as city attorney was a stepping-stone to his election as mayor at the age of thirty-two. Subsequent opportunities placed him in the New York state legislature and later in The Hague as the United States' chief diplomatic minister to the Netherlands. Throughout his distinguished career he wrote articles and texts that focused on his scholarly interest in the Dutch settlement of the New World. In order to carry on the research that his writing required, he built an extensive scholarly library. The most important part of that library reflected his deep interest in the period of exploration and in those men who were first to record their impressions. Among those texts were the 'Jesuit Relations' and the great works of DeBry, Hakluyt, Hudson, and Champlain, to name only a few. As a complement to the texts on early discovery, Murphy had twenty-six early editions of Ptolemy's *Cosmographia* ranging in date from 1462 to 1600. In another section of the library Murphy gathered a large number of books and tracts on American Indian languages, customs, and beliefs ... His library held excellent documentation on the settlement of New England and the southern states, with particularly strong holdings of early statutes and constitutional conventions, proceedings of historical societies, journals and newspapers. Books from the presses of William Bradford, Peter Zenger, and Benjamin Franklin were prominent in many of these holdings ... Murphy was a knowledgeable bibliophile, an energetic collector, and a competent historian.

His library was one of the outstanding collections assembled in the late nineteenth century.

After Murphy's death, his famous collection was sold in 1884 at auction in New York, the catalogue prepared by John Russell Bartlett. It is a final record of a library dispersed to the winds, many of the books now scattered among prominent rare book libraries and others still sailing about in private collections.

Dr. Samuel Purple and his collections passed into unjust obscurity after his death, although he was well known to his contemporary collectors and book dealers. Purple is mentioned in Wynne's *Private Libraries of New York* (1860), "Dr. Purple's collection, which contains about five thousand volumes, is chiefly remarkable for its complete series of medical periodical literature, from its commencement in America to the present time." Dr. Samuel D. Gross in *History of American Medical Literature* (1875) exchanged correspondence with Dr. Purple and records, "The library of Dr. Purple, of New York, consisting of 6,000 volumes, contains a complete file of American journals, and the transactions of the American Societies, with an extensive collection of English, Scotch, and Irish periodicals, and many choice editions of the Greek and Latin fathers." These brief references are fortunately supplemented with a lengthy memorial tribute by his friend Dr. Stephen Smith, published in 1903 in *The Medical Library and Historical Journal*.

The tribute reveals a self-made man determined to overcome modest circumstances and a lack of early schooling. Dr. Purple was born in rural New York. He attended the local schools until the age of 13 and only sporadically thereafter because he helped his father in the manufacturing and selling of shoes. His father died when Purple was seventeen, writes Smith,

> [He] assumed the charge of the business and support of the family, now in reduced circumstances. That the task was difficult was apparent from the fact that it required three years of unremitting application of all his energies to relieve the estate of debt and secure for his mother a very humble home in the village. But his thoughts were not altogether confined to his business during this trying period, for we learn that he not only conceived the idea of

studying medicine, but actually began reading such books as were accessible to him.

This driven young man "obtained books from the village physician, Dr. David Ransom and devoted every leisure moment to their study. His habit was to rise at four o'clock in the morning and to study until seven o'clock, when he went to his shop and during the day studied, while working on the bench, with his book placed in a rack before him."

Purple's exertions did not go unnoticed. He garnered a number of scholarships that allowed him to attend medical school, and he graduated from the New York City University Medical College in 1844. At first, he planned to set up a rural practice near his family home. However, upon the advice and encouragement of medical school friends he decided to return to New York City. For five years he labored under extremely impecunious circumstances to establish his practice. His memorialist Smith notes that many young doctors under similar conditions gave up and returned to the safe confines of a less strenuous but not-as-fulfilling practice in the hinterlands. Dr. Purple persevered and became successful. During these early years, his literary bent led him to a position of assistant editor and then editor in 1848 of the *New York Journal of Medicine*. This appointment played a key role in giving birth to the budding bibliophile. Smith writes,

> [Purple's] connection with the Journal had brought him into familiar relations with many of the leading physicians of the city. The one who exerted the greatest influence upon him was Professor John B. Beck, of the College of Physicians and Surgeons. Dr. Beck was a very scholarly man and had a large and valuable library, which he had been many years perfecting, especially in the department of rare medical pamphlets. Commenting upon the importance of collecting and preserving the early medical literature of the country, much of which was originally printed in pamphlet form, he concluded by urging the young editor to avail himself of the opportunity which his position afforded him of securing and preserving every early publication obtainable. At the same time he gave him a

large number of pamphlets, which really formed the nucleus of the enormous collection which he subsequently made. These suggestions of Professor Beck stimulated into the greatest activity the latent passion for bibliography, which was finally to absorb so much of the time and means of his young friend.

From this time onward his business satisfactorily increased, both in quantity and quality, and though he never attained to a large and lucrative practice, his income satisfied every ambition except the single one of providing all the means he craved for the purchase of books. But when the opportunity offered of securing rare works he did not let it pass on account of a momentary want of money. His credit was good with all classes of book dealers and with most of the purveyors of old books he had standing orders for the purchase of rare editions. For the period of half a century he maintained a close personal acquaintance with all dealers in old books, and no quaint volume in the second-hand book stores or in the auction rooms escaped his careful scrutiny. At first his attention was especially directed to rare medical books and pamphlets, but constant association with the dealers in old books drew his attention to other inviting fields of bibliographical research. He was thus led to the study of American historical literature, and his collection of rare books and pamphlets relating to the early history of New York was very valuable. It very naturally happened that these investigations into the history of the early families drew his attention to the important and enticing department of genealogical research. To these subjects he finally devoted a large amount of his leisure time, and his collection of books and pamphlets relating thereto was probably not surpassed by any private library in this country.

Dr. Purple's life-long pursuit also created a strong desire to preserve his collection. In 1875, he became president of the New York Academy of Medicine. During the four years of his presidency and beyond he worked diligently to build a large reference library for the Academy. He also gave them his unique collection of serial medical literature. Smith writes,

> What that collection cost him in time, money and patient toil no one can have the remotest conception. For more than a quarter

of a century he ransacked every collection of old pamphlets accessible to him in this and other cities. Many were the occasions when he despaired of completing sets, but by correspondence with dealers in old books, with the older physicians and by advertising in medical periodicals, offering at the same time suitable payment, he succeeded in completing full sets of all the medical periodicals ever published in this country.

Dr. Purple's zeal in collecting was so great that he assembled a second set of rare medical journals and pamphlets. After his death, this material was acquired by the library of The Medical Society of the County of Kings, Brooklyn, thus establishing the foundation of two important medical collections. His extensive genealogy collection was auctioned by C.F. Libbie & Co., New York City, on February 16-19, 1909. The introduction to the auction catalogue records, "At an early date in his career (1850) he began collecting works on American Genealogy at a time when there were comparatively few collectors in these lines ... [and] until a few days before his death he was active in hunting and buying genealogies, and he left no stone unturned to run down any rare item that might come under his notice. It goes without saying that no such complete collection has ever been or ever will be again offered for sale."

The letter from Murphy to Purple glimpses Purple's generous nature and his ties to the rare book world. Murphy writes on May 16th, 1871, "My dear Dr. Purple, I have left the two volumes which you so kindly lent me at Mr. [Joseph] Sabin's for you and beg to return you my sincere thanks for their use. I learn this fact from them: that after all a patient must consult some good physician on the spot as to the necessity and mode of using any of these springs and especially the thermal ones. Repeating with you my obligations for the opportunity of reading these volumes I am ever Yours Truly, Henry C Murphy."

The utilization of thermal springs for health reasons has a long history. (One of the books lent by Purple may have been John Bell's *Mineral and Thermal Springs of the United States and Canada* [1855].) The circumstances of the letter are unknown, but a little imaginative conjecture places these two ardent bibliophiles in Joseph Sabin's bookshop, Murphy perhaps bending deep to examine those bottom shelves, Purple a few steps over straining skyward to reach a tome on the top shelf, Sabin in the background, knowing it is going to be a good day. Murphy suddenly lets out a groan as he tweaks his touchy back wrestling with a large folio. Purple feels a twinge in his shoulder on an overreach. The two men take a breather together, discussing with Sabin the issue points on various Americana rarities and eventually the aches and pains of a certain age. Purple is a bit awed by the mildly older Murphy, this former mayor of Brooklyn, Congressman, and generally famous collector. He offers to supply a couple of books that might just help Murphy rejuvenate what ails him. The thank you note becomes a memento, along with the rare catalogue and the dissected extract on Murphy from Wynne's book, all bound so finely together and shelved amidst Purple's other prizes as a token of biblio-friendship until Purple is no more. But the book itself carries on their connection, alternatively prized, forgotten, and now resurrected, the bond of bibliophiles remaining unbroken.

2017

✷ XIX ✷

J. Frank Dobie Meets Preacher, Gambler, & Book Collector E.L. Shettles

I WAS A book greenhorn when I first encountered J. Frank Dobie (1888-1964) and Elijah L. Shettles (1852-1940), two legendary Texas bookmen and personalities. My early discovery of Dobie and Shettles did much to inspire my interest in the history of book collecting and rare bookselling.

This momentous event happened while I was cataloging a collection of J. Frank Dobie material, the finest to appear on the market, offered in a 1992 Dorothy Sloan catalogue. (It was gathered by Dudley R. Dobie, J. Frank's cousin and a noted bookseller.) In Dudley's hoard I found J. Frank Dobie's eulogy "E. L. Shettles, Man, Bookman and Friend." Dobie read it at Shettles' funeral in 1940, and it was published in the January 1941 issue of the *Southwest Historical Quarterly*.

Dobie was an English professor at the University of Texas-Austin known for his outspoken liberal and wide-minded views that often clashed with the more conservative university administration. He taught a famous class on "Guide to Life and Literature of the Southwest." Dobie issued an influential guidebook under the same title identifying key works enhanced by his insightful comments. His fame as an author of non-fiction focusing on the Southwest has outlived him and his most important works remain in print. Notable titles include *A Vaquero of the Brush Country* (1929), *Coronado's Children* (1930), *Apache Gold and Yaqui Silver* (1939), *The Longhorns* (1941), *The Voice of the Coyote* (1949), and *The Mustangs* (1952). After his death his exceptional library of related material was acquired by the Ransom Center at the University of Texas.

Dobie's tribute to Shettles begins, "It was in the fall of 1925, nearly fifteen years ago, that I first came to know E. L. Shettles as a conversationalist, as a friend, and as a book man, and to realize the extraordinary riches within his mind. In my life I have not met more than two other men who possessed such a wealth of minute, accurate, readily available information. His memory was to me perpetually marvelous; his justness was comparable to his memory."

Dobie then recalls a recent interaction with the aging but still mentally limber Shettles,

> How Mr. Shettles loved to talk books to somebody who could understand and whom he liked! Last winter [1939] a book dealer from Kansas City came to Austin and expressed the wish to meet Mr. Shettles. What dealer of any consequence in America does not know his name? I took this one out [to meet him]. Mr. Shettles had been confined to his room from which he received us. The Kansas City dealer mentioned some rare pamphlet that he had come into possession of. He had forgotten the date. Mr. Shettles supplied it, told him where the pamphlet was printed, gave him more facts about the author, recalled how, when and where he, himself, acquired his own first copy of it, at what price, to whom he sold it and at what price. He went into the subject matter of the pamphlet, noted casually certain printed items that had preceded it, and then named a still rarer pamphlet in reply to it.

I ask Dorothy Sloan about the intriguing Shettles. She points me to historian Archie P. McDonald's entry for Shettles in the *Handbook of Texas* (the actual volumes, pre-internet). McDonald's brief essay is lively and pulls me in further, beginning thus,

> Elijah LeRoy Shettles, Methodist minister, magazine editor, publisher, and bibliographer, was born in 1852 in the Flatwoods country of Mississippi near Pontotoc, the son of Abner and Caroline (Browning) Shettles. His maternal grandfather, the family patriarch, was a Baptist minister and had a lifelong influence on Shettles. During his eighty-eight years Shettles worked as a teacher, a farm-implement salesman, a law student, a pressman for a newspaper, a freight agent, a public weigher, a coal supplier, a gambler, a

saloonkeeper, an insurance solicitor, a preacher, a church administrator, an editor, a book collector and dealer, and a representative of several university and public libraries. He was also a friend of the governors of two states, companion to men of prominence in business and letters, chaplain of the Texas Senate, publisher of books, and humanitarian. Shettles was over 6'5" tall and had the unlikely nickname of Shorty.

From 1881 to 1891 he traveled the Southwest as a hard-drinking, cheating, itinerant gambler, who frequently stopped long enough in a town to operate a gambling hall and saloon; most of these years he spent in Texas. He responded to a revival preacher on April 27, 1891, and soon thereafter felt a calling to the Methodist ministry. Shettles's ministerial career, all of it in Texas, spanned over thirty years. Always a devoted bibliophile, he revealed much of his secular reading in his early sermons.

Shettles was certainly a man with an uncommon bibliophilic focus—apparently not letting a gambling career or the call of God distract him from his book collecting and bookselling. I immediately warm to him and want to know more.

I cheekily ask Dorothy if Shettles is a role model for her as a bookseller. She smiles and says she only bets on rare books.

I soon found that Dobie revisited Shettles in a 1957 essay "The First Book-Seller to Enrich My Life." Dobie's book collecting is little-mentioned nowadays, but he assembled an exceptional collection of material related to ranching and the Southwest. Dobie utilized other notable booksellers besides Shettles to build his collection such as Wright Howes and Charlie Everitt.

Dobie writes in the essay of his beginnings as a collector and his fortuitous meeting of Shettles,

> About three years after a tide in human affairs made me aware of range life and folk tales of the Southwest as subjects for learning and writing, Oklahoma A&M College offered me the chairmanship of its Department of English at a salary beyond the barest subsistence level ... [In 1924] I began writing for *The Country Gentleman* for money ... Now a little book money was a wonderful addition to my life.

[In Guthrie, Oklahoma] I walked into a kind of racket store—as a store of odds and ends was then called. This one did not have much in it, but I noticed two books on a half-empty shelf. They were duplicate copies of Robert M. Wright's *Dodge City, Cowboy Capital* (Wichita, Kansas, 1913) in mint condition—a term I had just acquired ... the storekeeper [said] if I would take both copies I could have them for $2.50. I took both. They had no doubt been on his shelf since the year of publication. In my ignorance the title was new to me, but instinct plus knowledge of something else told me I had made a find.

The next year we went back to Austin for keeps, and I began spending an afternoon hour every week or two in H. P. Gammell's Book Store ... That ancient Dane was as rare as and a lot thicker than any of his quartos; he knew the prices of nearly all the scarce items but was not strong on the contents of many. If somebody told him his price was too high, he either moved the decimal point a figure to the right or put the book in what he called his 'private library' to wait for time to justify what he asked. One day in Gammell's store I met one of his best customers, E. L. Shettles. He invited me to come to see him.

Shettles had somehow learned that I had a duplicate copy of Wright's *Dodge City, Cowboy Capital*, and did not try to disguise his eagerness for it. I think it was selling for up to $25 or better at the time, and I am sure that he had an order for it from an unquibbling customer. Contrary to my practice in the stock market when prices are going down, I was not in a hurry to sell now, but finally Mr. Shettles got it for about $40 in trade. He was always generous with me and wanted me to learn and acquire books both....

Mr. Shettles did business, mostly by mail, in his cottage home out in a plebian part of town. He might have had three thousand, maybe more, books, not counting duplicates, mainly Americana, with emphasis on Texas, the West, and the South. He was an expert at acquiring remainders of privately printed historical material and then controlling the market on it. He was a great pamphlet man. He had been trained—as a professional gambler on cards—to remember concretely, precisely. He knew the bibliographical facts about almost every title stored in his capacious memory and knew an extraordinary amount of the contents of thousands of books and pamphlets. He could gut one very quickly. Some of the most knowing collectors in the nation were on his list. Once in a while one came to see him. He located tens of thousands of dollars worth of old newspapers, magazines, pamphlets and other material purchased through the Littlefield Fund for the University of Texas library.

Many times I would visit Mr. Shettles without buying anything, but never without learning something important to me. Almost anything that I took down from a shelf could lead to a revealing remark about its author, its relationship to another book, its pertinence to a patch—if not to a field—of knowledge.

In reading the Dobie essays, I learned that Shettles had written an autobiography, first published serially in the *Pontotoc Progress* newspaper from 1935-1936. Archie McDonald edited it for publication in 1973 as *Recollections of a Long Life*, reprinting Dobie's "E. L. Shettles, Man, Bookman and Friend" as the foreword. I acquired a copy quicker than a rousted paisano bird.

The whole work is robust and entertaining. Shettles devotes a chapter to "My Experience as a Book Collector." He provides a rare account of book hunting in the South from the 1890s-1920s including areas of Texas, New Orleans, Nashville, Mobile, Louisville, Kansas City, etc. He traveled often as a Methodist minister and he continued hunting after retirement, rarely passing up a bookstore or bookman.

Shettles particularly favored visiting a dealer named Paul Hunter in Nashville, "from whom I had been buying books and pamphlets and all sorts of material to be found in the South. I soon became very much interested in him, he was a jolly good fellow, all the time making out as though he did not know much about books and at the same time getting out of you all he could of what you knew about books . . . I bought extensively from him."

Shettles writes of another trip visiting Hunter ("I spent more than a week in Nashville"), then he adds, "I extended this trip to include Louisville, Cincinnati, New York and Washington, D.C., but about all I saw on the trip was old bookstores and old books. When I returned home and began to open the boxes I felt like my wife, from the way she looked at me, thought I had lost my head. In a way I had, for when a man gets to be a full fledged bibliophile, he is in a way, half crazy."

This half-crazed collector describes several interesting finds and broadly evaluates the book hunting opportunities,

> Next to Tennessee were Kentucky and Louisiana, both rich in early historical material . . . I always made a number of trips to Kansas City and always with profit. I liked the dealers, and I liked Mr. Purd Wright, Librarian of the Kansas City Library. I made several trips to Oklahoma and to Arkansas. I made nine trips to Arkansas in one year. I made two or three trips into Mississippi and Alabama, neither of these states was very good hunting ground, but Georgia was. But many of the states had been impoverished by the [Civil] War.

In 1921, upon retirement, Shettles transitioned from book collector to full-time book dealer. He had begun cutting books loose a few years earlier. He recounts,

> On a trip to Austin in 1918 I carried with me a long list of duplicates in my collection. I showed it to Mr. [Ernest] Winkler, then consulting librarian and buyer for the Littlefield Fund of the University of Texas. He bought most of them and said, "Why not sell us your Texas collection, that is, such as we do not have?" I agreed and began at once to list and ship over as fast as I could my collection; it was then I found out how deeply wedded I was to my books, but they must go. I sold to the University Library, the State Library, the Southern Methodist University library, the Rosenberg and the San Antonio libraries and to Miss Ima Hogg most of my collection that I had been many years accumulating. I have kept most of the invoices of these sales which would be a very good bibliography if arranged in alphabetical order.
>
> After I moved over to Austin and began anew to hunt for material I made an agreement with Mr. Winkler that if he would give me the privilege to represent the Littlefield Southern History collection of the University I would give him the first chance to pick over what I bought and buy it, if he wished. I think the plan worked out very well.

I have found little for my own Shettles collection in three decades of hunting. One gem did surface years ago, an undated Shettles catalogue, ca. 1930, possibly a proof copy in galley format, which had belonged to J. Frank Dobie and was annotated by him.

Then in 2022, I got a call to do an insurance appraisal for a small group of books in Beaumont, Texas. Beaumont isn't a typical destination city for tourism or travel, but I didn't mind the two-hour drive through East Texas, a mix of beautiful, wooded pines juxtaposed with pocketed poor areas that jar a suburbanite's senses. My fried catfish lunch at Fish Tales in Sour Lake, Texas was first rate.

A recently retired gentleman met me at the door of a spacious, newer one-story home with a landscaped backyard the size of a football field.

"My wife and I enjoy gardening," he said.

He also enjoyed books, but the ones I was there to evaluate were mainly from his father's Texana collection, formed decades earlier in the 1960s-1980s. Most of the rarities were sold at a notable sale in 2004 by Sotheby's New York. The few remaining did not meet the reserve at auction and were retained by the family. The son had sent me a brief list of the items before my visit. And what a list it was.

Books included Joseph Field's *Three Years in Texas* (1836), Arthur Ikin's *Texas* (1841), and David Woodman Jr.'s *Guide to Texas Emigrants* (1835), all potentially valued in the $20,000-40,000 range.

Most intriguing to yours truly, however, was a group of manuscripts and typescripts containing over thirty essays by J. Frank Dobie. Many had Dobie's notes and annotations. His father purchased them from Texas booksellers John Jenkins and Ray Walton in the 1970s-80s.

I began sorting through the essays, reliving my Dobie cataloging experience decades earlier at Dorothy Sloan's. I paused. In my hands, I held Dobie's original annotated typescript for "E. L. Shettles, Man, Bookman and Friend."

Dare I hope for more? Yes. A minute later, I found the typescript of "The First Book-Seller to Enrich My Life."

Oh reader, how I was suddenly overcome with the desire for possession. A hot flame burned within, and its heat was obvious to the owner. He had watched his father build a great collection and he knew the signs. He gave me a whimsical look. We talked. I have something else related, he added.

He soon appeared with a large, custom case that housed the very rare original *Pontotoc Progress* newspaper issues of *Recollections of a Long Life* that had published Shettles' autobiography serially. It was J. Frank Dobie's set with notes.

My car drive home found me in unusually fine spirits as I cruised through the Piney Woods. I don't sing often for good reasons, but on this occasion I was alone, the music was cranked up, and I belted out my favorite songs, glancing regularly at the Dobie-Shettles items in the passenger seat that would soon be on my shelves.

2023

❈ XX ❈

William P. Barlow Jr. (1934-2021):
Personal Rewards and Universal Benefits

WILLIAM P. BARLOW, JR. (1934-2021) collected books for almost 70 years—an admirable run achieved by few collectors, and rarer still was his ability to recall just about every acquisition going back to the beginning. A CPA by vocation, Bill was organized, and in case he needed to refresh his memory, he could consult his large, hefty ledger book in which he had written in chronological order each book acquired since the early 1950s. And there were thousands and thousands of them recorded within. I saw this ledger first-hand on a memorable visit with my friend Douglas Adams to Bill's home in Oakland, California in 2011. News of Bill's passing on October 21, 2021 at age 87 from a heart attack shocked me and stirred many thoughts.

I first met Bill in the mid-1990s while I was working at Butterfield & Butterfield auction house in San Francisco. He was of medium height, openly friendly, quick moving, and dressed well, if a tad unconventionally, almost always wearing the light-colored sport jacket and flashy tie, for example, at a formal gathering of dark-suited bibliophiles. He was easy to spot, and I don't think he minded that. We discovered we shared a common interest in book collecting history. By then Bill was already a legendary bookman with a long list of accomplishments: Grolier Club Council member, earliest elected president of the Roxburghe Club in San Francisco, winner of the Thomas More Medal for Book Collecting, teacher with Terry Belanger at Rare Book School of a class on book collecting and the disposition of collections, notable speaker on bibliophilic topics, and proprietor of his own private Nova Press.

Not long before we first met, I'd run across his talk published by the Library of Congress, *Book Collecting: Personal Rewards and Public Benefits, A Lecture Delivered at the Library of Congress on December 7, 1983.* (1984). Bill was an enthusiastic promoter of book collecting, and this essay proved inspirational to me. Using examples from his own collecting, he explained with wit and clarity the wide range of delights (and a few pitfalls) one could expect when rare book hunting was taken seriously. The following excerpt struck a particular chord for me as I progressed into collecting "books about books" association copies. He wrote,

> There is a species of books generally classified by antiquarian book dealers under the heading 'books about books,' which is supposed to be distinct from a related classification called 'bibliography,' although the distinguishing characteristics are not always clear. The species includes reminiscences of book dealers and book collectors, collections of essays allegedly of interest to book collectors, instructions intended to enhance a book collector's fun or profit, and books designed to encourage non-collectors to collect.
>
> Although described as 'books about books,' these are really 'books about book collecting.' I am always amazed that so many of these books are published and even more amazed that they are sold. But the most astonishing thing is that they are written! The collecting experience, it has always seemed to me, is so personal that it is both painful to write about and impossible to communicate.
>
> Nevertheless, that is what I have been asked to do, and I am going to do it in the same manner most 'books about books' are written: I will describe my own experiences as a book collector and hope that something universal may emerge.

Bill recalled how the purchase in ca. 1953 of his first collectible book, Milton's *Paradise Lost and Paradised Regain'd* printed by John Baskerville in London in 1758, shaped much of his future collecting. The collecting of Baskerville imprints and ephemera soon led to an interest in provenance of various copies, spurring the gathering of auction and bookseller catalogues offering Baskerville material. This evolved into a wider collection of catalogues numbering in the tens of thousands (separate warehouse space required), with significant offshoots of collecting fine examples of printing, a large Thomas Dibdin collection, in-depth holdings of private library catalogues, and the history of bibliography. Later in life he gathered a massive collection of material related to Duncan Hines and his travel guides dating from the 1930s. The wellspring was memories of traveling with his brother and parents across the country in the 1950s in the family Cadillac, using the travel books published by Duncan Hines as a guide to the restaurants and hotels they encountered along the way. Oh, and he had huge holdings of stamps and related philately items stored in rows of file cases. I believe fine wines also had a niche. But books and printing were his primary focus. No wonder he didn't retire early—acquisition funds were needed!

One highlight of my Barlow collection is a typescript of his "Adventures in Book Collecting," read before the Roxburghe Club, January 16, 2001. He sent me the manuscript with a nice note after one of our biblio-discussions. Presented as an overview of how he gathered his Duncan Hines collection, it is a tour-de-force example of a book collector at the height of his powers.

Bill gave a version of this talk a number of times. Andy Foster of Milton and Hubble Books in Pasadena, CA was present at one. He wrote on a memorial thread for Barlow,

> William Barlow's 2011 address to the California Rare Book School, detailing his Duncan Hines collection, its genesis and growth, must rank among the great bibliophile lectures of all time. Before his talk, with all honesty, I thought that Duncan Hines was a cake mix. Then, I was educated.
>
> Biography, methodology, and details guided my understanding of who Duncan Hines was, why he shaped history, and how Duncan Hines's particular actions produced thousands of printed artifacts.
>
> William P. Barlow Jr.'s lecture demonstrated how a masterful collector hones to a theme with alert intelligence and creates an asset with lasting utility and untold significance.
>
> Thanks Bill. I'll really miss you.

The Relentless Pursuit of Rare Books

When my book *Rare Book Hunting: Essays and Escapades* (2021) came out, I included Bill in my essay "Book Hunter Bypaths Explored and Exposed." Here I recalled my visit to see him and his surprising sporting activity that created some unusual private printings from his press. I wrote,

> Bill Barlow is very clubbable and is an active member of longstanding with the Grolier Club of New York and Roxburghe Club of San Francisco. He taught a class for many years with Terry Belanger on 'Book Collecting' at Rare Book School in Virginia. He's an active public speaker on bookish topics. His accomplishments are many. And he is the only private citizen I know of with a Hinman collator in his dining room—not just any collator, but the one used by Hinman himself in researching the printing history of the First Folio of William Shakespeare. But that is another story.
>
> Bill is also a printer. He privately prints whatever he finds interesting or amusing, usually in pamphlet form, typically under his Nova Press imprint. His printing shop is set up on the second floor of his house in Oakland. The weight of the machinery and type must be several tons. The books (and a large collection of stamps in file cabinets) add several tons more. A delightful visit several years ago resulted in a question about structural integrity. Bill just shrugged. There is a guest room on the first floor but I didn't stay there. If I had, I wouldn't have slept much thinking of the weight of the bibliophilic world literally above my head.
>
> Bill is the consummate host and over wine and an Asian meal at a nearby restaurant, I was surprised to learn something decidedly non-bookish about him. William P. Barlow, Jr. was a champion water skier in his youth (and beyond). The image of this tanned bookman on skis, deftly slaloming and jumping, waving effortlessly to adoring fans as he sped by was disconcerting at first. And it was revealed he had also printed a few items relating to water skiing. I will mention two examples, each combining his creative bent and sense of humor.
>
> The first is *A Playlet for Water Skiers [In One Actlet]* (1961). The playlet records the lively banter between a water ski judge and his assistant as they reflect on their underappreciated talents. Barlow writes in the preface, "For a number of years I have been distributing

Christmas booklets regularly dealing with printing or book collecting. This has been a bit unfair to my water skiing friends, who have been regularly mystified by them. This year, out of respect for them, I have written something about water skiing. They may still be mystified."

The second is *Songs for Water Skiers: Another in the Continuing Series of As-Yet-Unsuccessful Attempts to Inject Water Skiing into the Mainstream of American Cultural Life* (1967). Bill points out in the introduction that all popular sports have their own songs, a good example being baseball's "Take Me Out to the Ballgame." To remedy this for the sport of water skiing, Barlow wrote and composed two original songs included here—"Sweet Anna Lee," and "Go, Go Trickin' With Me." This second song incorporates water skier slang throughout.

Soon after my book appeared, I received an unexpected email from Bill Barlow. I'm reproducing it here in its entirety, as it is not only informative but also exemplifies Bill's continued interest and engagement in book collecting even as relentless aging took a toll.

March 30, 2021

Dear Kurt,

I got wind of your book *Rare Book Hunting* at one source, bought it on Amazon, received it today, and went straight to the index. What did Kurt have to say (if anything) about me, since it has been a couple of decades, I guess, since you last visited my home and saw some of my collections. Well there it was, two pages listed in the index (actually a page and a third to be honest). And a pretty amazing recollection of what you saw and we talked about considering the intervening period. I am flattered, which is almost always welcome (unless it precedes a pitch for a charitable contribution). And I am humbled to be so mentioned among the many great collectors you have seen and written about. I have only skipped around a bit so far, but I wanted to get something off to you as soon as possible.

Obviously you can now be assured that I am still alive. I reached 87 in February, and it appears I am going to get through the pandemic.

The collection is still pretty much as you described it. The Hinman collator has gone to the Bancroft Library. The Baskerville collection is stronger than ever (another Baskerville binding spotted on eBay and added to the dozen or so others last week). The Dibdin collection is also more nearly complete. The Duncan Hines material may actually have been started after you were last here. The auction catalogues continue to be acquired, although not nearly in the numbers that were previously common.

The Nova Press is more or less idle, as my eyesight is not great and my ability to stand in front of a press is similarly reduced. The Christmas cards or pamphlets are no longer being produced (so don't feel that you have simply been dropped off the list). And the weight over the heads of those downstairs has grown by another thousand pounds or so, I suppose.

When I last saw you, you were regularly coming to the SF/LA Book Fair each year. I don't know whether that is still the case (or was before they became virtual). If you are coming out this way, I would love to show you a few new things and perhaps enjoy a dinner together so we can share stories about book collecting.

I hope this finds you in good health, and I hope your book will get a wide and distinguished circulation. I know, of course, it was not written to provide funds for your retirement, but it would be nice if it at least managed to pay for itself.

With all best wishes,
Bill Barlow

Feeling very remiss, I immediately dashed off a presentation copy to him. He liked that, too. Bill always seemed timeless to me, both a living and historic figure in rare books, with his own recollections of earlier book hunters he had met in his youth stretching his connection with the bookish past back over one hundred years. Such a distinguished bibliophile certainly gained quick and well-deserved admittance to Book Valhalla. And there I imagine he is already collecting, printing, teaching, and regaling the group, much to the delight of his fellows. His hope that from his own story something universal would emerge was realized. *Vaya con libros,* my friend.

Postscript:

Barlow's collection was gifted to the Bancroft Library *en bloc.* With perseverance, I was able to acquire about five hundred "duplicates" that were deaccessioned by the library.

2021

✣ XXI ✣

A Blockbuster Deal: Nineteenth-Century American Literature Chased and Preserved

"IF YOU can get that," said Mr. Wakeman, "all right. But remember that the collection is to be offered to no one but Mr. Morgan…"

Surprises await the assiduous biblio-reader. I encountered this passage in George S. Hellman's largely forgotten book, *Lanes of Memory* (1927), a collection of autobiographical essays. Hellman (1878-1958) was a prolific writer and editor. He was also a dealer and collector of rare autographs, manuscripts, books, and art. In the early twentieth century, Hellman sold exceptional literary material to J. Pierpont Morgan and other prominent collectors. His discursive essays rambled down many literary bypaths, and gems of manuscript and book hunting surfaced regularly. None read better than his chapter on selling material to Morgan. It was Hellman who facilitated the sale of collector Stephen H. Wakeman's exceptional gathering of American literary manuscripts to Morgan. That episode, a quotation from which is dangled above as a prelude, is reproduced in its entirety below. Hellman's account is an unusually candid insider's view of a blockbuster transaction. Hellman had an advantage in his retelling. He originally supplied Wakeman much of the manuscript material including the famous Thoreau journals.

Even as Hellman has disappeared into history, Wakeman remains alive to specialists through the famous auction of his library of American literature in New York at the American Art Association in 1924 (sans the manuscripts sold to Morgan). The auction catalogue and its contemporary reprint served as a basic bibliographical tool for decades and even now is an astonishing record of a dedicated collector's achievement.

Stephen H. Wakeman (1859-1924) was a life-long New Yorker who made his fortune in produce, specifically as head of John Wakeman & Co., Beans and Peas. Bookseller John S. Van E. Kohn's biographical sketch of Wakeman in *Grolier 75* (1959) is illuminating, "[Wakeman] had three children, the last born in 1900. The same year Mrs. Wakeman joined the Roman Catholic Church and her husband found the consuming interest of his life in collecting books. In 1904 he ceased to traffic in beans and peas in order to devote all his time and energy to books." Kohn doesn't speculate whether three children at home and a newly devout wife may have spurred Wakeman in search of a distracting hobby. Kohn does write, "Wakeman's family life was on the whole not happy. He was generous but unsociable. Extremely taciturn, he liked best to spend his evenings in his second-floor library, reading or corresponding with booksellers and fellow collectors."

Wakeman is pictured in the frontispiece to the sale catalogue and Kohn describes him as "a slender man of medium height. His clean, rather delicate features and high forehead gave his face a sensitive, intellectual aspect ... with respect to clothes he was dapper, almost foppish. He collected paintings and owned several Corots. He was an enthusiastic operagoer and an amateur fiddler."

Kohn records that under the tutelage of pioneer American literature dealer P. K. Foley, Wakeman "began to form his collection of books, letters, and manuscripts of his nine favorite American men of letters, and in the twenty-three years of life remaining to him he attained his goal with brilliant success. The nine authors are Bryant, Emerson, Hawthorne, Holmes, Longfellow, Lowell, Poe, Thoreau, and Whittier."

An unidentified contemporary provided a more detailed view of Wakeman's collecting habits in an introductory essay to the auction catalogue. It is titled "Mr. Wakeman as a Book Collector, by an Intimate Associate" and reads in full,

When Mr. Wakeman set out in the year 1900 to acquire a library which was to contain the works of certain American classic authors, he brought to the task a penchant for collecting, a taste for good reading, a fund of experience in business affairs and a naturally incisive mind. For twenty years he devoted himself to the study of his nine favorite writers of fiction and poetry, conducting all the while an active search for copies of first editions of their productions and especially for examples bearing a personal association with their creators through autograph signatures or through accompanying letters referring to the books.

Mr. Wakeman was fastidious in securing fine examples. Many copies of many books received on approval were returned unbought because of slight imperfections. As a result of adherence to a standard of excellence, the collection is unique in the immaculate condition of the first editions comprising it.

That his relations with fellow collectors and with dealers were a source of keen interest and pleasure to him is evident when one peruses his copious and interesting correspondence with them.

Besides printed books, Mr. Wakeman acquired a remarkable collection of manuscripts of great American authors and poets of the nineteenth century, including among their number all of Thoreau's journals and important Hawthorne and Longfellow items. Most of them were purchased from him by the late Mr. J. P. Morgan in 1916, but some precious manuscripts remain in the Wakeman Collection.

It was his custom to insert in each of the important volumes of this library a slip of paper bearing in his penciled handwriting a description of the book calling attention to features of especial interest. These notes form an interesting contribution to American bibliography.

After twenty years of activity in assembling this collection, Mr. Wakeman found his task virtually completed. Around him—in his very bed-chamber—stood bookcases, shoulder to shoulder, filled to overflowing with the friendly books bearing within themselves the very touch of the vanished hands of their authors. Here he held communion with them during his days of declining health and here they stood about him when he was gathered to his fathers.

A Blockbuster Deal

A number of years ago, I was fortunate to acquire what I consider THE copy of the auction catalogue, Arthur Swann's annotated copy with ownership signature. Swann was director of the American Art Association book department at the time, oversaw the sale, and catalogued the material with the assistance of his staff. Prices and buyers are recorded. Correction slips for three lots are tipped in. Swann has also recorded absentee bidders and the price Wakeman paid for each lot. This latter set of annotations is particularly fascinating and reflects the frequent wide divergence between the auction prices and Wakeman's costs, sometimes to his favor and sometimes not. For example, he did very well overall on his Poe and Thoreau but took a beating on many of the Whittier items.

The manuscripts and letters *not* in the auction sale and sold to Morgan previously for a tidy $165,000 included all that survived of Hawthorne's *Scarlet Letter* manuscript, the complete manuscripts of *The Blithedale Romance, Dr. Grimshawe's Secret, The Dolliver Romance, Septimius Felton* and all the *Journals*. Emerson, Longfellow, and Whittier are represented in depth with manuscripts and letters, as is Oliver Wendell Holmes anchored by the manuscript of *The Autocrat of the Breakfast-Table*. Rare Poe material included the manuscript for *Tamerlane*. Kohn writes, "Thoreau must have been Wakeman's favorite. This group includes the great *Journal* in thirty-nine manuscript volumes, *The Service*, twelve notebooks, and fourteen letters to his mother and sisters, Emerson, Hawthorne, and others."

George Hellman in *Lanes of Memory* (1927) recounts the acquisition of Thoreau's papers and journal, much of which he sold to Wakeman. Hellman got wind of their location through

> a literary discussion with Mr. Bliss Perry—then editor of the *Atlantic Monthly*—one of the young men associated with the firm of Houghton, Mifflin Company . . . By the next train I was on the way to Worcester, the home of the owner of these precious documents, Mr. E. H. Russell, principal of the high school. Thoreau had left his manuscripts to his sister; she in turn to Blake, the editor of several Thoreau volumes; and from him they had been inherited by Mr. Russell. It was after ten o'clock when I stood in front of Mr.

Russell's door. A few moments later Mr. Russell was showing me the two wooden chests which with his own hands Thoreau had carved to serve as the repository of his manuscripts; and before the hour's pleasant conversation had ended, an agreement had been reached by which Thoreau's papers were to pass into my possession.

In addition to the Thoreau manuscripts acquired from Hellman and sold to Morgan, Wakeman had 103 jaw-dropping lots of Thoreau material in the auction sale. These included letters, additional manuscripts, inscribed books, and books from Thoreau's library. So, you can see why I was quite excited to acquire Wakeman's copy of Francis H. Allen's *A Bibliography of Henry David Thoreau* (1908). It has Wakeman's book label, ownership signature, and a letter from Allen to Wakeman, thanking him for his "pleasant note" about the book, and "glad you've got that set of proof-sheets." Wakeman is acknowledged formally for his help in the preface and mentioned in reference to a number of books in the text.

A brief perusal of the auction catalogue itself will give the best flavor of Wakeman's overall collection. Kohn writes, "The well-written and well-illustrated catalogue abounds in excerpts from manuscript notes that Wakeman had written and laid in hundreds of his books ... Like the catalogue of the Carroll Wilson collection [published in 1950], which draws upon it to a considerable extent, the Wakeman catalogue ... is a standard reference work for collectors and librarians interested in American literature."

Wakeman's efforts were the culmination, both in material and technique, of the first wave of American literature collectors. Most notable among these were Charles B. Foote, Owen Aldis, William Harris Arnold, Marshall Lefferts, Frank Maier, and Jacob C. Chamberlain. Wakeman's pursuit of association material, manuscripts, and letters, his insistence on fine, original condition, and his in-depth gathering of ephemeral items, set the standard for the great collectors to follow, particularly Carroll A. Wilson, Parkman Dexter Howe, and Clifton Waller Barrett.

Kohn's reference to Carroll Wilson and Wakeman's influence

upon him has a particular poignancy for me. I bought in 2008 a copy of Ralph Waldo Emerson's *Letters and Social Aims* (1876)—another favorite author of the two collectors—that bears both men's bookplates.

Let us conclude as promised with George Hellman's account (*Lanes of Memory*, pp. 42-47) of the sale of the Wakeman manuscripts to J. Pierpont Morgan. Reading Hellman's book inspired this essay, and he should not be forgotten. He writes,

> The addition to the Morgan Library of the preponderant portion of the American manuscripts was negotiated under circumstances that bear recounting. Mr. S. H. Wakeman, a cultured and wealthy New Yorker, had for many years been quietly collecting manuscripts and association books of the great American authors, and his acquisitions were rumoured to be superlative in the field of literary Americans. One evening, on walking up Fifth Avenue with Mr. Wakeman, after leaving the auction sale of the library of a Mr. [Jacob] Chamberlain, a collector who had recently died, I said to Mr. Wakeman: "It may be rather a tactless question, but what is going to happen to your collection after your death?"
>
> "I've often thought of that," he answered.
>
> "Why not let me place it now in the Morgan Library, where it will presumably be intact forever?"
>
> But Wakeman could not so quickly come to the decision to part with his treasures, and I left him with the suggestion that he should think the matter over. When next we met, some weeks later, the subject was again broached, and this time Mr. Wakeman said that though he would not commit himself, and would in any case wish to keep his first editions and association books, I might make a study of his manuscripts and suggest what price Mr. Morgan would, in my opinion, be willing to pay for them. So the next day I went carefully over two or three hundred manuscripts, including such star pieces as Hawthorne's *Blithedale Romance*, Poe's *Tamerlane*, and various great essays of Emerson. At the conclusion of the analysis I named a sum in the six figures as my estimate of the value of the collection.
>
> "If you can get that," said Mr. Wakeman, "all right. But remember that the collection is to be offered to no one but Mr. Morgan,

as his is the only library into which I should be willing to have my things go. I wouldn't accept fifty thousand dollars more for them from anyone else."

This last remark was made because I had suggested that another collector, W. K. Bixby, of St. Louis, might be willing to pay more than the sum I had suggested in connection with Mr. Morgan.

The manuscripts were accordingly sent to my office, there to be carefully catalogued. With these descriptions in detail, and with many of the more important items forwarded to his library, Mr. Morgan was able quickly to size up the remarkable character of the manuscripts offered. His interest was immediate, but though he did not question the price asked, it represented a sum larger than he had ever expended on a single purchase of manuscripts, and he asked me to return a few days later for his decision. At the second meeting Mr. Morgan was still undecided, and said that I should come back the next day. This was sometime in the month of May. On arriving at the library for the third time I was aware of a rather unwonted atmosphere of activity. Several gentlemen, presumably business associates of Mr. Morgan, were in conference with him.

After a little while Mr. Morgan came, with his energetic stride, into the librarian's room, where I was waiting, and said: "I cannot give you an answer to-day. I'm leaving for Europe to-morrow. I'll be back in July. Keep the collection for me, and I'll decide then."

"Very well," I answered, and returned to my office.

"A day or two later Mr. Wakeman dropped in to inquire concerning the progress of the transaction. When I informed him of its status, he said: "I am sure you have done your best, but please send the manuscripts back to my house. The collection is withdrawn."

"But I have promised to reserve the manuscripts for Mr. Morgan until his return in July," I replied.

"I am sorry," answered Mr. Wakeman. "Mr. Morgan has had his chance. The collection is withdrawn."

The situation thus became rather a difficult one. The owner of the manuscripts was a reserved and wealthy gentleman who at my solicitation had made the concession of offering America's greatest collector the opportunity of acquiring his cherished treasures.

His request for their return, could, of course, not be disregarded; but on sending them back I took the liberty of retaining just one manuscript, a poem by Longfellow. This I placed in a large envelope, writing on the outside 'Property of S. H. Wakeman'; and about the same time I informed Mr. Wakeman that I intended to resume the transaction with Mr. Morgan in July.

"You've heard what I said," he replied.

"You've heard what I said," I replied with a smile.

July came and the newspapers had recorded Mr. Morgan's return. Shortly thereafter I went to his library. He was alone in his room at the western end of the building, a room which opened into a fireproof chamber that contained his manuscript treasures. He was seated before a table on which he had been playing solitaire, a recreation that one could not help recalling had been a favourite pastime of Napoleon. In earlier discussions I had laid stress on various points which made the Wakeman collection the greatest in existence of its kind—finest in the world as regards Hawthorne, Thoreau, Poe, and Whittier, and exceedingly important as to the other authors. The obvious arguments had been used without convincing success and on this occasion I had determined to try another approach: and if that failed, I did not intend to bother further. It was with this in mind that I had retained the one manuscript alluded to above.

In reply to my inquiry as to how he had decided, Mr. Morgan said: "I'll go over the catalogue once more. Come in again to-morrow and I'll decide one way or the other."

"No, Mr. Morgan. I'm afraid it's no use my coming again. As a matter of fact I do not know whether today's visit is of any use." And I then told him that Mr. Wakeman had withdrawn the collection, but that I still thought that if he, Mr. Morgan, would come to an immediate decision, I could see to it that the manuscripts would become part of his library.

Mr. Morgan, of course, knew of Mr. Wakeman as an ardent collector to whom the money value in the transaction we were discussing was a minor consideration. As a man devoted to his own treasures Mr. Morgan could readily understand the sentiments that had prompted Mr. Wakeman first to offer and then to withdraw the offer of his collection. Mr. Morgan sat there for a moment, obviously considering the entire situation. It was then that I took up the one manuscript that I had kept.

"Here's one of the poems in the collection," I said; "and if you will excuse me for being personal, whenever I read it I think of you and your grandchildren."

"What's that?" said Mr. Morgan in his quick, incisive way. I fancy that he was not used to having his private sentiments brought into a business discussion.

"It's Longfellow's poem concerning his grandchildren, and it reminds me of you and yours."

"Let me see it," he said.

Mr. Morgan put on his spectacles and read that lovely lyric of grand-paternal affection whose opening verses are so familiar:

> Between the dark and the daylight,
> When the night is beginning to lower
> Comes a pause in the day's occupations
> That is known as the children's hour.

When Mr. Morgan finished reading the poem he hit the table with his fist. "I'll take the collection," he said.

What rare items, worth thousands upon thousands of dollars, had not been able to consummate had now been effected by a short manuscript of comparatively insignificant monetary value.

"The Children's Hour" had made this enormous appeal to Mr. Morgan because he was himself a lover of children; and in that stately library to which influential and distinguished leaders in all fields came, somewhat as courtiers came of old to a powerful prince, Mr. Morgan's grandchildren romped around with that freedom made possible by their grandfather's affection for them. They were among the comparatively few people who held in no awe whatsoever the masterful man who delighted to play with them.

Hellman was a salesman *par excellence* as witnessed here. (You earned your commission, sir! And history's gratitude.) His ability to facilitate the transaction between two hardened businessmen, both of whom went instinctively into sparring mode, resulted in the preservation of Wakeman's manuscript collection as originally desired. Otherwise, egos would have won out and the material potentially scattered to the winds at auction.

2014

✦ XXII ✦

In the Midst of It: A Book Hunter Down the Cataloging Rabbit Hole

THE story begins with a drowning, includes a fratricide, a sensational trial, and has no ending yet. But let us start anyhow.

Prominent book collector C. Fiske Harris and his wife are both recovering from illness in 1881. They decide to take a recuperative canoe ride with their servant Hedges on Moosehead Lake in Maine. The canoe capsizes in rough water "and for a time the Harrises clung to the craft. Hedges heard Mrs. Harris say, 'If Mr. Harris goes, I will go also.' She succumbed first, however, and Harris followed her." Thus wrote Roger Stoddard in his authoritative essay, "C. Fiske Harris, Collector of American Poetry and Plays" (1963).

This abrupt and tragic demise of a notable collector is not yet on my mind as I prowl the aisles of the recent ABAA Book Show in Pasadena, California. I am nearing the end of my Saturday all-day scout, my eyes strained and the need for food urgent. Serendipity comes into play as I browse the booth of Holly Segar and Jeffrey Rovenpor of Caroliniana Books, Aiken, South Carolina.

Propped up on a shelf in a sleeve is a modest looking pamphlet in plain original wrappers, with a neat ownership signature on the cover. I almost miss it, but I don't. Holly & Jeffrey's description reads, in part: "*Index to American Poetry and Plays in the Collection of C. Fiske Harris.* Providence, RI: Printed for Private Distribution, 1874 . . . Finely printed pamphlet listing the major American poetry and play collection belonging to C. Fiske Harris. The collection today resides at Brown University . . . This copy with the ownership inscription to the front wrapper of R. A. Guild."

Neither Holly nor Jeffrey is available to chat, so I continue to other booths, but I remain intrigued, the biblio-wheels spinning slowly then building up speed as the importance of the item soaks in. I return a short time later and buy the *Index* from Holly. I ask her where they found this elusive item. She doesn't recall off-hand, but Jeffrey will be returning to the booth soon. And he does. He and I haven't met before, but he knows me through my blog.

"Reading your blog posts inspired me to buy this at the Papermania show in Hartford," he says.

I am momentarily flummoxed.

He continues, "This is the first time we've had it out on display and in the back of my mind I thought by chance if you were here you might want it."

Well, Mr. Rovenpor, the Book Gods certainly put us together in one of those unexplainable instances that happens occasionally to dedicated collectors. But next time, let's not tempt fate and just send me a quote directly.

New friends made, I carry my prize off to show to a few other book people who would appreciate it, including Joe Fay & Nick Aretakis of Reese Co. and Bill Butts of Main Street Books. For what fun is it if one can't share with others?

I have big plans for a blog post about Harris' *Index*. Upon reviewing Stoddard's essay on Harris, I realize much of the heavy lifting has already been done. A shorter excursion is very much in order though. During the journey, I'm buffeted by a deluge of unexpected discoveries and find myself gloriously deep in uncharted territory and I push on, wondering where it will all lead. Come with me.

The importance of Harris' *Index* is summarized by Stoddard,

> In March of 1875 there was issued privately in Providence a small pamphlet which was without precedent in the annals of American bibliography ... it credited Mr. Harris with 4,129 volumes in a field almost totally unexplored by scholar or collector. Harris's contemporaries in the book world were historians and collectors in the field of American history, and it would be another decade before successors with Harris's inclination toward his native literature could appreciate his foresight and achievement.

C. Fiske Harris (1818-1881) was certainly a biblio over-achiever. He attended Brown University but pursued a business opportunity and didn't graduate, went to New York City in 1837, made his fortune, and returned to Providence, Rhode Island twenty years later, settling into an expansive home with his certainly patient wife near the Brown campus. Almost every room in his home was filled with books. Horatio Rogers writes in *Private Libraries of Providence* (1878),

> Go where you will in Mr. Harris' house, you will find books. They long ago overflowed the library proper, which holds but a small portion... They stand upon shelves: they are stacked in piles: they are packed in trunks and boxes: they are shut up in closets: they are bundled up in paper; and they are huddled on the floor. The owner has no idea of their number, and the writer estimates that there are, at least, 8,000 volumes and 5,000 pamphlets.

Harris formed three major collections: Early English literature, poetry, and drama including the Four Folios of Shakespeare and over 600 quarto plays up to the time of Dryden. This was sold at auction in 1883 after his death. He gathered over 8,000 items pertaining to the American Civil War, a remarkable assemblage covering virtually every aspect of the conflict. This collection remained intact and is now a gem of the Providence Public Library. His third collection of American Poetry broke new ground. Stoddard writes of Harris's collection,

> Its influence still continues to be felt in collecting, bibliography, and scholarship. John Russell Bartlett wrote for The Providence Journal in 1875: "Mr. Harris, who has always had a taste for English literature, and formed a very good library of the best writers, both English and American, conceived the idea a few years ago to make his collection of American poetry and dramatic literature as complete as possible, and having once made this a specialty, has pursued it with a zeal unsurpassed by any [other] American collector in this department. To form so large a collection would ordinarily be the work of one's life, but Mr. Harris has accomplished his work mainly within the last fifteen years.

Zeal is not the only factor involved. Harris was fortunate and astute enough to buy a large portion of Albert Gorton Greene's collection. Greene (1802-1868), a distant cousin of Harris, also lived in Providence and attended Brown. Greene's home was a meeting place for local writers and visiting authors. Greene himself was a minor poet celebrated for his once much-published and parodied poem "Old Grimes." Stoddard writes, "Greene's interest in American poetry is noteworthy in the history of American book collecting. He was the first collector to specialize in American poetry and, indeed, in any branch of American literature."

Greene's library was sold at Bangs' auction house in New York in March of 1869. Contemporary bookseller William Gowans comments, "It was presumptuously catalogued in 6,742 lots; for over 2,000 of the lots sold for less than the cost of printing their descriptions; and the total realized less than $8,000. Attendance never exceeded twenty-five and sometimes dropped below a dozen spectators."

Such can be the case when one is ahead of their time. C. Fiske Harris, seizing the opportunity, utilized Joseph Sabin as his agent and bought three quarters of the American poetry lots (over 1,600 volumes) at a cost of about $750. The purchase added quantities of minor rarities and ephemera to his collection. Harris pursued the more expensive desiderata such as Anne Bradstreet's works via the English and American booksellers and at auction. Stoddard writes of the collector who presciently bought Greene's books,

> Harris was not a gentle, quiet man who had retired to the solitude of his library. He was a hard competitor whose livelihood had in part depended upon exact knowledge of the minute details of textile printing. He demanded accuracy, promptness, and exact conformity to instructions from his agents, and when a fake or a cripple was delivered to him, he flung it back with a stinging letter. He reacted in similar fashion when an agent exceeded his limit at auction. His correspondence reveals him as such a difficult customer that one sometimes wonders why such established dealers as Sabin and Quaritch bothered to handle his account.

Harris was hard on booksellers, but Stoddard notes his openness to assist scholars who utilize his library. He also has a measure of charm when called for,

By 1874 he was a close friend of Mrs. Sarah Helen Whitman and she favored him with the finest memento of Poe which she owned and one of the great association copies in American literature: the 1845 *Raven* and *Tales* inscribed, "To Mrs. Sarah Helen Whitman, from the most devoted of her friends, Edgar A. Poe." Mrs. Whitman added her inscription to Harris, and in his letter of 30 Oct. 1874, Harris thanked her "for the precious volume you have so generously confided to my keeping."

And now to Harris's *Index to American Poetry and Plays* which I hold gently in my hand. Stoddard writes, in part,

> By mid-year of 1873 Harris, with the benefit of [John Russell] Bartlett's advice, was hard at work on the catalogue of his collection. In March of 1875 the *Index* was printed [in an edition of 255 copies, not all bound], and he sent copies to prominent librarians, scholars, collectors, and poets. Harris issued the *Index* as a temporary, short-title catalogue, stating that he might in the future "print a more comprehensive catalogue of his collection, with full titles and collations of all the more important articles, and with, perhaps, brief notices of the writers." . . . A few of the recipients sent him additions to his collection, but many more sent him notes of attributions or of further titles.
>
> Most of the recipients and reviewers were startled to learn that over 4,000 volumes of poetry, plays, and songs had been written by Americans. William Cullen Bryant's reply, though a bit unkind, was typical: "Your work, *Index to American Poetry and Plays*, has amazed me by showing me what multitudes of persons on our side of the Atlantic have wasted their time in writing verses in our language." But few of Harris's contemporaries were competent to see that he had made one of the most significant achievements in American book collecting.
>
> The *Index* itself was a careful piece of work. It was cross-indexed, and each entry included the author's name with initials, short title, place, date, format, and reference number. Where applicable, Harris included notes of paging, special title pages, and watermarks. It was not known generally that many nineteenth-century American books were signed in one manner and gathered in another until the publication of the first volume of the *Bibliography of American*

Literature in 1955, but Harris pointed out this discrepancy in several entries.

Harris added 120 titles during the printing of the *Index*, and by the time General [Horatio] Rogers published his account of the Harris library in June 1875, he had added 180 more. Indeed, in the six years following the publication of the *Index* Harris added over a thousand titles to the collection.

In 1871 Harris had written to Henry Stevens that "There is but one title of which I absolutely despair—the old Bay Psalm Book [1640]. Five years later, in October 1876, Harris had his chance when the Shurtleff copy came up at Leonard's in Boston. For $1,025 Harris bought what was perhaps the most desirable copy of the book he had despaired of finding. Not only was it in the original binding, not only had it been one of Thomas Prince's copies, but it had belonged to one of the translators, Richard Mather.

Harris's excitement upon holding the long-sought Bay Psalm book, the first surviving book printed in North America, is easy to imagine. Five years to the month after its purchase, Harris was gone, perishing in the canoeing accident, and his collection was up for grabs. According to Stoddard, "The American poetry ... was sent to the shop of Sidney S. Rider of Providence, an eccentric bookseller whose ethics were inscrutable to his contemporaries. Rider began by selling the Bay Psalm Book to Mrs. John Carter Brown for the library of her late husband. Then he let it be known that the remainder of the poetry could be purchased for $4,500."

Through various twists and turns, the collection was eventually acquired by Henry Bowen Anthony, a senator from Rhode Island, graduate of Brown, another cousin of Harris and an old friend of John Russell Bartlett. Anthony died a year later and bequeathed the collection to Brown University in 1884. Stoddard notes, "In his will he requested that it be kept together and that an inscription in Latin be placed over its alcove in the library:'The Harris Collection of American Poetry: Commenced by Albert C. Greene, Continued by Caleb Fiske Harris and Henry B. Anthony. By the Latter Presented to this Library.' Today a similar wording is used in the bookplate of the Harris Collection."

Now let us examine the ownership signature on the front wrapper of my copy of the *Index*, "R[euben] A. Guild." This is a fantastic association copy! Guild (1822-1899) was the librarian in charge of the Brown University Library when it acquired the Harris collection. It is he who oversaw the purchase and installation of the books as a separate special collection in a dedicated room—the first at Brown University and one of the earliest in the country. Guild was prominent and active in the library field, celebrated for his professional achievements and congenial nature. He was a founder of the American Library Association and wrote *The Librarian's Manual: A Treatise on Bibliography* (1858) as well as a number of works about Brown University history.

The Harris collection numbered approximately 5,000 volumes in 1884. An early endowment provided acquisition funds, and a lengthy honor roll of curators nurtured and built the holdings over the next one hundred and thirty-five years. The collection now contains approximately 250,000 (!) volumes and is unique in scope and effort.

While absorbing Stoddard's Harris essay for the above recounting, I see that he references a newspaper article from 1871 by Thomas Donnelly on "Prominent American Book Collectors" quoted by C. Fiske Harris in his correspondence. This is very early for the subject matter. Curious as to the article's contents, I immediately try to hunt it down online and find another reference to it in Paul Leicester Ford's "Bibliography of Private Libraries," an annotated checklist published in the July 1889 issue of the *Library Journal*. Ford's short and often pithy comments provide amusement. For example, he cites the Donnelly article, published in two parts under the pseudonym "Book Worm" and comments, "Better than ordinary newspaper work, but of little real value."

Ford's list leads me further afield from Harris, a full-on distraction that has me careening off course until I plunge down the proverbial rabbit hole. But before we get to that excitement, let's discuss the compiler Ford, for he leads a varied life, filled with rare books and writing, cut short by tragedy.

Paul Leicester Ford (1865-1902), was immersed in books from the beginning, his father being a prominent collector. He was also a great-grandson of dictionary maker Noah Webster, the subject of his first work, an edited volume of *Webster Genealogy* (1876). Ford was frail physically, small in stature, with a deformed spine and was obliged to wear a brace, but he persevered. He is best remembered today as the editor of *The Writings of Thomas Jefferson* (1892-1896) which set a new standard in editing historical texts. He had a strong interest in bibliography and rare books, particularly Americana. He published bibliographic work on Alexander Hamilton, the Constitution, Benjamin Franklin, George Washington, The New-England Primer, printer Hugh Gaines, and of course, Thomas Jefferson. He compiled several checklists of Americana references. Ford also had a creative streak and was a popular novelist of his day. He found time to edit *The Bibliographer: A Journal of Bibliography and Rare Book News*. Ford was married with a family.

Paul Ford's life stands in sharp contrast to that of his brother Malcolm, at one time the most famous amateur athlete in the country. During the 1880s, he was three times the American National Champion as "All Around Athlete," and in 1885-1886, Malcolm won National Championships in the long jump, and both the 100- and 200-yard dash. Malcolm married an heiress but after a divorce he experienced severe financial difficulties. The wealthy Ford family did not approve of Malcolm's devotion to athletics and the father disinherited Malcolm from the will. After their father's death, Malcolm expected support from his siblings including Paul. Friction between them increased over several years.

It was under these strained circumstances that Malcolm went to Paul's new home in New York City at 37 East Seventy-Seventh Street on May 8, 1902. They met in the library. Malcolm wanted money. A brief argument ensued, and the brimming bookcases surrounding the two men could only watch silently as tensions escalated. Ford's private secretary, seated on the other side of the room, was stunned by a sudden gunshot. Malcolm had shot Paul. Malcolm turned the gun on himself and committed suicide. Paul Ford, mortally wounded, died in a bedroom upstairs within the hour. An inquest ruled that Malcolm had been temporarily insane.

Thinking about Ford's sensationalistic death, I am drawn back to his "Bibliography of Private Libraries." His comments about the entries reveal a man not hesitant to express his opinion. I wonder if his forthrightness led to a miscalculated escalation with his unstable brother. But this is just a passing thought.

I discover a reference cited by Ford to a newspaper article by one Lewis Rosenthal, titled "Book Collectors of New-York," in the June 13, 1886, issue of *The New York Times*. Ford notes, "A very good newspaper account." This high praise (by Ford's standards) makes me very curious to read it, and pronto. Fortunately, my newspapers.com account is current and after a bit of hunting the article is before me.

Rosenthal frames his lengthy piece (some 5,000 words) as an interview with an old New York City bookseller of forty years' standing called "Dryasdust." This is certainly a composite figure by Rosenthal drawing upon his familiarity with actual booksellers and spiced with stereotypes. He writes,

> Antiquary Dryasdust was standing on a low ladder and putting an octavo on the shelf as I stepped into his shop on University-place a few days ago resolved to make him chat about some of the book collectors of New-York. Imagine a short, slight, bent figure; a head with a brown wig on it; a thin face, with a complexion like parchment; small, quick, gray eyes that seem to peer for bargains under their shaggy brows, and you an outline idea of the personality.

Rosenthal supplies via his bookseller character short descriptions of dozens of living collectors and their libraries, including famous bookmen such as Robert Hoe, Rush Hawkins, Samuel P. Avery, Samuel L. M. Barlow, Brayton Ives, Hamilton Cole, Thomas McKee, and Augustin Daly. He describes many of the libraries first-hand. He has a thorough knowledge of the nascent Grolier Club and the more obscure Book Fellows' Club. Rosenthal even notes, for example, that Henri Pène Du Bois's book *Four Private Libraries of New York* (1892) is in the works almost six years before publication.

He also comments on trends: the rage for extra-illustration of volumes, and the in-depth collecting of single authors. He has a good knowledge of fine bindings, material related to the theatre, and the collecting of French books, describing in detail for example the French library of M. Jolly Bavoillet.

Much to my surprise, Rosenthal rather boldly for the time records a reference to the widespread collecting of erotica,

> Even the most cursory account of the private collections of New-York would be incomplete without a statement that there are many collectors of suppressed and facetious works. John Quincy Adams, who somewhere in his diary speaks of a certain nobleman in Paris who had a private collection of such rarities under lock and key, could, in our time, find at least a score of bibliophiles with similar tastes in our good town of Gotham. I keep the names of these men a secret. The customs officials and the agents of the Society for the Suppression of Vice are active in suppressing such books and by their rigor push the prices of things of this kind to a fabulous figure. Generally, bound in bright colors—yellow, saffron, light blue—the publications of an erotic kind command an extensive though stealthy sale.

Lewis Rosenthal was very much in the thick of the book action of his day, both legitimate and under-the-table. I need to find out more about him. He is completely unknown to me before my encounter in Ford's checklist.

It is getting late in the evening, but there is no clock when my interests are stirred. I begin to hunt and remain tenacious. I focus on the journalist angle and facts emerge. I find a contemporary biographical sketch of Rosenthal in Isaac Markens *The Hebrew in America* (1888),

> Lewis Rosenthal was born in Baltimore, September 10, 1856. He was educated at Columbia Grammar School, New York and at Dartmouth College, N.H., where he graduated in 1877. He then removed to Paris where he was for four years a member of "The Parisian Staff," being at the same time engaged as tutor to a son of Hon. Thomas F. Noyes, United States Minister to France. In 1882 he published "America and France; the influence of the United States in France in the Eighteenth Century." Subsequently he was

a special contributor to various New York daily newspapers. Among his magazine articles are: "Poe in Paris," "Rosseau in Philadelphia," and "Bret Harte in Germany." He also wrote for the "North American Review" an article "Our Services to the French Republic" and for "The Theatre," a series of sketches on the Dramatic Critics of New York and the European Capitals.

Now I have a handle on him and find in a Dartmouth alumni publication that Rosenthal dies in Washington, D.C. in 1909. The brief bio above explains his Francophile tendencies and his theatre interests exhibited in the "Book Collectors of New-York." I am excited to see if he wrote other biblio-essays. Contemporary late nineteenth-century accounts of American book collecting are not plentiful, and any rediscovered tidbits are important historically.

By now the time is 2:00 am and I refuel with a jumbo rum and coke, light on the rum and heavy on the carbonated sugar / caffeine infusion. The waft of fresh, microwaved popcorn piled high in a University of Texas Longhorn bowl permeates my office. I toss a few kernels in the air, mouth open wide, a few make it, a few litter the floor. I'll pick them up later, probably. My wife Nicole has retired for the evening so I'm unsupervised.

A major discovery comes after half my drink is gone: *The Curio: An Illustrated Monthly Magazine Devoted to Genealogy and Biography, Heraldry and Book Plates, Coins and Autographs, Rare Books and Works of Art, Old Furniture and Plate, and other Colonial Relics.* (NY: R.W. Wright, 1887-1888), edited by E de V. Vermont. This short-lived publication (Vol. 1 only, Sept. 1887-Feb. 1888) contains four signed articles by Rosenthal including "Great Men Bibliophiles," "Hobbies of the Book Hunter," and "New York Dramatic Libraries and Their Owners." The last describes on-site visits with collectors McKee, Daly, Jolly-Bavoillet, William B. Dick, J. V. Arnold, and Charles C. Moreau. It is unlikely many, or any, biblio-historians have read these articles in over one hundred years.

The Curio also contains a lengthy, illustrated essay on "Book Binding as a Fine Art" by "The Grolierite" and four first-hand biographical sketches by Max Maury of "Great Booksellers of the World," including

Bernard Quaritch (London), Ludwig Rosenthal (Berlin), Damascene Morgand (Paris), and Edmund F. Bonaventure (New York). The European dealers are today still prominent in the annals of bookselling. Bonaventure is not. He was a specialist in rare French books and Maury calls him "one of the most famous of living American book dealers."

This plethora of biblio material in an obscure periodical becomes even more intriguing when I discover that "The Grolierite" and "Max Maury" are pseudonyms for Lewis Rosenthal. (Rosenthal was not a Grolier Club member but certainly knew several of them.) Figuring this out requires online gyrations I won't detail here, but suffice to say that Rosenthal publishes a novel, a work on Napoleon, and under "Max Maury" translates several French novels into English, pens a tourist guide to Paris, and compiles an English-French travel dictionary.

It's a fine and lengthy night down the cataloging rabbit hole. I am getting sleepy, but I'm not quite out of drink yet and there is one last jolt of discovery. I turn up another pseudonym used by Rosenthal: Lew Rosen.

Here is an entirely unexpected twist that has Rosenthal (as Lew Rosen) arrested by Anthony Comstock himself, the infamous anti-vice activist, United States postal inspector, and secretary of the New York Society for the Suppression of Vice, who is dedicated to upholding Victorian morality. The trial is a landmark one.

Josh Lambert writes of Rosenthal and Comstock in *Unclean Lips: Obscenity, Jews, and American Culture* (2013),

> Comstock's greatest legal triumph in the regulation of printed obscenity would be the Supreme Court's upholding of the conviction of one "Jew editor" in 1896, a judicial decision that defined obscenity in American constitutional law for half a century. Comstock deliberately and cunningly pursued this editor; whose name was Lew Rosen. Under a false name, Comstock dispatched a letter in April 1893 to the magazine Rosen edited, *Broadway*, a "witty New York society journal," complaining that he had received the recent issue but that "some boy or printer's devil has been playing a joke

on you, as the paper on three pages is marred with a black substance marked over them.'" "There has been no practical joke played on you at all," one of Rosen's employees quickly replied, following instructions from the editor. "It is only lamp black . . . and is easily removed with a piece of bread." When Comstock scrubbed away the grease, he discovered beneath it what the court later referred to as "pictures of females, in different attitudes of indecency." Comstock testified against Rosen, and the latter was convicted and sentenced to thirteen months at hard labor for sending obscenity through the mail. Rosen appealed his conviction all the way up the judicial ladder, but the Supreme Court finally upheld his sentence, condemning Rosen to jail because his aim had been, as Justice John Marshall Harlan wrote, "of course, to excite a curiosity to know what was thus concealed."

And *then* I discover that bookseller Edmund Bonaventure, profiled by Rosenthal in *The Curio*, has years earlier in 1883 been prosecuted by Comstock for selling racy prints.

But it really is getting late now, and I'd rather not be sitting here when the sun rises. My mind is full. A straightforward cataloging of my chance find in Pasadena has become a surreal plunge through known and unknown; a drowning, a murder-suicide, famous and forgotten bookmen, a brush with the underbelly of the late nineteenth-century book trade, and a desire to learn more about the intriguing Lewis Rosenthal, aka Lew Rosen, Max Maury, and "The Grolierite."

Would it surprise my readers that before bed I've already hunted down and ordered an inscribed Rosenthal item and a complete set of *The Curio?*

2020

✣ XXIII ✣

Trafficking, Fossicking, and Noodling in Old Books: The Partaking of Biblio-Pleasures

BOOKSELLER and writer Anthony Marshall, where art thou, kindred spirit? I discovered your two books by chance in an Austin, Texas used bookstore: *Trafficking in Old Books* (1998) and *Fossicking in Old Books* (2004), far from their place of publication in Australia. There may be copies in abundance in Australia, but they are pretty scarce here—my excuse for overlooking them these many years. And what an oversight! Your adventures running an antiquarian / used bookstore in Melbourne and ancillary essays are among the damndest, bestest, funniest biblio-writings I've encountered. Your prose enlightens and surprises: creative skills meeting a worthy subject. I must simply salute you.

But I'm just late to the party. Some sleuthing revealed you received accolades upon publication (and just as importantly, brisk sales) primarily in Australia and the UK, but also a foray into the US where you did a few book signings. Both books sold in the thousands of copies, not an easy achievement. (You record a sold-out print run of 5,000 copies for the self-published *Trafficking in Old Books*.) You even had a fan base and book signings in Tasmania! Admittedly, that was much closer to your bookshop in Melbourne than it would be to someone in America, but it sure sounds exotic and alluring as recorded in your delightful *Fossicking* essay, "Et in Tasmania Ego."

I find you were born in Scotland to a Scottish mother and English father, grew up in England where you taught school before becoming a bookseller, and then migrated to Australia, owning Alice's Bookshop there until 2012, when you sold the shop and retired to Germany. I've gleaned this information from your own writings and online searching. It all piques my curiosity, but this is secondary to your published works. The last of your essays that I can find appeared in 2016 in *Book Source Monthly*. The proprietor, John Huckans, speaks highly of you, but has not heard from you in years. He supplied me your email on file and copied you in his reply to me but no response as of yet. I fear none will be forthcoming but imagine nothing sinister or final, just that you have disconnected from the online discord and are relaxing with a giant stein of Hefeweizen in hand, listening to Wagner ("I think that as a man Wagner was a rascal, a cad and a bounder but as a composer, sublime."), and perhaps missing your bookselling days just a bit.

If you don't mind (and I doubt you will), I'd like to share my excitement about your writings. There are certainly others reading me who may have overlooked you as well. Your first book *Trafficking in Old Books* (1998), collects fifty-two essays relating almost exclusively to running an open bookshop. Every conceivable situation is described, reflected upon, laughed at, and occasionally grumbled about. Your own engaging character emerges throughout, adding unusual depth to the panorama that populates the essays: fellow booksellers, book buyers, book thieves, collectors, and other hangers-on, including bookstore pets and the taxman. Nowhere have I found another book that more fully explores the workings of an antiquarian/used bookstore. And it is accessible to the average reader—however that is defined—who simply enjoys good stories.

Your follow-up, *Fossicking for Old Books* (2004), collects thirty-seven additional essays. I find it more discursive and personal as you deftly weave bookish themes through essays about travel adventures, caffeine addiction, family lineage (including a number of Scottish castles), and the gum of the Eucalyptus tree.

The term "fossicking" was foreign to me, but I was enlightened in your introduction to the book,

> If ever, in the hope of finding treasure, you have rummaged through a heap of old books—at a school fête, a church bazaar or an opportunity shop—then, knowingly or not, you have fossicked

Trafficking, Fossicking, and Noodling in Old Books

for old books. Welcome to the club! Welcome to the Worshipful Company of Book Fossickers! And welcome to this book which celebrates the delights and dilemmas of book-fossicking as well as other pleasures and pitfalls associated with old books, old bookshops and old booksellers.

An excellent word, fossicking. For years it languished in the broom cupboard of an English dialect, until it was rescued and put on a stout ship and despatched to Australia. Here it has grown tall and strong; here it is a word that is widely used and understood. "To fossick" means to search or to rummage or to prospect. It implies—at least to my mind—that great treasure lies at the end of the quest. Also that this search is somewhat haphazard, lacking in system and method (especially bureaucratic method). A lone prospector, with a mule and a pick, may be said to fossick for gold but a multinational mining company with teams of experts backed up by whiz-bang technology cannot. No, fossicking is for individuals, fired with private hopes and dreams.

Bookdealers like me spend a lot of time fossicking for old books. Partly because it's fun, but mostly because our livelihood depends on it. And we tend to be focused. We do not always know exactly what we are looking for but we have a lively sense of what we are not looking for. Ninety-five per cent (no—let's be honest) ninety-nine per cent of all the books ever published in the world are from the bookdealer's point of view completely worthless. We pick them up and toss them aside. They are the dross, the spoil and the tailings, fit only for the mullock heap. But bookdealers are not infallible. Where they fossicked others may follow and "noodle" after them. "Noodle" is another good Australian word. "Noodle" is what you do at Coober Pedy in South Australia when you pick over the tailings of the professional opal miners in the hope of spotting overlooked opals. Many browsers in old bookshops can be said to be "noodling" through the books, hoping to spot a bargain or some treasure that the bookseller has overlooked. Try to incorporate this fine word into your lexicon. Use it when a family member reproaches you for wasting your time looking at books. Explain that you love to go a-noodling. There are many worse things you could be doing.

I see that many of your essays published in the two books first appeared in biblio-magazines. Most notably you wrote about ninety essays in a regular column for the *The Australian Book Collector* over the span of a decade before the magazine folded in 2002. In the last column "Signing Off" (reprinted in *Fossicking for Old Books*), you express some revealing thoughts on your writing,

> There is really no end to the subjects you can write about in a bookish sort of column. The challenge has been to make the topic of my fancy at least vaguely relevant to books and bookshops and bookselling. And part of the fun has been seeing what oddments can be dragged in; I often feel like a sort of bower-bird on the lookout for shiny treasures which I can stuff into my next article. People who know me know that anything they say (or do) may be taken down and used. I am not (I think) "mad or bad," but I may very well be "dangerous to know."
>
> I have generally been pretty conscientious about getting my articles written and sent in by the due date, but it hasn't always been easy. Other things (like the necessity of earning a living) have got in the way. I'm told (by one who loves me) that when wrestling with words, and with a deadline looming, I am apt to become cranky and withdrawn. Downright offensive even, for days. You find this hard to believe (as I do). Surely I have a sunny, cheerful disposition? Not at article-hatching time, I don't. It's easy to criticize the cook. But cooks know that it is not easy making souffles. You try to whip the words into a nice froth and all you get is stodge. And I know stodge when I see it.
>
> There was a time when I thought I could perhaps be a writer who did a bit of bookselling on the side. Nowadays I am happy to accept that I am a bookseller who does a bit of writing on the side. Fame, ambition, worldly success? I do not think so. I am a humble bookseller who has achieved a tiny amount of celebrity or notoriety. I enjoy visits and comments from people who have read my articles or my books. But it is all on a minuscule scale; not sufficient to turn my head. Which I am sure is how it should be.
>
> This exchange [about an essay] made me realize that one of the delights of writing is this: you simply hand readers a fork so

that they can start digging in their own gardens. Your words are just the catalyst that sparks off a reader's memory and imagination.

Writely so, Mr. Marshall, and easier said than done, my friend (may I call you a friend?—I feel like one after reading your books, and doesn't that make the point?) I'll bring this homage to a close for now unless I hear from you. But it's not necessary, really. Your books are enough.

2022

❋ XXIV ❋
Letting Go

MY mission has me breaking a sweat in a storage unit near Houston, Texas, with the air-conditioning set on survival, not comfort. I'm here to meet a university special collections librarian who has expressed interest in a unique biblio-archive, and I want to find it a home. I've rescued the archive from a highly probable shredder/recycle bin. The archive consists of the papers of rare book and manuscript appraiser John R. Payne. Payne's first career was as a rare book librarian, bibliographer, and administrator at the Harry Ransom Center, UT-Austin from 1969-1985. He then went on his own as a full-time appraiser. Over the course of his almost forty years of business he rose to the top of the profession, performing around 1,000 appraisals for private individuals and institutions. He appraised not only rare books, but archives, documents, and photographs.

John is a close friend and mentor. I took a class on rare books with him while still a pup in library school at UT ca. 1990. I assisted him with his appraisal business. I provided input and wrote the introduction to his magnum opus/labor of love *Great Catalogues by Master Booksellers* (2017). My wife and I visited him and his wife Ann in Austin regularly for over two decades. Their lifestyle in later years was insular outside of travel for work and family gatherings. They were enthusiastic to see us—our energetic visits filled with biblio-news and discussions of the rare book world. But that is past now. Ann has died and John is in a memory care facility with severe dementia. He doesn't remember Ann is gone for good, and he waits for her return.

These melancholy thoughts are interrupted by a sudden, mysterious loud pop coming from the attic which is adjacent to my office

Letting Go

upstairs. Alarmed, I enter the attic stuffed full of boxes of bookseller catalogues, reading copies, and other ephemera. Nothing seems amiss. Quiet and peaceful the items slumber, none admitting wrongdoing. Not long after, I'm in the garage below the attic. I let out a favored expletive, one reserved for special occasions. An attic joist has cracked under the weight of my boxes above and a gaping, fragmented section of sheetrock is dangling precariously over my near fine 2007 Chrysler 300 SRT 8. There's a coating of sheetrock dust on the hood. My response time beats any seasoned NASCAR pit crew, and I have my baby backed out of the garage pronto. (Who knew you could burn rubber in reverse?)

I grab a ladder and survey the damage up close. A wasp buzzes me, already looking to form a new home in the open ceiling cavity. The joist will need to be replaced and the sheetrock fixed but not today. I carefully rearrange the boxes in the attic to relieve the pressure, exhale, select a craft beer from the beer fridge, and get back to writing. Payne's situation has me contemplating the challenge of eventually dispersing one's library/archive. This now weighs even more heavily upon my mind after the attic incident.

All who have determinedly and perhaps obsessively built a library face the challenge of finding a future custodian(s). If an archive is involved another layer of complexity is added. Our instinct for collecting is usually associated with the urge to preserve what has been collected, a private hope for immortality, or at least a memorial of the effort. In most cases, an adequate catalogue is a realistic goal, even if the physical objects are dispersed to seed other collectors' or institutions' pursuits. Donations, private sales, auctions, and dealers all come into play. Not infrequently, dispersal plans are simply ignored by the collector. The decisions are then left to well-meaning but hapless family members or the whim of the book gods.

Payne made no formal arrangements for his reference library and a gathering of collectible books focusing on T.E. Lawrence, fine bindings, and important bookseller catalogues. Informally, he had told me he wanted to keep the catalogues together because they were the basis of his book. The rest of the library would be offered to his family first, but he provided no further guidance, and his archive was not mentioned at all. By chance or serendipity, his daughter discovered a note by Payne that led her to me after his condition worsened. I coordinated gratis the sale of his collectible books to a reputable bookman, and I acquired the catalogue collection and the core of the reference library. The family was going to shred the business archive, but I realized its importance as a unique gathering with many research opportunities including provenance studies, private libraries, history of the book, history of collectors, history of antiquarian bookselling, history of libraries, economics of the book trade, the transition of material from private to public institutions, and more. The sheer bulk of sixty-five boxes caused the first few institutions approached to hesitate, even when offered as a gift by the family with no strings attached. Dispersal in this case has been stressful for all involved.

Then there is my friend Mike Cox, notable and prolific author of books on Texas history, journalist, bibliophile, and bookseller in his earlier days. His recent work *Book Hunter: How to Collect Books, Sell Them, and One Day Let Them Go* (2022), is a delightful memoir filled with his adventures and advice for the book collector. He addresses the "letting go" part of his collecting with a blend of humor, realism, and pathos. You'll enjoy his "book collector's prayer": "Oh, Lord, when I die, please don't let my wife sell my books for what I told her I paid for them."

Cox recounts, after many frustrating years of effort, finding a home for his 6,000 volume Texana library via donation to the San Marcos Public Library in central Texas. The solution was serendipitous: the library had a bond issue pass, was expanding the facilities, and was able to devote a new separate room to his collection christened the "Mike Cox Texas Collection." Cox writes,

> When I first began delivering books to San Marcos, each box going out the door seemed like a little bit of me going away. I mourned the loss of each book, even though intellectually I knew I would always have preferred access to them at the library.
>
> So, while I've gotten a measure of peace in finding a willing recipient for my Texas collection, the psychological fallout has had a

longer shelf life. The overriding issue, of course, is that disposing of my books is more than the ending of a chapter. It's the beginning of the ending of MY 'book'...

At least I know that my books will live on as I assembled them. I can be further pleased that they will be of benefit to future researchers from genealogists and students to writers and historians.

Nicole and I attend the dedication ceremony of Cox's library. Mike and his family and many friends are there. A stirring speech by Dr. Arro Smith of the library expresses their appreciation of the collection. An assortment of other speakers rounds out the occasion. There is even a book-themed cake to replenish our sugar levels. We give hearty congratulations to Mike, and we step aside for a line of other well-wishers. I watch from a distance, distracted somewhat by his books on long shelves in front of me, irresistibly pulling a few titles of interest, wondering why I hadn't talked him out of a few before his donation. But then I see him overwhelmed with emotion, a joyous emotion, a tipping point reached, and his tears begin to well up, and I have to look away, for I feel sympathetic stirring, and Nicole and I soon make a soft exit.

I have no pontifical advice on the eventual dispersal of your library. There are too many variables. But let my thoughts stir your thoughts. Barring a disaster, your books will outlive you, and as much effort as you have put into gathering them, enjoying them, and caring for them, they also deserve a quiet moment or two in contemplation of their future.

2024

✤ XXV ✤

A Biblio-Bender in the Northeast

THE flight to Philadelphia is spirited and direct although running late. Nicole and I have tickets on this discount airline express. I reason that the savings on the flight cost can be applied to book purchases on our two-week trip. But as we sit on the plane waiting to embark, the time grows lengthy, the air stifling, and strange noises can be heard coming from the plane itself. What looks like tear gas shoots out of the a/c vents in a futile attempt to cool us overheated passengers. Nicole has turned decidedly negative on my budget flight choice. Her own snacks have already run out and the airline wants to charge us a ransom for theirs. I tell her it isn't my fault she didn't bring more.

After about an hour, the flight attendant's voice crackles over the speaker, "We are just waiting on our pilots, and we'll be ready to go."

There's a lot to sift through with such an announcement but suffice it to say I *imagine* the pilots hurriedly closing out their tab at the airport sports bar, slurring to each other why neither has been paying attention to the time. But I have flight anxiety, and we do make it safely to our destination. Thank the deities for Dramamine and autopilot.

We spend the first two nights at the Terry House Bed & Breakfast in New Castle, Delaware, in the old section of town dating from 1651, a beautifully preserved area of history on the Delaware River, and not coincidentally the home of Oak Knoll Books established in 1976. Oak Knoll specializes in books about books, both as a publisher of new titles on the subject and as a seller of used and rare items. Rob Fleck, just shy of forty years old and the son of the founder, is carrying on the business admirably. His mother Millie, who is a part-owner and assists with daily operations, greets us warmly upon arrival with wine and good conversation. There are two full-time staff members, Erin Desmond and Arianna D'Avolio, both young and energetic. The business is housed/stuffed within the top two floors of the former Opera House built by the Masons in 1879. The sight of tens of thousands of biblio-books momentarily inspires me to leap onto the still-preserved opera stage and sing. But I resist the urge, wanting to keep the visit a positive one.

During the day, Nicole and I visit the nearby Winterthur Museum, Garden, and Library. The museum and estate were the home of Henry Francis du Pont (1880-1969), Winterthur's founder and a prominent antiques collector and horticulturist. In the hallway entrance to the library, we encounter Allie Alvis, curator of Special Collections, setting up an exhibit. I recognize Allie and her distinctive, pink-colored hair from her YouTube channel "Book Historia" covering various aspects of rare books. This is a celebrity sighting for me! The last time I'd heard, she was a cataloguer in the rare book trade, but she's transitioned to the curator position at Winterthur, creating more opportunities to interact with people. She has an outsized personality, and the cataloging of books as a focus became too confining, although it remains a favorite aspect of her duties. Nicole and I visit with her for about half an hour, all of us discovering we have many mutual book friends.

We make one more stop at Baldwin's Book Barn before heading back to New Castle. Baldwin's is a huge, five-story stone barn built in 1822 that houses an estimated 300,000 books. It is reminiscent of a medieval fortress with two-foot-thick stone walls, massive arched wood doors, numerous rooms and nooks, and aging bookshelves that have become organic extensions of the building itself. Frankly, we find little in the tired stock that interests us, but the atmosphere proves entrancing on our brief visit.

Back in New Castle, we have two stellar dinners with Rob & Millie Fleck including rare Belgian beers on tap at Jessop's Tavern and a sentimental meal at Zollies Jazz Cucina located in the space that housed the original Oak Knoll Books. Rob is a foodie and orders things unfamiliar to me. My taste buds bloom with surprises as Millie & Rob tell us delightful biblio-stories, many centering around various Oak Knoll Fests, an annual gathering of fine press printers and their works.

Oak Knoll founder Robert Fleck was an ardent supporter of the fine press community. One close friend was Henry Morris (1925-2019) of the Bird & Bull Press. Morris' many publications centered around the history of the book. His sense of humor was legendary, but he could be opinionated and cantankerous. Navigating his personality was part of the challenge and it was one topic of our dinner conversation. Bob Fleck's extensive personal collection of Bird & Bull publications is housed in his office as he left it, his son Rob proud to show it to interested visitors.

Rob has recently acquired several large collections, a significant amount of them uncatalogued. The thought of this stirs my collecting instinct. I anticipate good hunting and I'm not disappointed. The first night after dinner, Rob and I are up until midnight as I dig through the material. On my previous visit during the pandemic in January 2021 he had gone home and left me in the store to lock up. This time our bantering and booking keeps us both revved. The next night we don't leave the store until 1:30 am. And supposedly he goes to bed early. Not when the Zman is in town!

I buy three boxes of material including association copies from the general stock, items from the reference library of Ken Karmiole and the collection of Herbert Johnson, the first black Grolier Club member. I am particularly pleased to acquire Henri Pene du Bois' *American Bookbindings in the Library of Henry William Poor* (1903), this example from Poor's library and inscribed by Poor himself.

Before we leave New Castle for Philadelphia, we walk along the waterfront Battery Park that hugs the Delaware River. This once bustling port welcomed many visitors and immigrants in the eighteenth and nineteenth centuries. A working reproduction of an eighteenth-century sailing ship moored at New Castle pier dominates the scene. Little remains of the actual dock but there is a wide expanse of lawn leading to Packet Alley and the old town section of restored homes, buildings, and a church with a graveyard of weathered tombstones. While I think of Benjamin Franklin huffing up the hill, Nicole is nearby ziplining in the play area of the park, the zipline designed for kids but adult friendly, her zipping along about two feet off the ground, her hair blowing in the breeze, one arm outstretched in a circus pose, as a small crowd cheers her on.

Next up is a bucket list item for me. Our drive to Philadelphia follows, not zippy in speed, but we arrive by early afternoon at the Rosenbach Museum & Library founded in 1954 by Dr. A.S.W. Rosenbach (1876-1952) and his brother, Philip (1863-1953). It was their home and often a place to meet clients. Rosenbach is generally regarded as America's most famous rare book dealer. But he was also a collector and once an item went into his private library it was rarely relinquished. This exceptional private collection is housed at the Museum/Library. I collect material by and about A.S.W. Rosenbach as my regular readers are aware. At last count, I have over seventy important association copies inscribed by Rosenbach himself.

Finding a place to park is a real pain in the arse as the museum is in a residential neighborhood and every spot is taken as far as we can see. (I find out later that there is a parking garage a fair distance away that is normally used.) I circle the block twice and then, magically, a spot opens right in front. I pull in not fully realizing my luck. Soon after, our Rosenbach tour guide Justin Borkowski is in disbelief. I've managed the nearly impossible. In eight years of volunteering, he's never been fortunate enough to snag such a parking place. It is then that I realize A.S.W. Rosenbach senses my presence. And I would have certainly freed up a space for him if the situation were reversed.

The Museum/Library consists of two adjoining townhomes, part of which served as the last residence of Dr. Rosenbach. The rooms are filled with art and antiques gathered by the Rosenbach brothers. Our tour is a revelation to me. I expected something more grandiose in size, but the museum is intimate and feels like a visit to a personal space. Rosenbach's original collection and additions are housed in two rooms upstairs in glass front bookcases, most of them the same ones that he used. The library has a huge contemporary dining / work table that has been the scene of many book gatherings. Above the fireplace is Rosenbach's portrait. I briefly think I'd like a biblio-portrait of myself above our fireplace, but I don't mention this to Nicole.

I feel at home in the surroundings, and I wouldn't have been surprised if Rosenbach himself appeared from around the corner, whiskey in hand, ready to show me the greatest rarities you ever saw. Among the early printed books, rare Americana, and fine copies of the literary classics is the manuscript of James Joyce's *Ulysses* purchased by Rosenbach only a few years after publication at the John Quinn auction (1923-24), Quinn being a patron of Joyce who sold him the manuscript. This unexpected sale caused Joyce indigestion not so much from the sale itself, but because Joseph Conrad's manuscripts in the same collection sold for more. There would have been a magnificent collection of early Shakespeare folios and quartos, too. But near the end of Rosenbach's life his brother and business partner Philip, more motivated by money than preservation, sold the lot in a blockbuster deal to Swiss collector Martin Bodmer.

The entrance of the current librarian Elizabeth Fuller brings me back to the present. She shows our small tour group a curious new acquisition, an early printing of Joyce's *Ulysses* concealed using the binding of another contemporary book because the work was initially banned for its obscenity. Some things never change. She opens the case and simply slides the book into position next to the other copies. A reminder that the collection is not static although the new acquisitions are normally supplemental rather than blockbusters.

Our next stop is the home of collector David Klappholz and his wife Lisa in Berkeley Heights, New Jersey. I've been looking forward to this. Dave and I have known each other for over twenty-five years. We first met crossing swords on Ebay. Dave began collecting in the early 1980s after discovering the writings of the famous book collector A. Edward Newton (1864-1940). Newton's best-known work is *The Amenities of Book Collecting* (1918). Dave was browsing for a book on Sir Isaac Newton when he serendipitously noticed an Eddie Newton book adjacent on the shelf. Curiosity took over and a bibliophile was born. Dave was certainly not the first collector to be inspired by Newton's writings, but he went all in and decided to collect the man himself. In 1986, he purchased much of Oak Knoll Books founder Robert Fleck's exceptional collection of A. Edward Newton described in Oak Knoll catalogue 86. This purchase established a foundation. The collection has been added to at every opportunity and the result is awe inspiring: dozens of superb association copies, many unique items, hundreds of letters, manuscripts, photographs, and ephemera. He even has in his garage the large metal entrance sign to Newton's "Oak Knoll" Pennsylvania estate, a rare relic of the now gone property. Dave is a computer science professor and has a memory to match. His knowledge of Newton and the rare book world of that time (ca. 1880-1940) is exceptional.

We all enjoy a memorable lunch together at Goodman's Deli established in 1943, the corned beef *almost* as tasty as the best of Texas barbecue. Dave's wife Lisa is great fun, more demonstrative than her husband, and quick to flesh out stories briefly alluded to by Dave. Until recently, they spent many summers in the Los Angeles area. Dave also collects material related to the early development of L.A. His knowledge of the city's history is encyclopedic. He and Nicole discuss prominent West Coast architects during lunch. We recall an exceptional day with Dave and Lisa in Los Angeles years ago when Dave served as our private tour guide.

Back at the house, Nicole and Lisa leave the two of us alone. I follow Dave to the garage and narrowly avoid tripping over the Oak Knoll sign. There are boxes of miscellaneous material, including many biblio-periodicals. He is open to letting them go. I wade through and select a few items, the sheer mass of it almost overwhelming. In the dining room are dozens more boxes. His Newton collection is normally upstairs in bookcases, but a painting project has required it to be packed and moved downstairs. I admire that pallet size stack. However, these boxes are off limits. He does point to ten boxes of related material and says he is open to parting with it. I get a tingle. The boxes contain many association copies and reference material directly connected with the rare book world of Newton's contemporaries—collectors, dealers, and scholars. An assemblage that fits perfectly into my collection.

I go through the items, eventually selecting five boxes worth. We spend time with a few individual pieces. One item that is irresistible to me is collector R.B. Adam's private library catalogue *Printed Only for a Few Friends* (Buffalo: 1925) inscribed to his close friend Charles G. Osgood. The book was later in the library of Donald & Mary Hyde with their bookplate. This is a book with a sublime combination of rarity and provenance. Osgood was a famous Princeton English professor and specialist on English writer Samuel Johnson. He wrote the introduction to R.B. Adam's *Catalogue of the Johnsonian Collection of R. B. Adam* (1921). He was a dedicatee of the revised edition *The R. B. Adam Library Relating to Dr. Samuel Johnson and His Era* (1929-1930). Prominent collectors Donald & Mary Hyde would later purchase the fabled R.B. Adam Johnson collection while forming their unmatched library of Johnson material now at Harvard.

Dave found many of these books and pamphlets in the pre-internet days by hunting in bookstores. I see a number came from Dawson's Books in Los Angeles. I don't think Dave has looked at this material in a long while. But even so, parting with things is rarely easy for a serious collector and I imagine what he is feeling. Finding an appreciative home for one's books can be a challenging task and is often ignored or delayed to the detriment of posterity. I think about it myself now and again as years accumulate.

Dave and I talk further, both enjoying the exchange. I want to be sure that he is ready to let this stuff go. The visit reinforces our common interests, and I wish he lived closer. This is the third time I've been to his house. He's seen my collection once. I'm already missing his companionship before we've even left. He and I reach an amicable agreement on price, and Lisa is pleased to see five boxes in the hallway ready to load into the car. Nicole's happiness level is not quite as high as hers.

Dave has a quirky sense of humor that can materialize at any moment. As we are about to leave, he gifts us two cowboy hats that he's picked up in the distant past from a dollar store. We find out he can't resist collecting such hats any more than books. (Dave likes wearing hats.) Lisa encourages us to accept more accumulated hats, but we demur. Dave and I put the cowboy hats on, and I must say we looked like some serious book-slingers ready for action. Nicole promises that when we have a book person visit our home, she'll take pictures of me and the lucky book guest wearing Dave's gift hats. This may cut down on visitors if the word gets out.

The finale to our visit is a random question from Dave, "You're pretty tall, but I think I'm still taller." I'm left speechless for a second. I suggest we stand back-to-back and let the ladies decide. Dave's a big guy but he's eighty years old and has shrunk a tad. The match-up is close. I'm going to claim victory. Let's just say relentless collectors are competitive and sometimes it spills over in special ways. We bid Dave and Lisa a fond farewell, our new cowboy hats worn sporadically the rest of the trip.

If you are keeping track (and I know Nicole did), I'm up to seven boxes of new acquisitions already. But you can't have too many *good* books can you? Or can you? We'll leave that touchy subject for another lifetime and hopefully a bigger house.

Next, we meet our friend Rebecca Rego Barry to browse Hobart Book Village of the Catskills in Hobart, New York. The seven bookstores of mostly used and rare books beckon the bibliophilic traveler. They are walkable and symbiotic in creating anticipation in the book hunter. The quality and depth of stock varies widely but all are worth a look. As we park, we watch a few bibliophiles squint and stumble from a nearby shop into the bright sunshine like spelunkers emerging from a cave.

I spot Rebecca in front of a bookstore waiting for the Zman and my better two-thirds. Rebecca, her husband Brett, and their two teenagers live about forty-five minutes away. Two years ago, we had a fabulous visit with them at their home nestled into a picturesque patch of the Catskills, a postcard scene with soaring greenery and a rocky stream. We ate lunch on their screened porch, the sound of the running water a background symphony. Rebecca reminded us then that GPS was unreliable in their area, and we arrived late after a dash of lostness, Nicole forcing me to ask directions at a convenience store.

Rebecca is one of the rare book world's notable personages. For many years she edited *Fine Books & Collections* magazine before taking a position in the trade with the Raab Collection, a well-known autograph and manuscript dealer in New York City. Her editorship of the magazine was widely admired for the breadth of stories offered, the balance maintained between readability and scholarship, and the reports on the news of the auction houses and trade. Rebecca also understands that the promotion of book collecting in general is key to long-term stability of the great sport. In this vein, she authored *Rare Books Uncovered: True Stories of Fantastic Finds in Unlikely Places* (2015), a gem of inspiration, and the recent *The Vanishing of Carolyn Wells: Investigations into a Forgotten Mystery Author* (2024).

We explore the bookstores. (Brett couldn't make it because he was working.) It's not long before our hunting is in sync, and we cover ground quickly. The result is a Carolyn Wells title for Rebecca, a couple of Latin American things for me, a few items for Nicole, and a book I unearth for Brett's John Burroughs collection. A bookcase of books about books tempts me with offerings in W. H. Adams' Antiquarian Books, the most impressive of the bookstores. But I've got to be awfully picky, or so I tell myself. Then Rebecca comes over and points out a sleeper I missed, *Simon & Schuster: The First Seventy-Five Years, 1924-1999* (1999).

"That's my first book. I did it while working there. You'll see my name's not on the title page, nor did I receive much credit, just a mention here," and she points to the reference at the back of the book.

I can tell this still nettles her, but she is mostly amused to find it randomly in Hobart, "It's pretty scarce and was done for in-house use."

Well readers, is there any universe where I'm not going to buy such a book found by the author herself? If there is, I won't be staying long. Her book is now on my shelves graciously inscribed by her to commemorate the Hobart occasion.

My hungry stomach begins to make embarrassing noises, and the women are ready to eat, too. We meet up with Brett for dinner at the Jagerberg Beer Hall and Alpine Tavern in nearby Hunter, New York. Brett is well-known in the region for his award-winning podcast "Kattcast" featuring Catskills culture, history, sustainability, local interviews, literature, and the arts. He is also a professional reader / creator of audio books with a studio in their home. We haven't spent much time together, but I quickly note that he is a shy introvert like me. We work through it by talking a lot. He also likes good beer, for example hosting a podcast in 2024 featuring three local breweries. Just listening to his perfect ten voice is strangely mesmerizing.

We reluctantly part with Rebecca and Brett, the rapidly darkening sky intruding and the corralling of their teenagers beckoning while our meal of Deutsch delights, Bavarian draft beer, and Brett's surprise round of dessert schnapps lingers. Come see us in Texas sometime we say, as this is simply a pause and not an ending.

That evening, we stay at Moore's Motel in Prattsville, highlighted by fresh flowers, mountain air, and a basketball goal outside our room in the parking area. The next morning, I shoot hoops with Nicole, my once feared jumper clanging off the rim with regularity, my vertical leap non-existent, and my layups resembling slow motion replays. But I still beat her, barely. She'll return the favor next time we play pool.

Then the real dash of a trip begins. We motor to Cooperstown, New York and plunge into Willis Monie Books run by Willis Monie Sr. and Jr., an open shop for over twenty-five years with hundreds of thousands of temptations. The building used to be an auto dealership and garage in the 1930s. The bottom floor is the retail shop for walk-in customers. The second floor, conveniently reinforced with heavy pillars built to support the earlier autos, is accessed by an old concrete car ramp, and contains over 100,000 catalogued books and pamphlets that are searchable online.

The store is a favorite of ours with an expansive books about books section and plenty of architecture and decorative arts books for Nicole to browse. This is our second visit. We are so focused on book hunting that we skip the famous baseball Hall of Fame nearby, again. On the first visit, Nicole's innate sense of bringing order to chaos came into play. The architecture section was quite a mess with stacks of books on the floor and the shelves disheveled. She organized the entire section. Will Monie, Jr. upon seeing this gave her a hearty thanks and an open-ended invitation for her to work at the store.

A few years ago, when the Reese Company in New Haven, Connecticut cleared out their warehouse after Bill Reese's death, many boxes of miscellaneous material were sent to Willis Monie. Bibliotreasures large and small have surfaced from the hoard. I find, for example, the important reference *Bibliography: Its History and Development* (NY: The Grolier Club, 1984), published in conjunction with a Grolier Club exhibit, this copy owned by Marjorie Wynne (1917-2009), highly regarded rare book librarian at Yale's Beinecke Library. Another item is bookman Terry Halladay's copy of Wright Howes' *U.S. IANA* (1962), a bedrock reference of Americana, with his early ownership signature dated "Dallas, TX, 1974." Halladay is most well-known for his decades of overseeing the literature division of Reese Company, but he cut his teeth working for various Texas booksellers in his formative years. Nicole and I ship two boxes of goodies home from Willis Monie Books. Many finds are hers this time.

We drive north the next day into Vermont, Green Mountain country, the home of famed nineteenth century rare book dealer Henry Stevens (1819-1886), who spent much of his career in London but proudly trumpeted his "Green Mountain Boy" (GMB) roots on the title page of most of his books. We play tourist for an afternoon at the Trapp Family Lodge & Resort near Stowe, Vermont. The family's escape from Nazi Germany to America is immortalized in the movie *The Sound of Music* (1965) starring Julie Andrews. For a fee, you can frolic in the surrounding fields channeling Andrews, but this is a waste of book money, and we simply explore the lodge, enjoy the free views, and visit their beer garden. We top this off with a stop at the Ben & Jerry's Ice Cream factory nearby. The company's inventive "graveyard" of dead ice cream flavors is a high spot of the tour, each flavor represented by a tombstone. We eat premium ice cream at a premium price while enjoying the mountain ambiance.

We shake off the carb-load and get ready for another one later that day—an Italian dinner at Mimmo's in Essex, Vermont with gregarious bookman Kevin Graffagnino and his wife Leslie. Kevin, raised in Montpelier and a graduate of UVM, spent a distinguished career curating/directing the Vermont, Wisconsin, and Kentucky Historical

Societies before becoming director of the Clements Library at the University of Michigan. He retired in 2019 and has returned home. Rare books are hard to shake, and he is already involved in an upcoming local auction of a collection of Vermontiana owned by a friend. Kevin was a bookseller in his youth, and he feels the long slumbering return of nervous energy and uncertainties that accompany the selling of rare books. We chat about this and lots of other bookish topics in a too short dinner.

Kevin and I share a common interest in the history of American book hunting, particularly Americana. He's written and / or edited over twenty-five books at last count. Two published by the Clements Library shortly before his retirement are catnip to me: *The Pioneer Americanists: Early Collectors, Dealers, and Bibliographers* (2017), and *Americana is a Creed: Notable Twentieth-Century Collectors, Dealers, and Bibliographers* (2019). Most recent is his *Vermontiana* (2024) that describes his selection of 154 essential pre-1900 works about the state. His introduction to the book, "Vermontiana: Collecting the Green Mountain State" is a master class in biblio-history.

Kevin sends us off with a tip to visit The Country Bookshop of Ben Koenig in Plainfield, Vermont. It's not often I've taken an unpaved road to a bookstore, but part of the drive to this tiny Vermont town is decidedly off the beaten track. We pull up to the Victorian two-story house/bookstore. It looks unkempt, and that is charitable. Weeds of prehistoric size grow tall, and a half-hidden path leads to the porch / side door which serves as the main entrance, the front door inaccessible unless you have a machete and courage. Ben is not a yard guy, but he's gathered a lot of books over forty plus years crammed into every corner of the store. I ask him about his foreign language section, but a huge stack of boxes currently blocks the entrance to that area. He apologizes and I sympathize. Ben is mild-mannered and friendly and doesn't intrude on our scouring of his store. The climate control is mostly left to nature and there is a mustiness to the whole place that is so strong even I notice. Nicole browses and then retreats. I find one nugget that appears to have been there forever in his rather substantial books about books section. It is John Russell Bartlett's signed and heavily annotated copy of bookseller Alfred Russell Smith's *Bibliotheca Americana: A Catalogue of a Valuable Collection of Books, Illustrating the History and Geography of North and South America and the West Indies. Collected by John Russell Smith.* (London: 1871).

Bartlett (1805-1886) was one of America's first great bookmen, initially working as a rare bookseller in New York City then as private librarian and bibliographer to John Carter Brown (1797-1874), the founder of the Brown Library at Brown University. In fact, Bartlett went through this Smith catalogue closely checking holdings and ordering books presumably for Brown. Bartlett was versatile as well, serving as secretary of state for Rhode Island, and accepting the role as U.S. commissioner to survey the disputed Mexican-United States border shortly after the 1846-48 Mexican-American War. His resulting book *Personal Narrative of Explorations and Incidents in Texas, New Mexico, California, Sonora, and Chihuahua* (1854) is a classic of Western Americana. He also found time to compile *Dictionary of Americanisms* (1848), an assemblage of slang terms that ran through several editions.

We wish Ben Koenig farewell, and I ride the high of the Bartlett find the rest of the day. What follows the next morning is an excursion to indulge one of Nicole's passions, architect Frank Lloyd Wright. We arrive at the Currier Museum of Art in Manchester, New Hampshire, and Nicole practically skips to the entrance to pick up our tickets to tour the Zimmerman House (built in 1951, no relation), and the Kalil House (built in 1955), two Wright-designed residences now owned by the museum. Although constructed within a short time of each other, they exemplify two radically different versions of his Usonian style. After an in-depth tour of both with an estimated four million photos taken by Nicole, we finish with lunch in the Currier's Winter Garden Café. I'm ready for our big push into Maine.

We first visit Scott Vile, proprietor of the Ascensius Press, well-regarded for quality fine press work, typecasting, and book design. His press is named after Jodocus Badius Ascensius (1462-1535), a scholar and printer who played a central role in the French Renaissance. Scott has been in business since the late 1980s. The shop is located in Bar Mills, Maine, a small town outside of Portland. He knows we are coming but still asks on arrival rather incredulously, "Why are you *here?*"

"To see you!" we respond. We sense he doesn't get many out-of-town visitors.

We receive a grand tour of his impressive print shop with many projects obviously afoot, the intoxicating smell of ink and paper filling our senses. The four-thousand-foot space is crammed with printing equipment dating back over one hundred years, all of it is functional and utilized. For example, in one corner is a linotype machine, in another a Heidelberg Cylinder Press, in another a group of monotype casters. In contrast, he also utilizes the latest design software for his clients.

I see one type caster machine from the 1930s with hundreds of intricate working parts that look like a mechanic's nightmare. I notice lots of tools present, and I'm reminded of my earlier days when I worked on cars and engines.

"Yes, I'm pretty good at fixing things," he replies.

We finish with a tour of his substantial book collection and reference library accompanying a long wall. He has gathered examples during his career of fine printing from the 15th century onward. It is not a rich man's collection, but one assembled by a printer in the thick of it, indulging occasionally in an admired relic of his predecessors.

He shows us an association item given to him that has been owned by at least three previous printers of stature. His own works are there too, ranging from humble pamphlets and well-designed trade publications to superb fine press titles. His latest fine press production is John Milton's *Areopagitica*, an impassioned defense of freedom of the press originally published in 1644, this edition beautifully printed in a small edition of twenty-six copies for the cognoscenti. He shows us the proof in a trial binding. The noted Maine binder Gray Parrot will be doing the binding of the finished copies.

Scott first reached out to me after I gave a zoom talk to the Baxter Society of Maine, a bibliophilic organization based in Portland. He is a member. He then invited me as a guest via zoom to a meeting of the Club of Odd Volumes in Boston. He's engaged in the wider book world and has a passion for printing that he hopes to pass on.

"If I could find an apprentice willing to learn the trade, I'd leave the shop to him or her," he says, rather wistfully.

We exit his shop, a steady rain not dampening the experience, and I think about his comment. There is a lot of ballyhoo about the resurgence of appreciation for books and fine printing, but deep-down serious bibliophiles know the future is uncertain.

My solemn thoughts dissipate as we make our way to Alfred, Maine, the home of DeWolfe & Wood bookstore. Proprietors Scott DeWolfe and Frank Wood, both veteran dealers, joined forces and opened the store in 1993 "during a snowstorm on April Fool's Day." It is located in yet another building well over one hundred years old reflecting the age of many of the thousands of books within. The main floor is stuffed but well organized, as is the downstairs basement area. DeWolfe and Wood advertise themselves as the successor to Tuttle Antiquarian Books, a fabled Vermont bookstore with roots back to the 1830s. Many years ago, they acquired the stock of Tuttle's, a literal barn full of books which took years to organize and process. Frank Wood recounted early in this endeavor being greeted aggressively by a neighbor who was fully armed with rifle in hand asking not so politely why he was there and removing things. Police soon arrived and the whole near-death experience ended amicably.

I'm eager to dig into the stock. I've bought online from them, and I know from other book people who have visited the shop that there are uncatalogued goodies to be had. I discover a dozen interesting items including the bound page proofs of bookseller Merle Johnson's *You Know These Lines! A Bibliography of the Most Quoted Verses in American Poetry* (1935). This is Johnson's own copy with bookplate and annotations, the book later passing to his friend, client, and formidable collector Paul Seybolt (1903-1991) with correspondence between the two laid in.

Johnson (1874-1935), who was a rare book dealer in New York, is best remembered for his influential books written during the 1920s and 30s including *High Spots of American Literature* (1929) and *American First Editions* (1929 and later editions). He also collected Mark Twain and produced the first significant bibliography of Twain's works in

1910 (revised in 1935). Less known is the fact he did delightful illustrations for many books and magazines including Howard Pyle's *Book of Pirates* (1921). Seybolt, a Boston collector, specialized in first books of literary authors. His *Catalogue of the First Editions of First Books in the Collection of Paul S. Seybolt* (1946) is an important reference source.

This Johnson is discovered in the basement. Upstairs, I spot on the top shelf of a wall of miscellaneous nineteenth century material a copy of Henry Stevens' famous *Bibliotheca Historica: A Catalogue of 5000 Volumes of Books and Manuscripts Relating Chiefly to the History and Literature of North and South America* (1870). I reach high to retrieve it, mildly pulling my latissimus dorsi muscle in the process, and I find it inscribed to William F. Poole (1821-1894). A fantastic association item! Poole was the groundbreaking librarian and bibliographer who directed in succession The Boston Athenaeum, The Chicago Public Library, and the Newberry Library. Stevens and Poole were close friends since their undergraduate days at Yale. Poole's rise in the library world mirrored Stevens' rise in the rare book trade, each supporting the other in various projects spanning publications to acquisitions.

The book is not cheap, DeWolfe & Wood know what they have, and the rather stiff price does not deter me. Book collectors all love bargains but a collector who is unwilling to stretch and pay retail on occasion, or even a record price, will never have a great collection.

Unsurprisingly, Nicole has also found treasures, and two more boxes are shipped home.

Maine continues to provide pleasantries as we visit bibliophile and collector Michael Burd in Kennebunkport. Mike has read my work and reached out with kind comments and common interests. He suggests stopping to see him if we are ever in his area. And we do, not long after this first communication, our Northeast trip already planned. I email him this opportune news and he remains welcoming and undeterred.

Mike is retired from a banking career, and he and his wife have beautifully restored and updated their home on Maine Street, located literally next door to the public library, preserving many of the home's eighteenth-century features and creating a space both expansive and warm, no easy feat. His massive, custom-designed library at the rear of the house contains over 20,000 books. He also has a substantial collection of books in the family room.

This is the home of a book lover, an enthusiastic student of whatever subject interests him, and these subjects are many, both literary and historical, each represented in depth with important works, the collection not focused on rarities—although there are some—but a scholar's library reminiscent of the huge personal collections assembled in the nineteenth century, yet here present in our own time. It is stunning to experience first-hand.

Mike is a voracious reader but no introvert. We have a lively pre-dinner discussion in his kitchen with wine for Nicole and me, and then he takes us to a restaurant within walking distance. It was a favorite spot for him and his wife. She passed away earlier in the year, and this is the first time he has returned since then. Nicole tries his wife's favorite dish. We get to know each other over that dinner, our new friendship and the solace of books hopefully easing a time of challenging transition.

After dinner, we enjoy an evening stroll back to Mike's house as he gives a historical tour of the neighborhood along the way. If we lived closer, I'd make Mike's place a regular stop. Perhaps my unofficial Maine clubhouse. I'd even bring snacks and attempt to surprise him with a biblio-book he might be unaware of. He generously invites us to stay with him on the next visit instead of a hotel. His home is built to accommodate big family gatherings and there is usually space available—unless Mike eventually converts it into more library shelving.

Serendipitously, our next visit after viewing Mike Burd's mighty library space is with Reid Byers, author of the bestselling *The Private Library: The History of the Architecture and Furnishing of the Domestic Bookroom* (2021). Reid and his wife Patty live in Portland, Maine, and we look forward to meeting them in person for the first time. Reid is a retired programmer and IT specialist who is immersed in the book world. He is a mainstay of the Baxter Society and technical guru of their zoom presentations. He is also a Grolier Club member with an exhibition there in 2024 of his collection entitled "Imaginary Books:

Lost, Unfinished, and Fictive Works Found Only in Other Books," accompanied by an extensive catalogue. The Grolier Club description will help those scratching their heads,

> Part bibliophilic entertainment and part conceptual art installation, *Imaginary Books: Lost, Unfinished, and Fictive Works Found Only in Other Books* features a collection of books that do not really exist. Curated by Grolier Club member Reid Byers, the exhibition includes approximately 100 books and associated arealia from his collection—all simulacra created with a team of printers, bookbinders, artists, and calligraphers—of lost books that have no surviving example, unwritten books that were planned but left unfinished, and fictive works that exist only in fiction. Highlights of the exhibition include William Shakespeare's *Love's Labour's Won*, the lost sequel to *Love's Labour's Lost*; Ernest Hemingway's first novel, stolen from his wife's bag on a French train in 1922; and the *Necronomicon*, John Dee's copy of the eldritch grimoire that has been kept sealed in a Wells Fargo strongbox, as a precaution, since the Krickle accident of 1967.

It is this subject we focus on during our visit. Reid and his wife have downsized in retirement. What was a large library in their former home is now compressed into a smaller, more vertically integrated space within Reid's office. We are fortunate to see his imaginary books shortly before he packed them up for the Grolier Club exhibition.

This physical manifestation of the imaginary books illustrates Reid's strong creative streak and bookish wit. His tour brings witness to his theatrical talents. He hands us examples of various titles and explains if we open them to look for contents they lose their magic so to speak, and one will find nothing for they exist only in the imagination. This is entertaining as we admire the different formats of the items, and the efforts involved in producing them. I attempt to talk with him about the production details, but he will have none of it. His persona is now that of a complete believer in this biblio-scene, the books real, the stories alive, the emotions felt deeply, a curatorial tour unlike anything we've experienced. Surreal is too strong a word, but it is immersive and mesmerizing, interrupted only by his need to take a conference call. He ends with a wry smile. I tell him I'm going to need an inscribed copy of the exhibition catalogue, and we laugh.

Nicole and I hit the reality button after this as we fight traffic and get closer to Boston and the Brattle Bookshop. Brattle was established in its current form by George Gloss in 1949. His son Ken Gloss and his wife own it, and they have developed the shop into one of the best antiquarian bookstores in the country. Ken is now in his 70s but his energy seems endless. He is always promoting the store and hunting books. Ken's a regular on *Antiques Roadshow* and social media. His talks are filled with entertaining stories of finds, and sometimes near misses. A not-so-secret ingredient to Brattle's success is a willingness to take on large quantities of books *en masse* whether it be an estate, a downsizing collector, a dealer shedding stock, or a voracious reader/gatherer who must let go. Brattle's stock is estimated at over 250,000 volumes.

The main bookshop occupies two large floors. The day we visit it is teeming as usual with general readers, students, and bargain hunters. The third-floor rare book room contains the better material and is fertile hunting ground with temptations in just about all subject fields. New items arrive daily. Turnover is brisk. I'd suggest that for an open shop, Brattle has the most vibrant collectible book selection in the country.

We are fortunate that Ken Gloss is in the office that day. Ken and I have met before, but I re-introduce myself. We discuss his most recent adventures as well as my interest in the history of the rare book world, including him. Also present is store manager Zachary Marconi. Zach is friendly, knowledgeable, and has a good memory. A couple of years earlier, when I found out that famed Harvard bookman Roger Stoddard sold a portion of his library to Brattle, I asked Zach to be my onsite scout. He pulled together about thirty Stoddard association items for me. This was a favor much appreciated, and I was now able to thank him in person.

Unbeknownst to me since that time, Zach has been assembling a further box of biblio-association items he thinks I might like. My unexpected arrival interrupts his imminent email to me, and I browse the box first-hand. He and I are bemused by the timing of this, and

Nicole just shakes her head. I buy most of his finds including biblio-books inscribed to Philip Hofer (1898-1984) the highly regarded collector/curator of the Houghton Library at Harvard. One high spot is *The Houghton Library 1942-1967: A Selection of Books and Manuscripts in Harvard Collections* (1967) presented by Arthur Houghton himself to Hofer.

Doing my own search that day amongst the shelves, I discover a long-sought title, William Brotherhead's *The Book of the Signers: Containing Facsimile Letters of the Signers of the Declaration of Independence* (1861), a large folio in the original cloth and a rare presentation copy.

William Brotherhead (1824-1893) was an enterprising and creative Philadelphia bookseller specializing in Americana who eventually built a stock of over 50,000 items and numbered among his clients the prominent collectors William Menzies, Samuel Pennypacker, F.J. Dreer, and E.D. Ingraham. He first came to my attention when I read his memoir *Forty Years among the Booksellers of Philadelphia* (1891). It is an opinionated and entertaining view of his fellow dealers and collectors. *The Book of Signers* with facsimiles gathered from collectors and "antiquaries" represents the surge in the collecting and preserving of autograph material related to the famous figures of the American Revolution. The book was ironically published during the first year of the Civil War when the country had just plunged into chaos.

I show Nicole the book with glee, and I see she has also had a successful hunt at Brattle. Our books are paid for and will be shipped home. We reluctantly leave as Brattle closes, Ken Gloss himself outside, securing the bookcases of discount books that draw in passersby during open hours. He waves and thanks us for coming.

We do not want to brave rush hour traffic from Boston to Cape Cod, so we sightsee in downtown Boston to kill time. We discover Democracy Brewing Company at 35 Temple Place. The food is tasty, their Red Ale equally so, and the pub theme is perfect for our location in a historic neighborhood. I acquire a brewery tee shirt. Our frenetic two-week trip is nearing an end.

Later that night we cross the Sagamore Bridge leading to Cape Cod and arrive in Mashpee at the summer home of our good friends,

Bill & Pat Allison. Bill & Pat are retired lawyers from Houston. Pat grew up on Cape Cod and still has family there. Bill decided that she had suffered enough through four decades of Houston summers during her law career. Pat was quick to approve the idea of a summer home on Cape Cod, one in which they could not only escape the Houston heat but also have a convivial meeting place for family gatherings.

Bill collected Western Americana for over three decades, first focusing on famous Texas author J. Frank Dobie then expanding into books on the history of ranching along with other rarities related to Texas and the West. Upon retirement, he thought it would be fun to switch hats and become a part-time dealer and slowly sell off the collection he had so industriously gathered. This was about twelve years ago. His taste in books combined with an opportunistic market quickly resulted in unexpectedly large sales of the original collection, and Bill summoned his book hunting skills to replenish his rapidly depleted stock. Fast forward to now, Bill is a full-time ABAA dealer with a second career. He issues monthly catalogues and attends numerous book fairs. His catalogues are filled with a wider variety of subjects than he gathered as a collector, but all are centered around the West –railroad maps, promotional ephemera for westward expansion, nineteenth century Mexican documents related to Texas, and a selection of uncommon and rare books. Clients include many prominent universities, dealers, and collectors. He witnesses first-hand that maps, manuscript material, and ephemera have eclipsed books in interest mirroring a larger trend.

"I'm working almost more now than when I was working," he says, but I know it's not really work to him, and one would be hard-pressed to find a better retirement gig for a book collector.

Over the years, we've had many biblio-adventures with Bill and Pat, and I'll recount the latest addition to the stockpile of memories as a fitting end to this escapade.

Our ferry ride with Bill from Cape Cod to Oak Bluffs on Martha's Vineyard is a smooth one, the bright sun shimmering on the waves, the harbor entrance picturesque, my only regret is standing at the back of the ferry pretending I'm Captain Hook as I inadvertently suck in a blast of diesel exhaust. I am still coughing spasmodically as we disembark. The upside is my hacking creates a wide buffer around me as people scurry to avoid a perceived germinator. Through my watering eyes I make out eighty-year-old Nicholas Basbanes waiting for us. He's wearing his distinctive Navy service cap commemorating his Vietnam tour of duty on the aircraft carrier *Oriskany*.

Basbanes is a journalist by trade and renowned author of ten highly acclaimed works, most of them focusing on aspects of books and book culture. A few of my favorites include his classic history of book collecting *A Gentle Madness* (1995), *Patience and Fortitude* (2001), *Among the Gently Mad* (2002), and *A Splendor of Letters* (2003). His works have had an inspirational influence on my own book hunting and writing.

Nick gives Nicole a hug. He shakes hands with Bill, the first time the two have met. He greets me, probably wondering why I am teary eyed.

"You guys hungry?" he asks after a pause.

Yes indeed, and we are all soon seated for lunch at Lookout Tavern, a popular spot close to the ferry landing. Nick's charming wife Connie joins us. He, like me, has married above his pay grade. The place is boisterous and crowded and wafts of fresh fish and the ocean. I'm seated next to Nick, and we are soon engaged in biblio-talk amidst the din. Nick and I haven't spent a lot of time together in person, but we've communicated regularly for over a decade, and we skip any formalities, and chat as long-time friends do picking up wherever we left off, any lapsed time inconsequential. But it is hard for all of us to hear as a group and after lunch we adjourn to Nick & Connie's cottage home close-by.

The home has passed down through Connie's family. What was a summer retreat for them has become a more permanent residence since the pandemic, though they still retain their primary home in New Grafton outside of Boston. I spent a memorable time there in

2014 with Nick, selecting a few hundred items for my own collection from his books about books library, most utilized by him in the writing of *A Gentle Madness* and other works.

Nick settles into his recliner and we gather round, the conversation expanding in many directions; talk of Nick's new book in process *Before Paper: Unlocking the World's Earliest Writings*, his biography of Henry David Longfellow *Cross of Snow* (2020) that fell victim to the pandemic in terms of promotion, his archive at Texas A&M, my own collection of Basbanesiana and my essays, the sale of a large portion of his general library to Brattle Bookshop, and the career of his daughter Barbara Basbanes Richter who is following in his footsteps as a writer. Our time is up too soon for we must catch the last ferry of the day back to Cape Cod. Our group piles into two cars for the short ride to the dock; Nick's late '80s Cadillac, the size of a well-fed dinosaur, and Connie's petite Toyota Prius making quite a contrast.

We wave goodbye from the deck of the ferry and Oak Bluffs recedes from view leaving a panorama of Martha's Vineyard and the surrounding sea bathed in the late afternoon sun. I avoid diesel fumes this time and sit with Nicole, and I talk less than usual. She seems appreciative. I'm adding up boxes of books in my head. Twelve is the count. I tell Bill Allison this when Nicole briefly leaves to stretch her legs. He laughs and congratulates.

I neglect to discuss something important with Nick. Back in Texas, I contact him about using his essay about *me* as the prologue to this book. The essay first appeared as a column in *Fine Books & Collections*, Autumn, 2021. His gracious approval is self-evident. Now Nick and I get to hang out together in perpetuity. The thought is pleasing but passes quickly at the sound of the mailman.

I eagerly bring in the first box of books to arrive and open it with a ceremonial flourish. Nicole retrieves her portion of the contents and nestles beside me. We rediscover our finds and relive an epic bibliobender of a trip, tired but happy. Then we spend much of the night reading quietly together until she falls asleep, and I head upstairs to catalog, feeling rejuvenated, my mind relentlessly roaming amongst books.

2025

Afterword

I'D LIKE to especially thank Nicole Zimmerman and Jennifer Larson for reading the manuscript. Their input has been extremely helpful and improved the book in many ways. Nicole as wife and supervisor has the daily joy of overseeing this wild-eyed bibliomaniac. Jennifer's immersion in the rare book world generates keen insights and welcome feedback.

I also would like to thank Nick Basbanes for allowing the use of his *Fine Books & Collections* column about me as a prologue. His friendship is a high spot of my relentless pursuit.

The fortuitous friendship of Scott Vile led to his design and layout of the book for which I am most thankful. If I ever issue a large paper, extra-illustrated edition printed on vellum, he will be the man for that, too.

The Book Hunters Club of Houston provides biblio-nourishment at a local level. Our gatherings always leave me invigorated. Douglas Adams, Bill Allison, and Jay Rohfritch should be singled out as particularly stimulating. We've spent many hours together with rare books. Two other honorary members not so close-by but always willing to participate in lively biblio-exchanges are Bill Fisher and Joe Fay. They've all enriched my life more than I should admit. (But don't expect any man-hugs.) I'm additionally comforted and confident that if I ever needed bail money, they would come through for me.

My library is an ever-growing organism and space is getting scarce. I just cracked that joist in the attic because of excessive book weight. Our planned library addition above the garage has run into a snag. Remodeling has gotten dang expensive. And how can I continue to write fresh biblio-stories if I don't have room to store the new acquisitions? So, if my fellow bibliophiles feel inspired to help, they will receive something very special in return.

Contributors to the Zimmerman Library Expansion Fund will receive a personalized photograph of me in the new library wing (various poses available). More generous donors will receive a biblio-tote bag emblazoned with the Zimmerman Library logo to take on book hunting trips. VIP donors will garner an overnight stay complete with unlimited browsing of the stacks, cuisine cooked by yours truly, and an open bar. The Platinum Donor will additionally have their likeness reproduced in a special stained glass library window that I will gaze upon daily.

I look forward to hearing from you.

SELECTIVE INDEX

Adam, R.B., 196
Adams, Douglas, 46, 134, 151, 213
Adams, Marion W., 103
Adams, Ramon, 135
Adams, W.H. Antiquarian Books, 198
Adler, Elmer, 16, 19
Aguirre, Carlos, 87
Ahlquist, Elizabeth, 85
Aldis, Owen, 162
Allen, Francis H., 162
Allison, Pat, 210
Allison, William (Bill), 93, 94, 105, 210-212, 213
Alvis, Allie, 191
American Antiquarian Society (AAS), 110-112
American Council of Learned Societies, 101
Andrews, Julie, 200
Andrews, William Loring, 22, 24-25
Annmary Brown Memorial Library, 94ff
Anthoensen Press, 101-102
Anthony, Henry Bowen, 173
Arcadian Books, 88-89
Aretakis, Nick, 44-45, 169
Arnold, J.V., 178
Arnold, William Harris, 162
Ascensius Press, 202
Avery, Samuel P., 176
Avini, Theresa, 56
Austin, Richard, 113
Bain, Vernon, 5
Baldwin's Book Barn, 191

Barlow, Samuel L.M., 176
Barlow, Jr., William P., 151ff
Barrett, Clifton Waller, 162
Barry, Rebecca Rego & Brett, 197-199
Bartlett, John Russell, 138, 170, 172, 173, 202
Basbanes, Connie, 211-212
Basbanes, Nicholas, i-iv ,12, 47-48, 211-212, 213
Battery Park Books, 113
Bauman Rare Books, 124, 128
Baxter Society of Maine, 203
Bay Psalm Book, 173
Beck, John B., 139
Beckham's Bookshop, 87-88
Beggs, Eric, 57
Belanger, Terry, 154
Ben & Jerry's Ice Cream, 200
Berland, Abel, 12-13
Bixby, W.K., 164
Black, Erin Mae, 124
Black, Jeannette, 103
Blacque, Valentine, 22, 27ff
Blue Cypress Books, 85
Blumberg, Stephen, 36-37
Bodmer, Martin, 194
Bonaventure, Edmund F., 179, 180
Book Fellows' Club, 22ff, 176
Book Hunters Club of Houston, 213
Book Source Monthly, 182
Borkowski, Justin, 193
Boyd, Andrew, 75
Brattle Bookshop, 93, 208-209
Brennan, Francis & Geri, 6
Brevoort, J. Carson, 137

Brotherhead, William, 209
Brown, Charles, 127
Brown, John Carter, 44, 173, 202
Brown University, 77, 94ff, 174, 202
Buffalo Bill Historical Center, 61
Burd, Michael, 205-206
Burns, Paul, 57
Butler, Lafayette, 115-116
Butler, William, 72
Butts, William, 169
Byers, Reid, 206-208
Caroliniana Books, 168
Caxton Club, 12
Cerf, Bennett, 20
Chamberlain, Jacob C., 162, 163
Chrysler 300, 2007 SRT-8, 187
Clements Library, 201
Clifford, Henry H., 59-60
Club of Odd Volumes, 203
Cole, Hamilton, 176
Comstock, Anthony, 179-180
Cotner, Robert, 13
Country Bookshop (VT), 201
Cox, Mike, 188-189
Cowan, Robert E., 118
Crescent City Books, 87
Crocker, Templeton, 119
Currie, Barton, 5, 38ff
Currier, Richard, 99
Currier, T. Franklin, 99
D'Avolio, Arianna, 191
Daly, Augustin, 176, 178
Dana, John Cotton, 108
Dannenberg, Tom, 6
David, Dorman, 58
Dawson's Books, 196
DeSalvo, Joe, 86
DesMarais, Nat, 118
Desmond, Erin, 191
Desmond, Russell, 88-89
DeWolfe & Wood Bookstore, 204-205

DeWolfe, Scott, 204
Dibdin, Thomas, 34
Dick, William B., 178
Dickinson, Don, 137
Dobie, Dudley R., 51, 57, 143
Dobie, J. Frank, 51 ,57, 143ff, 210
Doheny, Estelle, 59
Donnelly, Thomas, 174
Downtown Books, 6
Dreer, Ferdinand, 209
Dumont Andre, 45
Duprat, Alphonse, 22, 25-27
Driftless Books, 1ff
Dunaway Books, 5
DuPont, Henry Francis, 133, 191
Eames, Wilberforce, 104, 136
Eberstadt, Edward & Co., 55, 119, 135
Eckel, John C., 39ff
Erotica, Collecting of, 177
Evans II, Montgomery, 11-12
Faulkner House Books, 85-86
Fay, Joe, 93, 115, 169, 213
First Folio Books, 121
Fish, Daniel, 75ff
Fisher, Otto O., 117-118
Fisher, William (Bill), 87 ,213
Fleck, Millie, 190-192
Fleck, Bob (father), 192, 195
Fleck, Rob (son), 190-192
Florida Antiquarian Book Fair, 121ff
Florida Bibliophile Society, 127
Foley, P.K., 159
Foote, Charles B., 162
Ford, Malcolm, 175
Ford, Paul Leicester, 174-176
Foster, Andy, 153
Frick Museum, 133-34
Fuller, Elizabeth, 194
Gaeta, Dan, 115
Gallup, Donald, 133
Gammell, H.P., 146
Gilliss, Walter, 25

Selective Index

Ginsberg, Michael, 36
Gleichenhaus, Stuart B., 60
Gloss, Ken, 208-209
Gnarly Barley Peanut Butter Porter, 86
Goetzman, William, 55
Goff, Frederick, 93ff
Good Books in the Woods, 122
Gowans, William, 171
Graffagnino, Kevin, 88, 200-201
Grayshelf Books, 121
Greene, Albert Gorton, 170-171
Gresh, Richard, 40
Gribben, Alan, 91
Grolier Club, 22, 25, 32, 47, 154, 176, 200, 207
Gross, Dr. Samuel D., 138
Growoll, Adolph, 22-23
Guild, Reuben A., 174
Gura, Phillip, 112
Hale, Edward Everett, 127
Halladay, Terry, 200
Hanna, Archibald, 133
Harris, C. Fiske, 168ff
Harry Ransom Humanities Research Center, 90ff, 132, 143, 186
Hart, Charles Henry, 75
Hawkins, Rush, 94ff, 176
Heartman, Charles F., 52
Heber, Richard, 34
Heckscher, Gerard, 114-115
Hellman, George S., 158, 161-162, 163-166
Henderson, Jennie Crocker, 118-119
Heritage Book Shop, 61
Herndon, William, 75
Hertzog, Carl, 57
Hill, Walter M., 69
Hinton, Harwood, 52
Hobart Book Village, 197-198
Hoe, Robert, 176
Hofer, Philip, 209
Hogg, Ima, 134, 148
Hollywood, Hustler, 83
Holman, David, 57, 60
Holman, William, 56, 58
Holstein, Mark G., 10-11, 15, 17-18, 19
Houdini, Harry, 66
Houghton, Arthur, 209
Houghton Library, 209
Howard, Peter, 1
Howe, Parkman Dexter, 162
Howell, John—Books, 55, 56, 119
Howell, Warren R., 53, 55, 119
Huckans, John, 182
Hunter, Paul, 147
Huntington, Henry, 31, 77
Hyde, Donald & Mary, 196
Imerman, Jacob, 122
Ingraham, E.D., 209
Jackson, William, 103-104
Jagerberg Beer Hall, 198
Jay, Ricky, 112-113
Jenkins, John, 55, 56, 58, 135, 149
John Bale Company, 115
John Carter Brown Library, 95
Johnson, Herbert, 192
Johnson, Merle, 115-116, 204-205
Jolly-Bavoillet, M., 177, 178
Joyce, James, 194
Kahn, Ely J., 20
Karmiole, Ken, 192
Keiffer, Selby, 113
Kent, Henry W., 108
Kent, Rockwell, 19
Kern, Jerome, 20
Klappholz, David & Lisa, 194-197
Klopfer, Donald S., 20
Knowlton, Harold R., 101
Koenig, Ben, 201-202
Kohn, John S. Van E., 159
Kraus, H.P., 117
Kretzmann, Edwin M.J., 101
Kurutz, Gary, 60

217

Lakin, Bob, 128
Laird, Michael, 93
Lambert, William Harrison, 76
Larson, Jennifer, 213
Leland, Waldo G., 101
Laveau, Marie, 87
Lefferts, Marshall, 162
Lenox, James, 44
Levison, Lois C., 17, 19
Levy, Newman, 17, 20
Lewis & Clark College, 36
Libbie, C.F. & Co., 141
Liebert, Fritz, 133
Lilly Library, 77, 91
Lincoln, Abraham, 75ff
Lincoln Historical Research Foundation, 77
Littlefield Southern History Collection, 148
Locker-Lampson, Frederick, 22
Loveman, Amy, 71
Lowenstein, Solomon, 20
Lydenberg, Harry, 98
Lyrical Ballad Bookstore, 109
Madden, Sir Frederic, 35
Maier, Frank, 162
Main Street Books, 169
Marconi, Zachary, 208
Marshall, Anthony, 181ff
Martin, R. Eden, 12
Martin, Robert S., 60
Masi, Peter, 93
Mathes, Michael, 60
Mathieson, Roger, 105
Mayer, Roberto L., 55
McBride Rare Books, 115
McClurg's Bookshop, 17
McCorison, J.L., 75ff
McCorison, Marcus, 110ff
McDonald, Archie P., 144-145, 147
McKee, Thomas, 176, 178
McKinney, Bruce, 116

McLellan, Woodberry, 76
McMann, Preston, 36
McMurtry, Larry, 2, 63ff
Medical Society County of Kings, 141
Melhouse, Dennis, 121
Menzies, William, 209
Meserve, Frederick Hill, 81
Milton & Hubble Books, 153
Miranker, Glen & Cathy, 47ff
Monie (see under Willis Monie Books)
Montgomery, Charles, 133-135
Moosbrugger, Steve, 124, 128
Moreau, Charles C., 178
Morgan, J.P., 158ff
Morgand, Damascene, 179
Morris, Frank M., 79
Morris, Henry, 192
Morris, Jerry, 14, 127
Morrow, Jr., William H., 51-52, 57
Murphy, Henry C., 136ff
Mysterious Bookshop, 48
National Book Auctions, 38
Nettell, Andy, 45-46
New York Academy of Medicine, 140
Newton, A. Edward, 5, 9ff, 40, 70, 73, 194-195
Nix, Eddy, 1ff
Nova Press, 154, 156
Oak Knoll Books, 190-192
Oakleaf, Joseph, 75ff
Ong, George, 93
Orcutt, William Dana, 5
Osgood, Charles G., 196
Paul, John R., 5
Parrish, Morris L., 40-41
Parrot, Gray, 203
Payne, John R., 186, 187-188
Pearson, Edmund, 108-110
Pène du Bois, Henri, 23-24, 26-28, 176, 192
Pennypacker, Samuel, 209

Selective Index

Penzler, Otto, 48-49
Phillipps, Sir Thomas, 34-35
Poe, Edgar A., 172
Poole, William F., 205
Poor, Henry W., 29ff, 192
Posey, Tom, 124,128
Prairie Archives, 5
Prospero's, 6
Providence Public Library, 170
Purple, Dr. Samuel, 136ff
Quaritch, Bernard, 179
Quarto Club, 11,15ff
Queen, Dairy, 130
Quinn, John, 194
Raab Collection, 198
Randall, David, 91
Redoute, Pierre-Joseph, 72
Reese, William, 36, 43ff, 113, 132ff, 200
Rich, Obadiah, 44
Richter, Barbara Basbanes, 212
Rider, Sidney S., 173
Riesenfeld, Victor S., 20
Rockefeller, Jr., John D., 77
Rogers, Bruce, 20
Rogers, Horatio, 170, 173
Rohfritch, Jay, 121ff, 213
Rose, Alfred L., 20
Roselund Rare Books, 93
Rosenbach, A.S.W., 40, 66, 116-118, 119, 193-194
Rosenbach Museum, 193-194
Rosenthal, Lewis, 176ff
Rosenthal, Ludwig, 179
Rosenwald, Lessing, 105
Rovenpor, Jeffrey, 168-169
Roxburghe Club (California), 153, 154
Roxburghe Club (England), 34
Rudge, William E., 16
Rum House, 84
Sabin, Joseph, 141-142, 171
Sachs, Howard J., 20

Saints and Sinners Club, 17
Samuel, Ralph E., 19
Samuels Lasner, Mark, 19
Scott, Temple, 20
Segar, Holly, 168-169
Sessler, Charles, 10, 40
Seybolt, Paul, 204-205
Shettles, Elijah L., 143ff
Shipton, Clifford K., 111-112
Shurtleff, Nathaniel, 173
Simons, Gary, 127
Simpson, Bill, 58
Skiff, Frederick W., 5
Skillings, Warren, 101
Sloan, Dorothy, 50ff, 107, 143, 144, 145
Sloan, Jasmine (Julie), 57
Smith, George D., 31, 66, 119
Smith, Dr. Stephen, 138ff
Staley, Thomas F., 90ff
Steinhardt, Amos, 19
Steinhardt, Maxwell,19
Stern, Peter, 47ff
Stevens, Benjamin Franklin, 127
Stevens, Henry, 44, 127, 173, 200, 205
Stewart, Judd, 76ff
Steyne, Alan, 20
Stillwell, Margaret, 93ff
Streitfeld, David, 87
Stoddard, Roger, 168, 169, 171-173, 208
Stroganov, Earl G.A., 72-73
Strouse, Norman, 127
Swann, Arthur, 30-31, 161
Talcott, Edward B., 114, 115
Taper, Louise, 75
Taylor, W. Thomas, 57ff, 60
Tegge, Tim & Barbara, 7
Thielman, James, 71
Thomas, Isaiah, 111
Tuttle Antiquarian Books, 204
Tweney, George, 36
Updike, Daniel Berkeley, 16
Urban, Valerie, 57

Vader, Darth, 39
Vandale, Earl, 58
Vile, Scott, 202-204, 213
Volkmann, Jr, Daniel G., 60-61
Voodoo Museum, 86-87
Wakeman, Stephen H., 158ff
Walpole Society, 19
Walton, Ray, 149
Wells, Carolyn, 198
Wells, Gabriel, 66
Weintraub, Stanley, 116
Wendlick, Roger, 35-36
White, Jr, Fred, 45
Whitehill, Walter Muir, 112
Widener Library, 99
Wiley, Ben, 127
Willis Monie Books, 93, 110-111, 199-200
Wilson, Carroll A., 162
Wind River Press, 57
Winkler, Earnest, 148
Winship, George Parker, 94ff
Winship, Michael, 44
Winterich, John T., 20
Winterrowd, Will, 68ff
Winterthur Museum & Library, 133, 191
Wise, Thomas J., 6
Wolf, Edwin, III
Wood, Frank, 204
World, Frog Capital, 130
Wright, Frank Lloyd, 1, 4-5, 13, 202
Wright, Purd, 148
Wroth, Lawrence, 102-3
Wynne, James, 136, 138
Wynne, Marjorie, 200
Yezer, Frank, 90
Young, Bryan & Kelly, 121-122, 128
Zahn, Mabel, 10
Zamorano Club, 59
Zamorano 80, 59-60, 118
Zimmerman, Kurt, i-iv
Zimmerman, Nicole, 1, 4-5, 83ff, 110, 190ff, 213
Zimmerman Library Expansion Fund, 214

www.ingramcontent.com/pod-product-compliance
Lightning Source LLC
Chambersburg PA
CBHW040235110526
44582CB00020B/204/J